*BOOKS FOR WARTIME*

FREEDOM'S BATTLE
by J. Alvarez del Vayo

THE JAPANESE ENEMY
GOVERNMENT BY ASSASSINATION
by Hugh Byas

ASSIGNMENT TO BERLIN
by Harry W. Flannery

MEN ON BATAAN
by John Hersey

DESERT WAR
by Russell Hill

INDIA WITHOUT FABLE
by Kate L. Mitchell

PRELUDE TO VICTORY
by James B. Reston

BERLIN DIARY
by William L. Shirer

DESIGN FOR POWER
by Frederick L. Schuman
maps by George D. Brodsky

LAST TRAIN FROM BERLIN
by Howard K. Smith

MOSCOW WAR DIARY
by Alexander Werth

THESE ARE BORZOI BOOKS

# APPEASEMENT'S CHILD

# APPEASEMENT'S *CHILD*

## THE FRANCO REGIME IN SPAIN

*Thomas J. Hamilton*

NEW YORK

ALFRED · A · KNOPF

Manufactured in the United States of America

Published simultaneously in Canada by The Ryerson Press

FIRST EDITION

TO

*My Wife*

The real permanent and standing cause of Spain's thinly peopled state, want of cultivation, and abomination of desolation, is BAD GOVERNMENT, civil and religious; this all who run may read in her lonely land and silent towns. But Spain, if the anecdote which her children love to tell be true, will never be able to remove the incubus of this fertile origin of every evil. When Ferdinand III. captured Seville and died, being a saint he escaped purgatory, and Santiago presented him to the Virgin, who forthwith desired him to ask any favours for beloved Spain. The monarch petitioned for oil, wine, and corn—conceded; for sunny skies, brave men, and pretty women—allowed; for cigars, relics, garlic, and bulls—by all means; for a *good government*—"Nay, nay," said the Virgin, "that never can be granted; for were it bestowed, not an angel would remain a day longer in heaven."

—From Chapter iv of Richard Ford's
*Gatherings from Spain* (1846)

# CONTENTS

## PART I

## FASCIST CASTLES IN SPAIN

I · *On Loving Our Enemies* 3

II · *Wages of Civil War* 19

III · *The Rise of Spanish Fascism* 51

IV · *The Fascist El Dorado* 69

## PART II

## AWAKENING TO REALITY

V · *Conflict within the New Order* 91

VI · *Franco and the Spanish Laval* 109

VII · *Neither Guns nor Butter* 131

VIII · *Special Privileges and the Black Market* 162

IX · *"Bread, Motherland, and Justice"* 177

X · *Some Notes on Daily Life* 197

*Contents*

PART III

## THE FRANCO REGIME AND THE OUTSIDE WORLD


XI · *The Last Exit from Nazi Europe* 215

XII · *The Germans Fight Us in Spain* 234

XIII · *Franco Fights Us in Latin America* 255

XIV · *Britain and France Try to Appease Franco* 271

XV · *The United States Takes Over the Job* 292

XVI · *Spain and the Second Front* 308

BIBLIOGRAPHY 324

INDEX *follows page* 327

# *Part* I

# FASCIST CASTLES IN SPAIN

# *Chapter* I

## ON LOVING OUR ENEMIES

"Naturally," Señor Serrano Suñer told the *Völkischer Beobachter* during his visit to Germany in September 1940, "we contend that the Spanish war was the preliminary phase of the present conflict." Today there are few Americans who would disagree with him. The foes of the Spanish Republic then are our foes now. And Soviet Russia, its ally, is now our ally. Today it is clear that the so-called non-intervention policy which permitted the triumph of General Francisco Franco was one of the cardinal blunders committed by England, France, and the United States in the last years before the guns went off.

Spain has taken its place with Manchuria, the Rhineland, Ethiopia, Austria, Czechoslovakia, and other names that come hauntingly out of the past. Each was a Pearl Harbor, a monument to the divided councils of the democracies, an omen of self-destruction.

For a long time, however, it seemed that Franco's victory did not affect us directly. We have been absorbed in the stupendous events set in motion by the German invasion of Poland, and as long as Hitler did not formally take over Spain, there seemed no reason to lose any sleep over the fascist regime he had installed in Madrid. Time enough for that after the war.

The Allied landings in French North Africa, however, have

changed all that. They have opened our eyes to the extraordinary strategic importance of Spain and to the possibility that at any moment Hitler or Franco, or both together, may carry the civil war to its logical conclusion and strike a crippling blow at our exposed lines of communication. The Franco regime matters more to us today than perhaps any other not actually in the war.

For we must realize that whether they are sent from England or the United States, every tank and every airplane that our forces in French North Africa receive must pass within a few miles of Franco's naval and air bases. We tend to picture the grey mass of Gibraltar as completely dominating the most important supply route. We forget that with the exception of the Rock, Spain now controls every foot of territory on both sides of the narrow Strait, which, between Gibraltar and the fortress of Ceuta, in Spanish Morocco, is barely twelve miles across.

Gibraltar itself is probably safe against capture, but it is to be feared that the powerful German cannon which Franco has installed above Algeciras and La Linea could seriously impair or destroy its usefulness as a naval base. The great dockyards of Gibraltar, and the anchorage at which most of the North African expedition assembled, are perfect targets for Franco's batteries as well as for planes operating from the numerous air fields near by.

For the British, duplicating their error at Singapore, constructed their base on the land side of the Rock, directly across the small Bay of Algeciras from Spanish territory. Gibraltar's capacity to defend itself is limited by the fact that its pocket-size air field, built on the former racecourse and only a few hundred yards from the Spanish frontier post of La Linea, is too small to accommodate modern fighters or heavy bombers. Oran and Casablanca are now available as alternate bases, but there is no question of the fact that Axis attacks from Spanish territory would greatly diminish the volume of shipping that we could send through the Strait.

The only alternative is to land most of our reinforcements and supplies at the Atlantic ports of French Morocco and send them on to the fighting zone by the railroad connecting Rabat and Casablanca with Algeria and Tunisia. But it may be conjectured that this line is already loaded to capacity, and as it runs for a considerable distance within a few miles of Spanish Morocco, it also is highly vulnerable to attack.

Nor do these complete the list of Franco's opportunities to cause serious trouble. The Canary Islands and the Spanish colony of Río de Oro, on the southern frontier of French Morocco, constitute a menace to both land and sea communications between Africa and the Western Hemisphere. The Balearic Islands are strategically placed athwart the principal shipping lanes in the western Mediterranean, and the great base of Port Mahon, at Minorca, is on a direct line between Toulon and Algiers and half-way between them. We cannot invade the Mediterranean coast of France or northern Italy until we are sure that it will not be used against us.

Fortunately, there is little to be feared from the armed forces of Franco himself. His navy, consisting of six cruisers (one of which is the excellent Vickers-designed *Canarias*), a dozen destroyers, and six submarines, is relatively modern and efficient. But unless large German reinforcements have arrived recently, he has only three hundred or four hundred planes. These are mostly obsolete German and Italian aircraft left behind after the civil war, and he has no factories with which to make more. His army, which in recent months has approximated 500,000 men, could be raised to one million by calling up trained reserves. But it lacks supplies and equipment for anything more than a short campaign, and the Spanish people today have no stomach for a war of conquest.

The danger, of course, is that the Germans will take over Spain and do the fighting themselves. The advantage of Spain's strategic position has been obvious to them from the first, and I became fully aware of their intentions during the civil war, when it was my assignment to cover the fantastic proceedings of the London Non-Intervention Committee for the *New York Times*. Later, during the two years that I was *Times* correspondent in post-civil-war Spain, this possibility was the one unchanging guide to the policy of the Franco regime. The three months I spent in Chile after leaving Spain, which gave me an opportunity to study the Franco question from a different angle, confirmed my belief in the importance of Spain to the Axis.

Everything leads to the belief that Hitler, if he does take over Spain at last, will not send hundreds of thousands of troops pouring over the International Bridge at Irún. That would be to put both Spaniards and ourselves on our guard. Instead we may expect the Nazis to repeat their tactics during the civil war and rely principally on aviation units and tank crews, who would be in such small numbers that they would not put too much of a strain on the inadequate transportation system. The Spanish armed forces, with German officers and commissars, would be expected to do the heavy fighting.

Franco's co-operation is essential, of course, if the Nazis are to avail themselves of Spain's geographical position at minimum cost. Whether Franco will fall in with these plans is a question which will be examined later in this book. But the threat of an Axis attack through Spain and Portugal (which is defenceless and probably not defendable) is one of the most serious which we have to face before we can come to grips with the Germans on their own ground.

It is long since time that the people of the United States awoke to the realities of the Spanish situation and understood that the mistakes that we have made cannot be wiped out by repeating them. It is not within our power to take from the Nazis the benefits that they derived from their use of Spain as the proving ground for all phases of the Blitzkrieg; it was in Spain that the Nazi general staff learned the lessons in co-ordinating mechanized units and aviation which they have applied so successfully in France, in Yugoslavia, in Egypt; it was in Spain that Hitler and Mussolini found that together they could overawe the democracies. And it is equally impossible to cancel the advantage to the Axis resulting from the combination of German troops at Hendaye and an avowed pro-Nazi regime in Madrid.

If we bring ourselves to face reality, however, there are important advantages to be gained which may even counterbalance the difficulties that we created for ourselves by allowing Franco to capture—and retain—Madrid. As we shall see later in this book, there is nothing to prevent us from taking *now* the indispensable steps necessary to assure determined underground resistance to Hitler when he does occupy Spain. The same people who fought Franco and Hitler for nearly three years are ready to do so again if only they are assured that they will obtain a democratic government as a reward for renewing the battle against fascism.

In order to carry out such a policy we must, of course, remove the scales of class prejudice which have blinded us ever since the outbreak of the civil war in 1936. This very awareness, in fact, will be more valuable to our cause than the entire Iberian Peninsula. It will mean that we are really fighting a people's war. It will mean that we have the relentless will to win which will be satisfied with nothing less than the extirpation of fascism and militarism throughout the world. It will mean that we have no lingering belief that Hitler "has got something" and that perhaps a little domestic fascism would help us overcome our fascist enemies. And while recognizing fully the efficiency of the German military machine, we will know that it is the product of German, not fascist efficiency, and that when fascism is attempted in a country like Spain, it only makes inefficiency worse.

Above all, the lesson to be learned from Spain will straighten out the psychological kinks which thus far have kept us from giving wholehearted support to two of our most valuable allies, Russia and China. As this is written, the China front is calm, but the loss of Burma, cutting off General Chiang Kai-shek from help, may mean that the Japanese can finish him off at their leisure. And although the valour of the Russians saved Stalingrad in 1942, they have been weakened considerably by the struggle. We must face the possibility that both China and Russia, whose tremendous strength should have made them unconquerable champions of our cause, may yet be knocked out of the war.

We should not be confronted with such disasters if we had given Russia and China adequate help. Successful as the isolationists had been in preventing us from making adequate war preparations, we had the tanks and the airplanes a year ago which would have saved the situation if we could have brought ourselves to let them go. Numerous explanations can be brought forward now that the damage is done, but the real reason why Russia and China did not get the help they needed was simply our class and colour prejudices. Our leaders, reflecting only too well the warped outlook of a nation which had its eyes fixed on the Communist bogy, delayed sending the necessary matériel. We rationalized our refusal to do so by prophesying that Germany would knife through the "incompetent" Russian armies in six weeks, or that the Reds would "sell us out"—thus unconsciously betraying the course we would have taken if the roles had been reversed. And although Great Britain, under pressure from Stalin, did declare war on "brave little Finland" in December 1941, to this day the Finnish Minister in Washington continues to circulate among our well-padded Communist-haters while Finnish troops fight our Russian allies.

The Japanese, to be sure, are too much now for even our appeasers to swallow. But for Simon and the rest of the British Tory clique, the United States might have done something effective to stop the Japanese when they invaded Manchuria in 1931. Nevertheless we did little to help Chiang Kai-shek while the Burma Road was still open, and for years American soldiers will continue to be killed by bombs and shells made from the materials with which we so accommodatingly supplied the Japanese. We disdained a formidable enemy and a friend who could have given us powerful help because both are members of the yellow race. In the same way the British at this moment are engaged in making India, another potential ally, into another Burma.

It is not by chance that we have come so near to digging our own graves. And it will not be by chance that we correct these tragic mistakes in the future. Before we can cure ourselves we must diagnose the disease and recognize that these prejudices of class and race have been cunningly nurtured by Hitler and his Nazi propagandists. The virus already existed, for the Führer takes full advantage of existing cancers and does not seek to implant an entirely new infection. But these hateful and fatal diseases have been spread by his propagandists, and millions of Americans who have never read a Nazi propaganda sheet or heard even a Silver Shirt lecturer are as much his dupes as the master race itself.

It will be a long time at best before the cure can be completed; over a year after Pearl Harbor there are still Americans who, although they would deny that they are traitors to the cause of freedom, seem to be more worried over the possibility that the Russians will hold off the German onslaught than the probability that we also will lose the war if they are defeated. Our blindness is the more incredible in view of the fact that Hitler revealed in *Mein Kampf* not only his technique but the actual content of the propaganda which he has used to split united nations into mutually hostile classes and races. Unless we can learn to destroy, or at least to control, these prejudices, and make winning the war our sole aim, we shall be beaten and we shall deserve to be beaten.

Hitler's efforts to divide us have been made so skilfully that it may be a long time before we can see our own way. To guide us at first we need a case in which the issues are clear beyond all dispute, and we have it in Franco Spain. For the policy that allowed fascism to overthrow a friendly republic is a chemically pure demonstration of the subordination of national interests to class prejudice. No warning signal was absent as German and Italian troops on the one hand, and Russian troops on the other, made the civil war what Serrano Suñer accurately described it: the first campaign of the world-wide conflict.

For anyone who desires a clear statement of the crushing defeat that Spain represented for the democracies, I can recommend no better source than the authoritative *Reivindicaciones de España* [1] by José M. Areilza, a member of the Council of the Phalanx, as the Spanish fascist party is called, and Fernando M. Castiella, a fascist professor of international law. This book, which was published in Madrid in 1941, is an excellent example of fascist rhetoric as well. I enjoyed its denunciation of "the decadent and worm-eaten structure of the French and British Empires, which were stuffed with wealth, rotten in their moral fibre, unwilling to consent to an indispensable social adjustment, and shut up within frenetic egotism. . . ." It deviated into sense, however, when it began to take up the significance of the Spanish war, which it called the "invisible war" that had made it easier for "the young and strong foreign policy of Germany to resolve meanwhile the problems of Austria and Czechoslovakia—indispensable prelude to the great historical rectification of the Versailles frontier."

As the authors said only too truly, Franco's victory was "a triple and formidable defeat" for the democracies in strategy, policy, and morale. "Because," they explained, "triumphant Spain was above all a nation which had recovered herself, with her will to Empire fully restored, ready to impose her desires in

1 *Reivindicaciones* goes much further than a mere "claim"; it is a legal term for the process by which property taken from the rightful owner is recovered.

the vital space to which strict justice entitled her. Because she was inspired by a new political mentality—the Phalanx—which was destined to associate itself in a singular and harmonious way with German National Socialism and Italian Fascism. And, finally, because the double conjunction of geographical and political interests necessarily would lead Spain, voluntarily and spontaneously, to increase her solidarity with the Axis powers in their opposition to the tortuous Anglo-French manœuvres, intended once more to encircle Germany with a ring of strangulation and death."

This is not the mere scribbling of fascist hot-heads, but an authorized declaration of Spanish policy. The Institute of Political Studies, which published the book, is a sort of political general staff for the Phalanx party. Its director, Alfonso García Valdecasas, was one of the founders of the Phalanx, and would hold one of the supreme positions in the party today but for the fact that his temperament was not considered fiery enough; of course the government censorship, now as in the days of Philip II, would not have permitted the appearance of the work if its statement of Spain's aspirations had not been in full accord with official policy.

These aims, in fact, were abundantly clear from the outset of the civil war. And yet millions of Englishmen and Frenchmen and Americans forgot their loyalty to their country when the subject of the "Spanish Reds" was brought up. Many of those who were awake to the Nazi peril could not see that Franco, "Christian gentleman" or not, was a Hitler pawn. Whenever I think of this tragic blindness my mind turns to one of the most zealous of the Franco partisans, Sir Walter Maxwell Scott, a descendant of the great romanticist, whom I went to visit at Abbotsford in July 1939, just before leaving for Spain. Lord Lothian, who was then preparing to take over the Washington Embassy, suggested that I go to see him, but warned me that I would find him a fanatical supporter of Franco.

He understated the case. An ardent Catholic, Sir Walter Maxwell Scott had made two visits to Franco Spain during the war and had made contacts which afterwards resulted in his election to the board of directors of a British company which owned mines at Huelva, in Franco territory. He had also brought away a burning hatred of the Republicans and the conviction that the Nationalist cause was identical with that of religion and civilization. Nevertheless, his great ancestor had been a staunch patriot, and the present laird of Abbotsford had risen to the rank of general in the British Army; I expected him to show some concern at least over the German and Italian troops that he had encountered in the Franco armies. But he was quick to tell me that the Axis influence over Franco served England and France right.

Naturally enough, General Scott did not believe that the Danzig crisis, then becoming threatening, would bring war. To allow it to do so would be a great mistake, he said, for England and France were not prepared to fight Germany and could not reach Poland anyway. I suggested that Russia, after all, was an ally of France and could help the Poles if Allied diplomacy could win over Stalin. With eyes flashing, the old general told me that if war could not be avoided, he preferred a thousand times to "see the British Empire go down in honourable defeat" than win with the help of the Bolsheviks.

In France, with its larger proportion of Catholics, the pro-Franco sentiment among the well-to-do was even more fervent. When I stopped off in Paris the Quai d'Orsay officials were still pleased that Franco had won out. They acknowledged a certain amount of German penetration, but that, they assured me, would be taken care of by the French Ambassador, Marshal Henri Philippe Pétain. Frenchmen in general were equally convinced that Chamberlain had stopped Blum's covert assistance to the Spanish Republicans just in time, and that there would be a deal over Danzig. After reaching Spain

I drove from San Sebastián to Burgos with a young Alsatian count, the son of a high Army officer, and the godson (he told me it was unique) of two marshals of France. He condemned the *canaille* of the Popular Fronts in the two countries with equal violence, and he said that if war came and Frenchmen had to "die for Danzig," they would not have tanks or even rifles because everything had been sent to the Spanish Reds. One knows without asking that he is with Laval today.

Marshal Pétain, it goes without saying, was pro-Franco, but even General Maxime Weygand, from whose first-class mind one would have expected better things, also was blinded by the ideological dust thrown in his eyes. For centuries the policy of France had been to maintain a friendly government in Madrid, leaving her free to face the Rhine without fear of a blow from the Pyrenees. Yet, in an introduction to *Leçons de la Guerre d'Espagne* (published in 1938), by General Maurice Duval, an ardent Franco sympathizer, General Weygand praised Franco and damned the Republic in language which could not have been more effective if it had been written by Goebbels himself.

"We are concerned," General Weygand wrote, "with the struggle between an established government and a little group of men who are determined to free their country from insupportable servitude [presumably a reference to Soviet Russia, France's ally]. At the beginning, the government possesses all the elements of superiority, army and matériel, the larger territory, gold, ports and almost the entire fleet, thereby enabling it to receive help from outside. But this government has no unity, it is labouring under a foreign influence. It may have passions, but not an idea. Thus it shows itself inapt at organizing an army; under its colours it assembles only a mob. This fundamental weakness is found again in the strategic sphere when it is a question of establishing a plan; the weakness of planning and organization appear with fatal effect, despite the bravery of the combatants, in the conduct of operations."

On the other hand, General Weygand found everything admirable on the Franco side, and most of all Franco himself, whose success, he was convinced, was due to his patriotism, his knowledge, and his will. Franco's foreign policy was "upright and courageous," while as a general he had the "creative gift" of organizing an army, was "persevering and wary in fixing his strategic objectives, methodical and bold in the conduct of operations."

"Victory," concluded the general who in less than two years was to be vanquished by Franco's Nazi allies, "cannot be attained by anarchy and ignorance."

We need only to refer to any chapter of *Reivindicaciones de España* to realize the calamity that this judgment represented. Afterwards, during his service as proconsul for North Africa —until the Nazis told Marshal Pétain to dismiss him—General Weygand's primary responsibility was to keep his troops ready for a joint attack by the Spaniards and the Germans. I have often wondered if he changed his views, for the failure to attack certainly was not due to lack of desire by Franco. *Reivindicaciones de España* is explicit on this point: "Now nothing can hold back the irresistible force of events. Oran will return very soon, for the third time, to the bosom of the Spanish community. The old English leopard will be turned out of his lair at Gibraltar, and the French threat from Algeria no longer will threaten the independence of a country which, like ours, has recently regained its strength."

It was quite understandable, of course, that not merely zealots of the type of General Scott, but a man of the importance and distinction of General Weygand disliked the Spanish Republic. I can sympathize with Catholics throughout the world who were revolted by the burning of churches and monasteries, and the slaughter of priests and nuns, which were allowed to take place under the Popular Front government. The cabinet which was in office when the Franco revolution began did not have a Communist member, but there is no doubt of the fact that Communist influence increased steadily during the war and that the clenched-fist salute became the standard greeting in the Republican zone, corresponding to the fascist salute in Franco territory. I can understand why a business man in South Bend who feared Communism would have preferred a Franco victory. Certainly anyone, regardless of his political views, must condemn the indiscriminate slaughter of suspected Franco sympathizers in Madrid and elsewhere in Republican territory. There is considerable merit in the Republican contention that these excesses took place only during the first months of the war, when the government was powerless either to keep internal order or to put down the revolution, and that the massacres virtually ceased when the Republic regained authority in November 1936. Nevertheless, it is obvious that the Popular Front victory in the February 1936 elections marked a definite swing to the Left. The avowed aims of the victorious coalition were perhaps no more extreme than those of the New Deal in the United States. But most Americans who had enough money to belong to a country club were against the New Deal and it was their privilege to dislike the Spanish Republic, too, if they chose. Well-to-do Englishmen and Frenchmen naturally were entitled to do the same.

But no citizen has the right to allow his personal preferences for one foreign government or another to imperil the existence of his own country. Many of these people obviously felt that the cause of the Spanish aristocrats and fascists was their own, but if they lacked sufficient patriotism to support a foreign policy which was in the interests of the democracies, regard for their own skins should have taught them better. We have found in these years of fascist victories that no country can afford the luxury of a foreign policy based upon mere likes and dislikes.

This does not mean a cold and selfish regard for our own interests alone. The armies of the French Revolution swept over Europe as liberators, not as conquerors, and men still fight hardest for ideas and ideals. But we must make these great intangible forces serve our purpose, not be their slave. Hitler used the Spanish war to turn them against us, and while the democratic appeasers were still exulting over this blow to Communism, he was laying the ground for his alliance with Stalin. That he later turned on Stalin did not alter the cold realism with which he has played upon our failure to support our own cause wherever it is assailed.

But we could not see the trap, even though Franco's most loud-mouthed champions in the democracies might have provided some hint. In France it was Léon Daudet, editor of *L'Action Française,* known for years as a royalist and a spokesman for Mussolini, who denounced England in every issue of his paper from the collapse of France until his death in the summer of 1942. In England it was Captain Archibald Ramsay, a violent fascist and Jew-baiter, who was considered so dangerous an enemy of his country that his parliamentary immunity did not save him from arrest after the war broke out. In the United States such a choice is difficult, but according to the Franco government one Jane Anderson was the "paladin" of the Nationalist cause; she has found other suitable employment since Pearl Harbor as a speaker on the largest Nazi broadcasting station beamed on the United States.

Even without such clear warnings, however, no second sight was required to see where Franco's triumph would lead. The question of which side *ought* to have won could have been left to observers from another planet. Both regimes had a common defect—inefficiency—and in some respects, such as their grandiose planning and their failure to attain results in any way comparable, they were curiously alike. At their worst they both descended to cruelty which was unworthy of the Spanish people.

But there was never any need for an American or Englishman or Frenchman to ponder the abstract merits of the case. War with the Axis was clearly approaching and any sensible man must favour the side which would support free government. It was absurdly easy to determine which this was. If there was no other way, you had only to learn which the enemies of your country were for and then support the other. Hitler and Mussolini were doing their best to help Franco win, and it should not have been difficult to decide that we were on the Republic's side of the barricade.

This is such a simple piece of reasoning that it would not be worth setting down if it were not for the fact that millions of influential citizens of the democracies could not follow it. Some, who unfortunately are in positions of power, still cannot follow it, still permit their views to be determined by the fact that the aristocrats of Spain were on Franco's side, and the hated Russian Communists supported the Republic. They still retain an unfortunate tendency to denounce as Reds all persons who do not agree with them, but one would be glad to be put in a class with Winston Churchill, who urged unceasingly upon Chamberlain the formation of a "Grand Alliance," with Russia a leading member, in the last years before the outbreak of war. Mr. Churchill doubtless feels it is a compliment that the Franco press, like the Nazi and Italian press, has singled him out for attack. Every month or so, when other ammunition failed, the Madrid newspapers used to reprint with suitable epithets an interview in which he declared that although Franco's was "the right side," the "interests of England" required the victory of the Republic.

"The interests of England," and of the United States, and of all the United Nations, is so simple and old-fashioned a concept that it appears revolutionary. It is revolutionary, and it is time we had such a revolution, time we buried the Colonel Blimp mentality and no longer permitted ourselves to be swayed by any consideration but victory. We survive or go down to destruction together, and though Sir Walter Scott may prefer to lose Abbotsford rather than co-operate with Soviet Russia, he and people like him must not be allowed to pull down England and America.

When the war is won, perhaps we can afford a foreign policy that is dominated by our class prejudices. Now we can consider nothing but the most efficacious way to win the war, and if our cause would be helped by an alliance with the Great Cham of Tartary, let us send our ambassadors on their way. And if it suits our interests for the moment to cultivate good terms with Franco, let us do that too. But we must be sure in our own minds that such a course is really in our interests, and that no lingering affection for this self-proclaimed champion of Christianity against the "Red hordes" has made us adopt it. At least in time of war we must ignore the Biblical exhortation to love our enemies.

# *Chapter* II

## WAGES OF CIVIL WAR

Although a victorious foreign war, if not won at too great a price, is a good long-range investment—the wealth of England, for example, is still based upon the empire she wrested from the French—civil wars are invariably unprofitable. Spain herself, whose centuries-long decline was produced by internal conflict even more than by her wars with England and France and the United States, is the classic example of such disasters. The Franco uprising was particularly tragic because under Alfonso XIII's relatively peaceful reign she was just recovering from the two bitterly fought Carlist wars which followed the war against Napoleon; if the Republic had been left free to follow the policy of peace and internal reform enjoined in its Constitution, by now Spain might have begun to catch up with more advanced nations.

The Republic, however, lacked a leader of sufficient ability and force to consolidate democratic government and smash the ancient forces of privilege. After five years of bickering which only divided the nation still further, the two sides resorted to arms. The civil war would have been a tragedy even if it had been brought to a prompt conclusion without excessive loss of life. Instead, despite the relatively inadequate supply of modern matériel on both sides, it was fought with extraordinary violence for nearly three years. The result was a still larger crop of hatred, and the domination of Spain by the Axis and by the local fascists. The war settled nothing, and sooner or later the people of Spain will rise again to expel Franco and make another, and, let us hope, more successful, effort to obtain decent and democratic government.

Anything would have been better than the state of affairs resulting from the long war. Had either the Republic or Franco won quickly, much loss of life, destruction of property, and long-lasting domestic and international complications would have been avoided. If the generals who organized the revolt had worked out their course more skilfully, Spain would be ruled today by an old-fashioned army dictatorship, probably very similar to the Primo de Rivera dictatorship of 1923 to 1930. Unquestionably it would be tainted with fascism and would be under Axis influence. But the lot of the average Spaniard would be incomparably better, and the nations fighting for freedom would not now be under the constant threat of an Axis attack from the Iberian Peninsula. Apart from the fact that most of Spain's difficulties today are the result of the mistaken foreign and domestic policy produced by fascism, Hitler and Mussolini would not have been able to use Spain to split the democracies; there is, indeed, every reason to believe that but for the Spanish civil war Britain and France would have stopped Hitler while there was still time.

The Spanish Republic itself, plagued by the weakness and lack of decision that had permitted the Rightists to block its program of domestic reform, committed the original error which started the disastrous chain of events. It failed to take adequate steps to suppress an uprising which it knew was being carefully planned, and it missed the opportunity presented by the inexplicable blunders of the commanders of the Madrid and Barcelona garrisons, who failed to carry out the military *Junta's* plan to take over these centres of popular resistance at the very start. If the Republic had acted with the requisite speed and vigour, it could have smashed the uprising in the first month. But it was torn by factional disputes, and by November 1936, when it more or less regained control of internal affairs and repulsed the attack on Madrid, the fronts had been stabilized and it was obvious that only overwhelming outside help for one side or the other could prevent the war from going on for years.

England and France were, however, responsible for the Republic's final defeat. Afraid to take positive action to stop the troops and matériel which the Axis was sending to the rebels, they set up the London Non-Intervention Committee to "keep the ring." The theory was that if nobody interfered the Spaniards would not hurt anybody but themselves, and the Committee did manage in the end to stop the help that the Republic, in accordance with accepted international practice allowing a legitimate government to buy arms abroad for suppressing a rebellion, had been receiving from Soviet Russia and, surreptitiously, from France. The United States, although not even a member of the Non-Intervention Committee, invoked the Neutrality Act to accomplish the same purpose.

The Axis, on the other hand, had determined to give Franco enough help to win, and it proceeded to furnish it without regard to the Committee. If Hitler and Mussolini had desired to do so, in fact, they could have won the war for Franco at least a year earlier. The fact that they rationed their aid so carefully, and that the Nazis even sold arms to the Republicans,[1] seems to confirm the supposition that they were deliberately using the civil war to produce disunion in the

[1] This is on the authority of an Havas correspondent who covered the war on Franco's side. He told me of being present on several occasions when fascist soldiers brought in German war equipment which they had captured from the Republicans. As these rifles, cannon, and shells were new, this would exclude the possibility that they had been discarded by the Nazis and sold to some international arms dealer. It may be supposed, of course, that the Nazis used some intermediary instead of dealing directly with the "Communist" government that they had sworn to annihilate. I have no other direct evidence to support this statement, but in view of the fact that the correspondent was a supporter of Franco and fascism in general, I see no reason to doubt his evidence.

democracies. Certainly it was more important to them to keep London and Paris divided than to install a fascist regime in Spain; that, to be sure, was a useful secondary achievement, but here, too, the longer the war lasted, the more firmly would fascism be saddled upon Spain and the easier it would be to keep Franco under their control.

The general political strategy of the Axis assuredly was aided by the prolongation of the civil war, and the final liquidation of Czechoslovakia, for example, might not have been such a shock to Chamberlain and Daladier if they had not been so occupied with an attempt to range themselves on Franco's side before he actually entered Madrid.

Whether or not these were the reasons which moved Hitler and Mussolini, it was at their desire that the Spanish war dragged on and on. Those years of merciless combat were trebly unfortunate for Spain: the destruction of property, although not so great as has been believed, was a heavy loss to a country which already was so much poorer than other nations; the war took a frightful number of lives, drove some of Spain's ablest men into exile, and created a bitterness between *Blancos* and *Rojos* which will last for generations; most tragic of all, it committed the Franco regime to fascism and to dominance by the Axis.

When I arrived in Spain in early August 1939 to begin my work as *New York Times* correspondent, I expected to find the country a desert. As a Georgian I thought of civil wars in terms of Sherman's March to the Sea, and I supposed that with the exception of Galicia and Navarre, which Franco had held from the beginning, there would be scarcely a house or factory left standing. Each side had accused the other of the most bloodcurdling cruelty, and I did not believe that Spaniards would be any more careful with property than they had been with human lives.

My first impression of Franco Spain seemed to confirm these expectations. I had a three-hour wait at the Irún frontier while the officials were busy with lunch and siesta, and as I tried to eat some miserable peas and fried fish at a filthy little restaurant near the customs house, I reflected that just at the other end of the International Bridge there was peace and plenty. Within less than a year the Nazis were to destroy both, and many more important possessions of France as well. But at the time the contrast between conditions on the two sides of the Bidassoa River was an excellent symbol of the civilizations produced by democracy and fascism.

Once the numberless formalities at the frontier had been completed, I set out on a tour of the town of Irún, about half a mile away, which I remembered from my previous visit to Spain some nine years before as one of the unloveliest collections of buildings known to man. Nevertheless they had served to keep out the heavy rains prevalent in the Basque country, and from the viewpoint of the inhabitants the military importance of Irún, which controlled one of the two important land connections between Spain and France, was most unfortunate. General Emilio Mola had promptly led his Carlist Requetés down from Navarre to close this gateway, and they stormed Irún in September 1936 after hard fighting. It was not admitted, however, that the destruction of Irún had this explanation; my taxicab-driver informed me of the official thesis, which I was to hear repeated elsewhere, that Anarchist militiamen had blown up the town as they retreated.

A thorough job had been done by whoever was responsible. Only a few sagging walls were standing in the business district, and the hundreds of junked automobiles and trucks which were rusting in a military area just outside contributed to a scene of utter desolation. The work of rebuilding the town had not even started, though the Franco forces at that time had been in undisputed possession for nearly three years,[1]

[1] I drove through Irún for the last time in June 1941, on my way to interview American survivors of the Egyptian steamer *Zam Zam* when they were released from imprisonment by the Germans. By that time nearly five years had elapsed since the Anarchists left, and still no move had been made to rebuild it.

and there was an ample supply of stone and wood in the Basque area. Apparently the aim was to retain a warlike atmosphere for the benefit of foreigners, who visited the war zone by the hundreds in the summer of 1939 on excursions conducted by Franco's Tourist Bureau. On a slightly different principle, Republican prisoners, hardly distinguishable in their worn khaki and rope-soled shoes from their guards, were building a few machine-gun nests along the road from Irún to San Sebastián, and a military road to other fortifications farther inland. The nests, which were placed only a few feet from the highway, obviously were only of the smallest military value and the aim was to impress France with the might of the new regime rather than to do any real fighting.

Except for an acute shortage of hotel space, there were no signs of war in San Sebastián, a poor imitation of Nice which is frequented by those members of the Spanish aristocracy who are too hidebound or too poor to go to Biarritz. In the next two months I visited almost every province in Spain where there had been any fighting, and although some areas, particularly the coastal zone from Valencia to Barcelona, had suffered very heavily, it was clear that the amount of destruction had been considerably exaggerated. This impression was confirmed afterwards by a report of the government agency in charge of reconstruction, the *Dirección General de Regiones Devastadas,* which placed the total damage done to real property "in operations connected with the war, deliberately by the Reds, in their continuous retreat, or from sheer hatred or lack of patriotism," at 4,250,000,000 pesetas (about $386,000,000 at the official rate of exchange). This report stated that 150 churches had been totally destroyed and 4,850 damaged, including 1,850 which were more than fifty per cent destroyed. There was no estimate of the number of private houses destroyed, but the government said it was planning to build dwellings to accommodate 532,440 people out of a population of approximately 25,000,000. No less than 183 towns, including Irún, Guernica, Oviedo,

Belchite, Brunete, and others whose names once were world-known, had been so badly damaged that Franco had "adopted" them—meaning that the national government would pay the entire cost of restoring churches, public buildings, and municipal services. As I found on a long drive from Gibraltar up the Mediterranean coast all the way to Barcelona, there were many villages which had been so utterly wrecked that they were likely to remain abandoned.

Nevertheless, even after making full allowance for this destruction, it represented only one per cent of the total value of real property in Spain. Even University City, which until Warsaw and Rotterdam were bombed was a synonym for absolute destruction, had not been damaged as much as was at first thought. The board which is in charge of rebuilding it estimated that 120,000,000 pesetas (about $10,800,000) had been spent on it up to the outbreak of the civil war, and that the plant was worth 80,000,000 (about $7,000,000) when the war ended. In view of the fact that for more than two and a half years University City had been in no-man's land, this was surprising. One explanation was that the windows, furnishings, and other easily destroyed fittings had not yet been installed, while the Clinical Hospital, where most of the fighting took place, belonged to the city government and was not included in the survey. The principal reason, however, for the relatively small damage was that the buildings were of modern steel girder construction, which stood up well against the comparatively small cannon and bombs used during the Spanish war. University City was nevertheless a gloomy sight when I first visited it in August 1939. Except for the removal of the sandbags and barbed wire, it was just as it was when the fighting stopped. The trenches which ran through the campus were filled with rusting sardine tins, and the corpse of a Moorish soldier—embalmed in some way, supposedly, and left there as an exhibit—was lying exposed on one of the upper floors of the hospital. The twisted battle line, which emphasized how close Franco had come to taking Madrid at the outset, instead of two and a half years later, was marked by wooden boards with the lettering: *Nosotros* (We—i.e., the fascists), and *Ellos* (They).

In the working-class neighbourhood close by, the destruction was far greater. One narrow six-storey tenement was particularly impressive. A delayed-action bomb had penetrated straight to the basement before exploding, and the front of the building had collapsed. Steel beams which once had supported the floors were twisted like macaroni, but the bathtubs somehow remained in place. The small two-storey stone houses in the area were badly damaged, and repairs had been confined to bricking up the windows (window glass was available only on government orders). People were living in houses with gaping holes in the walls and roofs, or in caves burrowed out in vacant lots, and as there was no plumbing, water for cooking and bathing had to be brought from street fountains. Clothes were washed in the near-by Manzanares River, and in general life was reduced to its barest essentials.

Heavy damage also had been done in the neighbourhood of the Toledo Bridge, another working-class section, and the zone of destruction along the highway and railroad to Coruña extended for about ten miles. Attracted by the nearness of University City, middle-class Spaniards had built hundreds of suburban villas along this road in the decade before the civil war. It was their misfortune that this was one of the principal routes used by the Nationalists in their dash for Madrid at the start of the war. An extraordinary number of these villas had been equipped with open-air handball courts, and the fire-blackened ruins, with walls pockmarked by shrapnel or machine-gun bullets, were all the more depressing. Equally depressing were the ruins of the two country clubs, the Puerta de Hierro and the Club del Campo. The first nine of the Puerta de Hierro course was open, but play was hazardous. If you took too big a divot, there was a strong chance that you would hit one of the unexploded shells buried in the ground and blow yourself up. On the other hand, there was the compensation that you could pick up without penalty if your ball went into one of the trenches on the course. As for the Club del Campo, its course had been completely destroyed, and even its swimming pool was damaged beyond repair.

In the central part of the capital, however, it was necessary to search for any evidence of the war. The huge Central Post Office did not have a window-pane left when I arrived, although this was not Franco's doing but the result of the street fighting that raged before the Casado adherents, demanding surrender, overthrew the Negrín government in the last days of Madrid. The Telefonica, the American-style skyscraper which housed the American-owned telephone system, had been one of Franco's principal targets because it was used as a Republican observation post. But although Franco refused to allow the American management to resume control, all evidence that it had been hit over a hundred times by his artillery had been effaced. The Hotel Florida near by, where many American correspondents stayed during the war, also showed no signs of damage. Except for the wrecked Hotel Savoy, on the Castellana Avenue, a gutted apartment house on Alfonso XII Street, across from the Retiro Park, and another near by in Espalter Street, you could wander around for days without seeing anything to indicate that Madrid had just emerged from a war.

This was due primarily to the great discretion used by the Nationalist gunners and bombers in their choice of targets. They concentrated for the most part on the poorer sections on the outer fringe of Madrid—where, it should be pointed out, most of the military objectives were located—and left virtually untouched the Salamanca residential quarter, favoured by the wealthy, which was full of Franco sympathizers. Although the furnishings of many of the great town houses were ruined by poor families who moved in after their own homes were bombed, only two were destroyed. One of these was the colossal home of a wealthy merchant, a few hundred yards from the American Embassy, which itself was hit by a shell that penetrated the Ambassador's study but fortunately did not explode. The other was the famous Palacio Liria, belonging to the Duke of Alba, the first grandee of Spain and now Franco's Ambassador to London.

I was particularly interested in the latter because the Duke, whom I saw in London before leaving for Spain, had used its destruction as the text for a long denunciation of the "Reds." He was convinced that the Republicans had deliberately set it on fire and looted his famous art collection. Actually, as I was assured by a pro-Franco American who was on the scene, the palace was set afire by bombs dropped by a Franco pilot, who was aiming at a powder magazine near by. Crowds then rushed into the eighteenth-century building, but although they made off with some of the *objets d'art,* virtually all the Alba paintings were saved. Taken over by the Republican authorities, they were stored at the Prado with other valuable pictures removed from churches and other private galleries. Between 14,000 and 15,000 paintings were thus collected, and although their owners had grounds for complaint against this confiscation, there is no doubt that the Republic's efforts to save the art treasures of Spain for posterity were successful.

I went into this point thoroughly with responsible museum authorities and found no evidence whatever to support the Franco propagandists' claim that many priceless art treasures of Spain had been destroyed and that some of the greatest had been shipped to Russia or carried off by fleeing Republican politicians. To save them from bombing, nearly two thousand of the finest paintings from the Prado and elsewhere were, it is true, sent to France by the Republican government after the fall of Barcelona. They had first been removed from the Prado and placed in the vaults of the Bank of Spain, but they began to deteriorate in the moistness and afterwards they were moved to Valencia. Heavy bombings there decided the Republic to move them to Barcelona, and afterwards, in association with the League of Nations, the British and American governments, and the International Committee for the Preservation of the Art Treasures of Spain, they were transported to Geneva to be held in trust for whatever government finally won out.

Alvarez del Vayo, in *Freedom's Battle,*[1] has told how the hard-pressed Republican government used its trucks to get the paintings over the frontier. The Republic had considerable reason to fear for the safety of the paintings if they were allowed to remain in the Prado. It may be assumed that Franco had ordered his pilots and artillery men not to hit the Prado, but the Hotel Savoy, directly across the street, was destroyed and several incendiary bombs actually fell on the roof of the museum. It may be questioned whether the Republic's action was wise, since it is risky to move such priceless treasures about under fire. But in any case their preservation must be reckoned one of the few compensations that civilization received from the Spanish war.

By a particularly fortunate chance only two of the paintings were damaged when a truck turned over in the dash for France. These were Goyas that the world cannot spare: *Dos de Mayo,* depicting the uprising against Napoleon's troops on May 2, 1808, and *Tres de Mayo,* showing the savage reprisals taken by the French on the following day. They were only slightly torn, however, and they were so skilfully restored by the Prado's experts that it is only just possible to see where they were damaged. Otherwise the Prado collection is intact. The Goya room, with the *Maja Desnuda* on one side of the doorway, and the *Maja Vestida* on the other, is just as it was. The other masterpieces by El Greco, Velásquez, Titian, Rembrandt, and the masters of the Flemish school are also back in their original places of honour, none the worse for their travels. And the Prado is richer than ever because some of the

[1] New York: Alfred A. Knopf; 1940.

finest paintings from other collections, such as El Greco's *St. Maurice* (previously at the Escorial), were retained there on loan exhibition following the return of the paintings from Geneva.

Toledo, the city of El Greco, was similarly fortunate. The *Burial of Count Orgaz,* in the Church of Santo Tomé, is still where we may hope it will always remain. So are the paintings in the Casa del Greco. With the exception of the Mozarabic Chapel in the Cathedral, in fact, the principal damage resulting from the siege of the Toledo Alcázar was done to the fortress itself. This good fortune extended throughout the Republican zone. Many churches in the Republican zone were despoiled by foes of Catholicism—in addition, of course, to those destroyed or damaged during the actual fighting—but most of the altars, church plate, and images destroyed were of no particular artistic value. Throughout my travels in Spain I never discovered any damage to church furnishings that were sufficiently known to deserve more than cursory mention in a guide book. Gifts from British, French, and German Catholics made up for the loss if the Spanish hierarchy did not mind the fact that the Nazi donations came from looted Catholic churches in Poland. It would have been impossible for any country to make good the vast sums tied up in the solid gold and silver vessels, ornamented with pearls, diamonds, and rubies, which are guarded in the cathedrals of Toledo, Saragossa, and Salamanca, the Monastery of Guadalupe, and other church centres. But these, which were mostly in Franco territory, were unmolested, nor was any damage done to the collections of manuscripts at Seville and elsewhere.

Moreover, as a small token of the spoil that Franco could expect when he finally joined Hitler in dismembering the French Empire, the Louvre was compelled to give him two pieces of art greatly coveted by Spaniards: one was the best-known of Murillo's many paintings of the Immaculate Conception, which had been carried off by Marshal Soult in Napoleonic days; the other was the *Dama de Elche,* a pre-Roman portrait bust which was discovered in the Spanish village of Elche in the nineteenth century and was promptly bought for the Louvre by a discerning French connoisseur. The Spaniards in return were supposed to hand over French art of equivalent value, but a heart-broken curator of the Louvre finally gave up his efforts to obtain them and left Madrid in haste before Franco could think of something else for Hitler to give him at the expense of France.

But of more immediate importance to the recovery of Spain than painting and sculpture was the condition of her industrial plants. These were concentrated in Bilbao, the capital of the Basque Republic, which was captured by Franco in the spring of 1937, and in Barcelona, capital of the Catalan Republic, which held out until January 1939. The port works of Barcelona, like those of Valencia, had been damaged severely, but its factories were almost untouched. The lightness of the destruction in Bilbao, whose blast furnaces and machine shops are vital in Spain's economic life, was even more fortunate. Some of the Basque millionaires' homes near the mouth of the Nervion River had been destroyed, but damage to the economic functioning of Bilbao was limited to the six great drawbridges over the river, which were blown up by the retreating defenders in an effort to slow up pursuit by Franco's troops.

Franco's leniency toward Bilbao was understandable strategy, since he was confident of his ability to break the over-advertised "Iron Ring" of fortifications and wished to save its war plants for his own use. As I went over the well-equipped factories I found it difficult, however, to see why the Basques for that very reason had not destroyed them when they saw that they could not hold the city. As a result of their failure to do so, the factories were back in operation a few days after the capture of the city and were turning out the first matériel that Franco was able to provide for himself.

I found the explanation from people who had lived in Bilbao throughout the siege. Representatives of the Basques conferred with Nationalist generals in Saint-Jean-de-Luz, I was assured, just before the offensive was launched, and offered to make a separate peace if the Basque *fueros,* or local privileges, were confirmed. The offer was rejected, but it seems clear that there was some agreement between the Nationalists and the big business men of Bilbao whereby no scorched-earth policy would be carried out. At the last minute the militiamen sent by the Spanish Republic to aid in the defence of Bilbao did attempt to put some mines and factories out of commission, but they were stopped by Basque soldiers.

Very nearly total destruction, however, had been the fate of Guernica, which once was a little town of 5,000 people and in a few hours was reduced to little more than a heap of brick. The Basque Parliament building and the famous oak in its grounds, which are dear to the heart of every Basque, were not touched. Neither were some comfortable villas on the northern side of the town and, curiously enough, a pistol factory and a milk cannery which belonged to a known Franco sympathizer. But otherwise scarcely a building had a wall left standing more than waist-high, and most were piles of rubble, so completely demolished that it was difficult to tell where the streets had once run. One exception was the *jai-alai* hall, or *fronton.* But to stand inside the roofless buildings and look up at the blue sky was even more poignant than walking among the other ruins. Coventry and Cologne and other cities have been nearly destroyed since then, but Guernica was very near a record in its day. In my journal I wrote as follows:

*Guernica today would be a perfect illustration of the Biblical story of the Cities of the Plain. Who was responsible? The London* Times *correspondent says it was Franco planes, who dropped little bombs to drive the people into their houses, then used big ones to blow up the houses, and finally strafed the fleeing survivors with machine-gunfire. Franco says it was the retreating Basques, who at the last blew up the town with dynamite. His contention hardly accounts for the heavy loss of life or the fact that the pistol factory, certainly the most important military objective, was left untouched.*

*I have visited Guernica with a trustworthy person who tells me that he was an eyewitness of the bombing attack. He was on his way to Guernica for some reason and was about a mile away when he saw the planes circling very low. He claims that he doesn't know anything about any dynamiting. My guess is that a squadron of Göring's young men turned loose to see what would happen if they really put their Blitzkrieg theories into practice. As there were no defending planes or anti-aircraft batteries, they no doubt reported that it was like shooting fish in a barrel. Afterwards, I suppose, some of the Basque or Republican militiamen used dynamite to finish the job and prevent the Nationalists from using Guernica as a base.*

*Incidentally, despite the savage cruelty of the bombing, it was not the purposeless atrocity that it has been made out. Guernica controls one of the important crossings of the Mundaca River, which at the time of the attack stood between the Nationalists and Bilbao. Several highways and a railroad run through it, and there was the pistol factory as well. If you are impervious to feelings of humanity, these military objectives justified the attack. Even the killing of defenceless people had its use, for it seems to have softened up the morale of the troops in the "Iron Ring" considerably.*

The failure of both Basques and Catalans to destroy factories and public utilities of value to Franco was a grave disservice to the Republic's war effort, but their concern for their property greatly reduced the task of reconstruction when peace came. Some textile machinery had been ripped out in

Barcelona to make space for war industries, and what was left had deteriorated considerably from lack of adequate maintenance and the virtual absence of spare parts, but otherwise Spain's industrial equipment was almost as good as ever.

Farm land and buildings had suffered infinitely less damage than those of northern France during the World War. The irrigation works, on which production of vegetables and fruit in the rich land around Valencia depends, had remained intact. The war, it is true, cost Spain one third her livestock and considerable quantities of farm machinery. There was a deplorable shortage of insecticides, and the land had run down owing to the scarcity of fertilizer, which is used very extensively in Spain. Nevertheless, from the very nature of the case an agricultural nation can withstand wars and other disasters with more elasticity than an industrial country: the land was still there, and the landowners, who did serve the useful function of providing capital and equipment to work it, had come back as well.

On the other hand, Spain's transportation system, already inadequate, had suffered severely. Apart from blown-up tracks and bridges and deterioration from heavy war traffic, the railroads had lost sixty-one per cent of their passenger cars, twenty-two per cent of their freight cars, and twenty-seven per cent of their locomotives. The government estimated that it would cost approximately 325,000,000 pesetas ($30,000,000) to make good the damage, but the greatest difficulty was that Spain's own iron and steel industry did not have the capacity required to provide replacements, while the outbreak of the European war made it impossible to obtain the material needed from abroad even if Franco had had the foreign exchange to spare. To travel in unheated coaches, many without window-panes and infested with bedbugs, and all lamentably dirty, was uncomfortable. But the passenger trains did run; the difficulty was with movement of freight.

Even before the civil war trucks had begun to take over a

large share of the freight-carrying load because the railroads could not handle it. The excellent system of highways built by General Primo de Rivera has deteriorated considerably since peace came, but in 1939 it was in first-class condition with the exception of the Mediterranean coastal road. However, a large number of Spain's trucks and other vehicles were destroyed during the civil war, and although Franco bought hundreds from the United States during the war, they did not begin to replace those lost. In any case, most of those which he thus acquired were held for the use of the Army whenever The Day came; later the shortage of tires and gasoline, along with the bad state of the roads, aggravated these transportation difficulties.

There was also a serious shortage of labour. In addition to the hundreds of thousands of fighting men who were killed or crippled, between 300,000 and 400,000 Republicans managed to escape abroad. Most of these remained in France, and after the Armistice the majority decided to take a chance on Franco rather than be confined to a French concentration camp. Many of these were imprisoned as soon as they came back, however, and few of the remainder were permitted to work. In the autumn of 1939, according to an estimate by Vatican authorities, there were half a million political prisoners in Franco jails, and although some work was got out of them by shortening the terms of those who agreed to enter prison workshops, this was a long way from making good the economic loss resulting from their imprisonment. It was a particularly important question because the majority of the prisoners were skilled workmen. There was a companion shortage of raw materials and as a result there was at the same time a considerable amount of unemployment in certain industries.

The most severe economic difficulty was created by the fact that the Republican zone had been drained of stocks of food, raw materials, and all kinds of removable wealth that had accumulated gradually in the years of recovery from the Carlist wars. With the exception of stocks held by a few hoarders and speculators, there was almost literally no food left in the Republican zone when the war ended. It was all gone—the small amounts that a householder normally keeps in the pantry, the larger quantities in the retail shops, the still greater reserves that are maintained by middlemen. True enough, Spain usually produced more than enough to feed herself, and reserves had been accumulated in the principal food-producing sections, held by Franco throughout the war, for precisely this contingency. These, however, were not adequate. Even if they had been, the sudden responsibility of feeding Barcelona, Madrid, and Valencia was too much for the transportation and distribution system.

The shortage of raw materials also was pronounced. Here, too, stocks had been exhausted almost entirely, and large quantities of cotton, rubber, tin plate, coal, and other imported goods were needed. This condition was aggravated by the fact that in the Republican zone, at least, all sorts of things, from shoe laces to automobiles, had been missing for nearly three years, and there was a general rush to buy any articles of clothing or other consumers' goods which somehow managed to appear in the shops.

Even more disastrous for the future of Spain than these purely economic factors, however, was the loss of life during the war. According to an estimate by Franco's Census Bureau, the war cost Spain one million lives. Of these it has been estimated that only 400,000 died while in service with the armed forces on either side. The 600,000 civilians were killed in bombardments or air raids, died of hunger or privation, were executed for sympathizing with the side that was losing in their particular area, or were simply taken for a ride (Spanish has almost the same expression as ours, *dar un paseo*). As always happens in a war that is desperately fought, the death toll was especially high among the bravest on both sides. In relation to population, this was one of the highest casualty lists in modern times. Just how formidable it was may be realized by recalling that the entire British Empire lost less than a million men in the First World War.

It is true that the Spanish birth rate remained so high that Spain still had a larger population than ten years before. The 1940 census listed its population at 25,878,000, compared with 23,653,687 in 1930. This did not mean, however, that a husband or son was mourned any the less, or that his relatives hated the side that had killed him any the less. I do not believe that during the entire time I was in Spain I ever met a Spaniard, no matter what his politics, who had not lost a close relative in the civil war. The fact that black was worn almost universally was not conclusive evidence, for Spanish women, like French women, often wear black when they are not in mourning. But most of those in black were mourning. Black suited the mood of the people, grieving over their dead and the thousands of blinded and crippled soldiers.

This dark hatred that each side still felt for the other sometimes gave even visitors passing through Spain a sensation of outright fear. Civil wars are bad enough when a nation splits in two on a geographical basis. But in Spain the class issue split every section—except perhaps mediæval Navarre—and military capacity, rather than the views of the people, determined which side held a particular area. Andalucia, for example, stayed with Franco because of the superb audacity of Lieutenant General Queipo de Llano, who held Seville with 200 men. Yet the workmen of Seville, and the discontented peasants on the neighbouring estates, were Republican sympathizers. Each side therefore had a feeling of insecurity and a lack of solidarity, and to this must be attributed the primary responsibility for the large number of civilians killed behind the lines.

Another reason was the temperament of the Spanish people, who throughout history have shown themselves to be redoubtable and occasionally cruel enemies. Although generalizations about a nation's character must be made with caution, it is fair to say that Spaniards, having been toughened to endure suffering or death with more bravery than most races, also feel less pity for their foes. Even after making allowance for a certain amount of exaggeration by Protestant historians, we may feel sure that Philip II's Duke of Alba was not overgentle with the rebellious Dutch. Nor were Cortes, Pizarro, and the other conquistadores with the Indians that they fought more successfully in the New World. Little quarter was asked or given in Spain's national uprising against Napoleon, or in the two bitter Carlist civil wars of the nineteenth century. The "Bloody Week" at Barcelona in 1909 was marked by extraordinary violence on the part of the Anarchists and the soldiers who suppressed their uprising.

In the past few years, it is true, a more humane tradition had grown up. General Primo de Rivera exiled thousands of foes of his dictatorship but killed very few. Perhaps as a result, the right to start a small rebellion seemed to have become the heritage of any politically conscious Spaniard, and a short term of imprisonment or exile was the usual punishment. When I was in Spain in December 1930, almost the entire nation was protesting against the cruelty of a monarchy which had just executed two young Army captains, Galán and Garcia Hernandez, for attempting to lead a Republican uprising. (Curiously enough, Major Ramón Franco, then far better known than his brother because of a goodwill flight to South America during the Primo de Rivera regime, was the leader of a companion plot to win over the Air Force, but managed to escape to Portugal.) Humane practices seemed confirmed when the Republic displaced the monarchy in 1931 without a shot being fired. They seemed completely established the following year when the Republic smashed an attempt by General José Sanjurjo to restore the monarchy, then allowed him to go into exile in Portugal.

This more urbane tradition, however, came to an abrupt stop in the autumn of 1934, when the tough Asturian coal miners rose against the Rightist government in power. Franco, then chief of staff, brought over his equally tough Moorish troops to suppress the rebellion. Who was responsible for the ruthlessness with which it was put down is still subject to dispute. In any case, scores of the miners' leaders were executed and hundreds were sent into exile in the unhealthful Spanish colonies. As the years went by and the street fighting between Communists and fascists grew worse, so did the hatred on both sides. This hatred was aggravated by the murder of Calvo Sotelo, the ablest Rightist leader, shortly before the outbreak of the revolution.

With this bitter memory fresh in their minds, both sides showed little mercy. According to Nationalist writers, the entire garrison in the Montaña barracks, in Madrid, was slaughtered when a crowd fought its way in, a few days after the uprising began. Each side accused the other of similar massacres, and there was, unfortunately, far too much truth in these assertions.

After a time executions by Franco were placed on a more orderly basis, which was if anything more monstrous than the sporadic acts of private vengeance which prevailed on the Republican side during the first months of the war. Nevertheless, if the slaughter which took place in Republican Madrid between July and November 1936 was as it was represented to me by both Spaniards and foreigners, it also was one of the most deplorable passages in the history of a civilized country.

The evidence which I was able to obtain was convincing, though I paid little attention to the accusations made by the Franco newspapers, with their daily denunciation of "Red hordes," Marxist "assassins," "hyenas," "monsters," and so on, part of the deliberate effort by Serrano Suñer to keep alive hatred between victors and vanquished. But the testimony of many Americans and Englishmen who were in Madrid at the time, confirming the stories told me by Spaniards, seems indisputable. Several American families, in fact, lived in a relatively new real-estate development, off the northern end of the Castellana Avenue, which was one of the favourite execution grounds during this period. In this section the streets had been graded down fifteen or twenty feet below the original ground level, and in places there remain natural earth walls which are almost as straight up and down as if they had been made of brick. My friends told me of coming out morning after morning to see the ground littered with the corpses of suspected Franco sympathizers who had been stood up against the wall and shot at close range. Even today the indentations in these walls, corresponding to the height of an average victim's chest, are apparent. There are also indentations lower down from shots used to finish off the wounded. The bodies were taken down to the morgue some time during the morning. "Hæmorrhage" was usually given as the cause of death.

Over and over Spaniards have told me how they felt when they heard a car stop in front of their apartment house in the middle of night, then listened as the heavy tread of the posse came up the stairs, paused at their door, then perhaps went on to the luckless family living above them. The militiamen, pistols or rifles in hand, often were nervous when they were dealing with some grandee. Very often they could be bought off, or fooled by a trick. Many of them were simple labourers who did not relish slaughter and were impressed by a courageous bearing.

The prize story of some Spanish friends of mine was about a wealthy and eccentric old aunt who refused all offers to smuggle her out of Madrid and remained there throughout the war. This was because she had grown fond of a certain band of militiamen who often came to her house in the vain hope of finding her jewelry. She always upbraided them unmercifully, told them she had taken good care to send it to France so that the "dirty Reds" would not get it, then ordered them to stay and play a game of whist. The old lady, who had a deplorable habit of cheating at cards which long since had made her relatives stop playing with her, adored her partners. Either through timidity or stupidity the young soldiers never objected to her unscrupulous tactics, and she won their money away from them week after week.

A large number of the Spaniards I knew had been exposed to even greater danger and had extricated themselves only by displaying similar courage. Sometimes their escapes were melodramatic in the extreme. A Phalanx leader, for instance, had the presence of mind to fall as though he were dead when a firing squad failed to hit him, then made a successful dash for it. Others saved themselves no less effectively by telling a convincing story of their Republican sympathies and inventing a life history to back it up. One of my friends was a priest, member of a great Catalan family, who stayed in Barcelona for months despite the fact that a gang of anarchists was especially on the lookout for him. He simply dyed his hair, grew a moustache, dressed in workmen's clothes—and joined up with the gang which was pursuing him.

Of equal simplicity and courage was the stratagem of a grandee who worked out a method of escaping from Barcelona to France. He merely fitted himself out with a paint brush and a bucket of paint and walked north along the highway to France painting F.A.I., the initials of the Iberian Anarchist Federation, on the kilometre posts. Nobody bothered to demand the papers of a sign-painter with such zeal, and when he got near the frontier he left the road and went over the mountains with no difficulty. Some Americans who witnessed the scene told me about the device used to save a Rightist who had been smuggled to Valencia but had no papers with which to get on the ship which was to take him out of Spain. His rescuer, who was posing as a Republican official, hit upon the solution: as they approached the dock they started a loud argument. Republican soldiers immediately rushed up, as he had expected, and he explained that this man had committed a murder in Argentina, escaped to Spain, and was now challenging the authority of the Republic to send him back to pay for his crime. The soldiers immediately took the side of law and order and, without bothering to require any confirmation of the story, raised their rifles and forced the "prisoner" to walk up the gangplank to safety.

But the story I never tired of hearing was how a wealthy Spaniard had escaped being shot by the Republicans at Irún during the first week of the war. An ardent Franco supporter, he had been trying to win over an influential person to the cause. Unfortunately for him, he failed, and the incorruptible Republican had him arrested as he sped toward the border in a heavy downpour. A court martial was convened at once, and the death sentence was passed, to be carried out immediately. Seeing that it was useless, he made no appeal for clemency. But he pointed out that his clothes were wet and asked permission to change them so that he could face the firing squad in comfort. The request was granted, and with two guards accompanying him he went back to his little hotel at Fuenterrabia, a beach resort which is across a small bay from Hendaye, the nearest point in France. The militiamen, who felt shy about watching him change his clothes, lingered outside in the corridor. His window opened directly on the beach, and in a flash he raced to the water's edge and plunged in. He used to say that he had never been a good swimmer, but the shots from his angry guards gave him a strength he had never known before. He arrived on the Hendaye beach naked and exhausted but safe.

According to the Rightists whom I knew, during the early months of the war there was a reign of terror in both Madrid and Barcelona. Any servant, for example, who wanted to get even with an employer had only to go to a *Cheka,* one of the private prisons operated by some trade union or political faction, and denounce the "fascist." A squad would go out to bring in the accused, and if he was not there they were likely to bring back his son instead. Soon certain rules of safety were discovered. It was often fatal, for example, to obey the natural impulse to stay home; the concierge or a servant might notify a *Cheka* that the man who lived in such and such an apartment must be a fascist since he never went out. Any man who wore a tie or a hat, or seemed to take any particular pride in his appearance, was automatically suspect. On the other hand, women of the upper classes found that it was a mistake to wear an old tweed suit. No matter how old, its well-cut lines made them more conspicuous than if they had been wearing tawdry finery.

How many people were killed in Republican Spain in those months probably will never be known. A Franco official claimed that 40,000 were slain in Madrid and 30,000 in Barcelona, and although these figures were undoubtedly exaggerated, there is no doubt that the toll was very heavy until the Republican government reasserted its authority in November 1936. In extenuation, there is no doubt that a fifth column really was waiting within Madrid to take it over when the Nationalist troops reached the city, and that there were Franco spies everywhere who signalled to Franco's planes and fired from windows during the raids.

This terror, however, was as ineffective as it was horrible. Both Serrano Suñer and Raimúndo Fernandez Cuesta, his principal rival for control of the Phalanx, were imprisoned in those early months, but managed to get out and cross over into Franco territory. The Madrid Phalanx kept going throughout the war, and in Barcelona, which remained faithful to business principles, there was keen rivalry among the syndicates engaged in smuggling out Rightists to France; with a deplorable ignorance of the rules of fair competition, the contact man for one syndicate would claim that his organization had lost only five customers in the past month compared with ten captured from a rival who charged more.

Others escaped through the help of foreigners, for one of the strange things about Madrid during the civil war was the regard shown for foreigners and their property. The Republic, which was very lenient about this extension of the right of refuge, allowed Rightists to take shelter in embassies and legations by the thousands—Chile, for example, after filling up its Embassy, rented extra buildings and gave shelter to 1,500 Rightists until they could be evacuated. All this was done in the name of humanity, but diplomats from certain European countries required their guests to pay fantastic sums as "board." One way or another, thousands of really dangerous foes of the Republic remained hidden or made good their escape.

On the other hand, plain workmen who had offended somebody in power were taken for rides as though they had been grandees. Until my departure from Madrid the police were still publishing lists of unidentified dead who had been picked up on the streets during this period. The descriptions were of humble citizens with rope-soled shoes and cheap cotton trousers.

Thanks to the data prepared by hidden organizations of the Phalanx in Republican territory, Franco was able to make complete preparations to avenge the slain Rightists long before he brought the war to an end. He had, it is true, issued a statement that nobody on the Republican side need fear punishment if he was innocent of common crimes, such as murder or robbery, or had not held a position of leadership; those who had merely sided with the Republic and done nothing out of the ordinary were to have nothing to fear. Before the fall of Madrid, however, it was revealed that Franco had a black list of those marked for punishment. According to some versions this was composed of over a million names; according to others it was two million, but in any case this did not seem to indicate that only common crimes were to be punished.

These expectations were borne out only too well, for Franco proceeded to take a fearful vengeance. In the summer and fall of 1939 the firing squads were busy in Madrid, and I used to listen for the nightly volleys. Most executions took place in the East Cemetery, where prisoners were lined up before an open ditch, saving the trouble of throwing them in afterwards. I remember giving a lift to a Civil Guard who had just finished one of these details. His squad had killed forty, and he seemed impressed by the courage with which both men and women had met their deaths, shouting: *"Viva la República!"* Mostly, however, he was very tired of the whole procedure and wanted another assignment. Civil Guards, Assault Guards, and soldiers were all being compelled to serve on the firing squads, he said.

How many were executed by Franco after the end of the war I was not able to determine, but in the course of journeys throughout Spain I learned that operations were proceeding on the same scale throughout the former Republican zone, and that even in the provinces which were held by Franco since early in the war there were still occasional executions. Just before I reached Spain the killing of a Franco official produced the announcement that over fifty members of a "Communist plot" had paid for it with their lives.

Since 1940, however, the execution rate has declined considerably, although a number of prominent Republicans handed over to Franco by Hitler or the Pétain regime, such as Luis Compañys, President of the Catalan Republic, were shot. The collapse of France was, in fact, a great advantage to the Franco police, who were curiously slow in catching some of their most eagerly sought quarry. The Barcelona head of the Republican S.I.M. (military police), for example, was not found and executed until two years after the end of the war. And the mountains of Spain, which for centuries have hidden smugglers and guerrilla fighters alike, continued to shelter Republicans. Hundreds were at large in the mountains near Oviedo when I arrived in Spain, and the road between Oviedo and León was too dangerous to travel at night. Finally, after the local police found the task too difficult, Franco brought up a brigade of Moors who hunted them down. In the province of Pontevedra, in which Vigo is located, there were still more, and the military governor of the province finally had to issue a proclamation guaranteeing them against arrest if they would come down peacefully; they did so, and it was a bitter blow to the governor, who was an honourable man, when Franco had them killed or imprisoned despite the promise of safe conduct. There were others hiding in the mountains near Toledo, an hour's drive from the capital, as late as 1941. One day when Count Mayalde, then head of the police, was hunting partridges near there, a band of Republicans suddenly appeared and took his gun and money away from him. Fortunately for him, they did not learn his identity.

For the most part, however, the defeated Spanish people created few disorders. Except for an occasional demonstration when famine conditions became particularly acute in one region or another, they simply took what fate had done to them and waited for the day of revenge. They resented the executions less than the wholesale imprisonments, with years of waiting without trial and often without even disclosure of the charge. The wife of a Spanish journalist, imprisoned with 3,000 writers, teachers, musicians, and others in a prison outside Madrid, told me when she came to me for food that her husband had been in jail for two years without the slightest indication of what crime he was supposed to have committed.

Worst of all, however, was the system whereby every wage-earner or member of a profession, in order to obtain permission to make a living, was required to prove his unquestioned loyalty to the regime. The purifying or *depuración* was handled by the fascist syndicates, and of course encouraged vindictive and anonymous denunciations by a people already too prone to take hidden revenge. These denunciations affected only the rank-and-file Spaniards who had been entirely neutral, or, at most, mere Republican sympathizers; anyone who had really done anything to help the Republic was supposedly in jail or dead.

By this means a competitor could have a doctor or a teacher disbarred; a workman could satisfy a private grudge against another. On the other hand, there were many "Reds" (which in Franco Spain is an inclusive term applied to any type of liberal, Socialist, Communist, or otherwise, who does not approve of the regime) who managed to slip through the purifying process. The workmen were almost to a man against Franco, and it was pure caprice that disqualified one former Socialist or Communist and permitted another to become the head of his syndicate. As a matter of course, the political prisoners who by some means managed to obtain their release, and the exiles who returned to Spain after the collapse of France, also were barred from working.

The only possible recourse for these unfortunates, since emigration of men of military age was forbidden by Franco, was to obtain nondescript jobs, preferably with some foreigner who would not report them to the police. Such employment, however, was very badly paid, and at best there were few such opportunities. The remainder, with their wives and children, were condemned to idleness and hunger. Spain has no unemployment insurance system, and their only recourse was the Auxilio Social, the relief agency of the Phalanx party, whose resources were entirely inadequate to support this burden. Seldom in history has a government so deliberately set out to infuriate the conquered.

Not content with this, however, the Franco regime has set itself the task of keeping alive the hatred inherited from the civil war. Because Serrano Suñer was in charge of Press and Propaganda, he has usually been made the whipping-boy for this and other incomprehensible mistakes of the regime. But there has been nothing to show that Franco feels any differently or that his recent dismissal of Serrano Suñer indicated that the Spanish "Reds" could expect any better treatment from the Leader.

Whoever was responsible, the Spanish newspapers overlooked no opportunity to rub salt in the wounds of a nation that is more divided today than ever. Every bloody event connected with the war, including a host of engagements little known outside Spain, such as the siege of Oviedo, was recalled to illustrate the frightfulness of the "sub-humans" on the other side. Funerals of persons killed in political disputes are an accepted weapon of political warfare in European countries, and this device went to macabre lengths. Starting with José Antonio Primo de Rivera, eldest son of the former dictator and the founder of the Phalanx, Franco and Serrano Suñer ordered the remains of one dead Nationalist chieftain after another to be exhumed. Thus General Sanjurjo, who would have been chief of the Nationalist regime if he had not been killed in an airplane accident on his way from Portugal to lead the uprising, General Goded, whose blundering prevented the Nationalists from subduing Barcelona at the outset of the war, and numerous others were dug up and buried somewhere else. In addition, a huge monument to the slain was planned in a valley near the Escorial, and plans were made to preserve the ruins of the Toledo Alcázar as a memento of the strife. Each of these occasions provided an opportunity for still more speeches to remind the propertied classes how much they owed to Franco for winning the war.

When the supply of celebrities began to run out, the regime then turned to the unknown dead, and wells, ditches, and even a "death train" in which Franco sympathizers were supposed to have been entombed, were searched. With so much hatred and bitterness already poisoning the air, it might have seemed kinder to let the dead rest in peace and not rekindle the grief of parents, widows, and orphaned children. At each exhumation the public was called in to identify the remains of loved ones dead two or three years and more, and the newspapers prominently displayed photographs of the scene, with the bodies resting in their canvas sacks. They seemed to delight in such horrors, and they outdid themselves when General Moscardo, who had bravely defended the Toledo Alcázar after a captured son had been killed by the Republicans, went to Barcelona to identify the body of another son. Naturally, any father who had to go through such an ordeal would not be likely to advocate mercy for the vanquished Republicans.

Some Army officers, however, as well as a few Carlists, whose dauntless courage during the war entitled them to speak, did attempt to soften the implacable revenge taken by Franco. Always, however, their efforts were blocked by the Phalanx. This attitude of the Spanish fascists, which was at such variance with the efforts of the Nazis to win over German labour, was incomprehensible. Perhaps their unbending attitude was due in part to the desire of the many "Reds" who had obtained party membership to divert suspicion from themselves.

I remember one striking exception to this attitude. Most of the intellectuals of Spain were dead or in prison, but a few of those who had supported Franco met at the Lion Café, on Alcalá Street, facing the Central Post Office, for a few drinks and much talk before dinner. I was present one afternoon when they solemnly decided to ask Franco himself to commute the sentence of a young "Red" poet who was about to be shot. It developed that he was not only a "Red" but a bad poet as well, but they did feel a certain sympathy for him. And to the credit of the Catholic Church, many priests and nuns also testified in behalf of Republicans, although they were seldom able to obtain more than a lighter sentence, no matter what the record of the accused. No one could do more, for the slightest sign of preference for the Republic outweighed a score of positive actions, and though a father and six sons had been for Franco, the family was in danger of being listed as "Red" if the seventh had supported the Republic.

Just before Christmas 1939 I was taken as a special guest to a national congress of the S.E.U., the fascist students' organization, which met in a cold, depressing room deep within the Escorial. (Because of its connections with Philip II, the Escorial was a rallying ground for Spanish fascism even before the Founder was buried there.) A tall, black-haired youth from Murcia, a Mediterranean town south of Valencia which remained in Republican hands most of the war, got up and talked for a few minutes, then was abruptly ordered to his seat. Beginning with the chairman, almost every student present scornfully denounced him with the staccato eloquence possible only in Castilian. At that time I knew little Spanish, and after the meeting I asked what had caused the disturbance. A French-speaking student, rather embarrassed by the incident, explained to me that the Murcian had said it was time to forget civil-war hatreds and win over the anti-Franco youth of Spain. Every speaker had attacked this proposal as a Communistic device and some had pointedly warned the Murcian that he had best show more discretion in the future or he would be considered a Red himself.

Spain is the land of hatreds, where, as John Hay noted during his stay there half a century ago, a Spaniard is always ready to cut off his nose to spite the other fellow's face, and the Franco regime therefore will have a difficult task to justify its course. Both its economic and its foreign policy have been woefully misguided, but this can be ascribed to the Axis. Its policy toward the defeated Republicans is its own, and it went too far even for its fascist mentors, who on at least one occasion urged Franco to be more lenient. To this suggestion by the Axis may be ascribed the gradual decline in the number of executions and the gradual liberation of many political prisoners. But the poor who have endured these punishments so long are not to be placated, and the day of reckoning is inevitable.

# *Chapter* III

## THE RISE OF SPANISH FASCISM

When the civil war began in Spain the American public quickly jumped to the conclusion that here was a clean-cut battle between Communists and fascists. Accounts in American newspapers in fact gave these titles of opprobrium to the two sides. Later the terms "Nationalists" or "Insurgents" (whatever that was supposed to indicate) were evolved to describe the Franco side, and the Republicans were given the label of "Loyalists" by those who had accepted the Franco claim that this was not a rebellion against a democracy, but a crusade to save Europe from Communism.

It was apparent from the first that this was merely a dress performance of the Axis offensive against the democracies, but there is no question of the fact that at the outset the issues within Spain itself were much more complicated. At least a few liberals were on Franco's side because they thought the Republic had bungled the task of reform, and were confident that as soon as order and a stable government were restored, the reform program could be resumed. Many Leftist extremists in fact had joined the Phalanx, or Spanish fascist party, because they thought the Republic had been too timid in its handling of such important issues as the breaking up of the great estates. A large number of Army officers, including Lieutenant General Queipo de Llano and others who later rendered excellent service to Franco, had been ardent republicans at the start, but turned against the Republic because of its efforts to cut down the influence, and the pay, of the Army.

On the other hand, many Catalans and Basques, who were as Catholic as G. K. Chesterton and as conservative as Henry Ford, remained faithful to the Republic because it promised autonomy for Catalonia and the Basque provinces, with freedom from dictation by the Castilian bureaucrats. But as the conflict went on year after year, the influence of the moderates on both sides declined, and the fascists on the one hand, and the Communists on the other, unquestionably gained more and more control. The fascist and Communist salutes became the standard forms of greeting in the respective zones. Communism did not obtain complete control in the Republic, but by the end of the war there was no question of the fact that the Franco regime was at least as fascist as that of Mussolini. He had taken the title of *Caudillo* (Leader), corresponding to *Duce* and *Führer,* had adopted the Twenty-six Points of the Phalanx as the official program of the new State, and imposed the fascist aim of "discipline" and "sacrifice" upon ultra-individualist Spain.

This was a strange and paradoxical development, for by far the most important group of Franco's supporters cared little about discipline and were opposed to any kind of sacrifice, no matter what the regime. These were the moderate royalists, principally the landowning aristocracy, but with powerful support from the slowly developing big business interests. Associated with them were the other traditional forces of Spain, the Church and the Army. All envisaged a quick victory and a return to the good old times of the Primo de Rivera dictatorship, when strikes were suppressed and the forces of privilege had their own way.

In general, their aims went no further. Spain had been a comfortable place for them to live in before the Republic, and they asked nothing better than the restoration of the *status quo ante.* They did hope that order and good administration might be obtained simultaneously, and some of the relatively advanced Franco supporters realized obscurely that there must be a reason why Spain, with all her resources, was so obviously behind other nations: they had acquiesced in the overthrowal of Alfonso in the hope that the change of name from Monarchy to Republic was all that was needed. Their tolerant attitude, however, evaporated the moment they saw that the Republic was attempting to make some real reforms. Thereafter their attitude was more and more hostile, and the Rightist victory in 1933, while blocking for over two years any move toward abrogation of their vested interests, only increased their hostility to the Republic.

The Popular Front victory in the elections of February 1936 marked a definite turn in the tide. This time it really appeared that some effective action toward agrarian reform and a reduction in the privileges of the Church and the Army was impending. Most of the numerous strikes were settled by the new government in favour of the workers; the burning of churches and convents, and pistol battles in the streets between Communists and fascists, solidified almost the entire propertied class with the exception of ardent Catalans and Basques. The revolt of the Asturian miners in 1934 had convinced the men of property that the Communists were planning a *coup d'état* to overthrow the government, and the weakness of the Popular Front government, which seemed powerless to keep order, confirmed their fears.

On the other hand, these moderates, from the very fact that they were moderates, disliked the wild young fascists almost as much as they did the Communists. Their attitude was: a plague on both your houses, and Gil Robles, the leader of the CEDA, the strongest Rightist party, sneered that politics was too important a matter for "play-boys" (*señoritos*) such as José Antonio Primo de Rivera, the Phalanx leader. (For that reason he now finds the climate of Portugal better for his health than the fascist atmosphere of Spain.)

Although the Phalanx professed zealous regard for the Catholic Church, much of its inspiration came from Germany, where the Nazi determination to smash the Church was already becoming obvious. Other aspects of its domestic program, which in some respects went farther than any of the Republican parties, also were disquieting to the propertied class even though a few of the more sophisticated remembered that fascism always starts out with promises intended to win over the working class.

Most of all, perhaps, these moderates disliked the Phalanx's loudly proclaimed hostility to England and France and the determination to win back the *Imperio*. Being Spanish, they were convinced of their *personal* superiority over any Englishman or Frenchman—or anybody else, for that matter. But they were only too conscious that in both international and domestic affairs Spain was sadly behind both these countries. The culture and way of life of the Spanish middle class were mostly derived from France, while the more enlightened members of the high aristocracy were marked Anglophiles and wore as disreputable tweeds as you could find in the most stately homes of England. Many of them had their money invested in England and France, or in British or French enterprises doing business in Spain. The exchange of Welsh coal for Bilbao iron ore was the foundation of business life in the Basque provinces, while many of the Catalan business men had close ties with France. Whether this attitude was healthy realism or mere defeatism depends upon the point of view, but in any event most members of the propertied class were convinced that Spain was too weak to regain her position as a military power and should not bother about it.

Some of them, it is true, thought that despite the superiority of Spaniards to Portuguese, Spain could learn something from Salazar's corporative State. But they were not so much interested in the fascist technique which Salazar had used as the fact that he had restored order to turbulent Portugal, balanced the budget, and thoroughly overhauled the Portuguese bureaucracy, which hitherto had been perhaps even more inefficient and corrupt than that of Spain.

Few men are willing to die, however, for such things as a balanced budget or a well-run government, and the contribution of these moderates toward winning the war for Franco was scant indeed. Despite the charm of these people, their utter selfishness and lack of any feeling of social responsibility has justly been condemned by both the Republicans and the fascists. After Alfonso's flight into exile, for example, they roundly berated Count Romanones, Minister of Foreign Affairs in the last Monarchist cabinet, whose warning to the King that the people had turned against him finally decided Alfonso not to fight for his throne. But while the grandees of Spain were cursing both the Republic and Count Romanones from the comfort of Biarritz, the old statesman was fighting for his King and got himself elected to the Constituent Cortes as an avowed royalist. There he valiantly defended Alfonso at the "trial" of the former sovereign. And not a single member of the aristocracy that so dearly loved Alfonso had the courage to leave a card on Romanones to encourage him to keep up the fight. During the civil war only some fifty grandees of Spain died from service in the armed forces, although double that number were surprised in the Republican zone and killed before they could escape.

But there was no lack of fighting spirit among the Carlists, or Traditionalists, who constituted the next most important group of Franco supporters. The moment the war began they rushed in their red berets to Pamplona to join Mola's forces, and the Requetés were Franco's shock troops throughout the war. No softening spirit of the modern age had affected them, and their championship of the old-time Spain was so inflexible that to call them reactionaries would be sheerest understatement. They went back to Ignatius Loyola and the Counter-

Reformation; nothing less would satisfy them than the restoration of that unity of Christendom which had been wrecked by Martin Luther. By now they feared that this unity was gone for ever, but they were determined that Spain must remain as before, the sword of the Church and an unyielding foe of European and un-Christian influences. The Carlist belief in Spain's innate superiority over godless and debauched Europe had been a significant factor in the uprising against Napoleon's armies, and it had been exhibited in its pure state in the two bloody civil wars fought by the Carlists in the nineteenth century.

These wars resulted from the fact that when King Ferdinand VII died in 1833 he left the throne to his young daughter, Isabella. Whether a female had a right to inherit the throne is still disputed in Spain, but the important issue was that the regents who would rule until the young Queen's majority were too liberal and "frenchified"—which was about the same thing—for the more extreme clerical elements. They therefore put forward Don Carlos, the younger brother of the late King, as their contender for the throne, and bitter guerrilla fighting went on until 1839, when the last spark of resistance in the glens of Navarre was put out. Not even in the Jacobite uprisings, when some of the best blood in England and Scotland was spilled in behalf of the feckless house of Stuart, was so much heroism wasted on such a contemptible figure as the Carlist pretender, whose unbelievable stupidity alone prevented his cause from winning.

The Carlists rose again in 1870, two years after Queen Isabella, who had grown up to be as bad a sovereign as even Spain has known, was deposed for good. Navarre priests became some of the most noted of the great Carlist guerrilla leaders, but because of the stupidity of the new Don Carlos, a grandson of the first, six years of sporadic fighting only resulted in another lost cause. Another opportunity presented itself after the Spanish-American War, when Spain drank the cup of bitterness to the dregs, and a determined and able man might have ousted the Queen Regent.[1]

Long before the outbreak of the civil war, the restoration of the Carlist branch of the Bourbons had ceased to be a possibility. The male line did not become extinct until September 1936, but during the World War the last pretender, who was childless, quarrelled with the Spanish Carlists because of their pro-German attitude. With his death it was supposed that there could no longer be any question that Alfonso was the rightful ruler of Spain, and that the moderate monarchists and the Carlists would unite at once. But this was to ignore the depth of feeling of the Carlists, who hated Alfonso not only because he had given up the throne without a war, but because at the time he assumed the duties of King he had sworn to support the Spanish Constitution. They would have no king of Spain, ruling by divine right, who had defiled himself by making the slightest concession to constitutions and foes of the great Tradition, and his abandonment of the throne to the "godless Republicans" increased their loathing. They were no more enthusiastic over Don Juan, Alfonso's third son and heir to the vacant throne, because he had served in the Navy of their arch-enemy, heretical England.

Their "Tradition" is a concept so alien to American habits of thought that it is difficult to visualize at this distance from the Pyrenees. Probably France under the restored Bourbons, who lasted from 1815 until they were sent packing again in 1830, came as near the theocracy envisaged by the Carlists as is possible in modern times. Readers of Stendhal's *Le Rouge et le Noir* will remember what France was like in that era, when Louis XVIII and Charles X attempted to rebuild the edifice of privilege which had been shattered by the mighty upheaval of the French Revolution.

[1] One of the reasons why the government of the Queen Regent embarked upon the useless conflict was its fear that the Carlists would rise if it gave way without a struggle to the Yankee heretics.

But even Bourbon France—which lacked that admirable institution, the Inquisition, and no longer burned heretics—was too liberal for the Carlists. They were not to be placated by repeal of "Liberty, Equality, Fraternity," and could have been satisfied by nothing less than the abandonment of the whole tradition of humane letters and urbane civilization that France had brought to the world.

The Carlists, in fact, hated France almost as much as they did England, and this hatred was not so much political as religious and cultural. France and England in the course of the centuries had torn down the great Spanish Empire, but the Carlists detested them more for all that they symbolized: democracy and equal rights, no matter whether it was the Rights of Man or the Bill of Rights; the disunity of Christendom, which was equally violated by Protestant England and anti-clerical France; and the wealth and power which enabled the British and French to enjoy so many of the good things of this world.

The Carlists had a vague kind of social program, based mainly on the scriptural exhortation to servants to obey, but this was their sole concession to modern times and the Industrial Revolution. Basic in their thought was the necessity of holding fast to the old Spain, still faithful in her fallen greatness to the eternal verities. Time was when Spanish black, rather than the fripperies of Versailles, had set the style for Europe, and they demanded a return to this sobriety untainted by foreign novelties of any kind.

A certain amount of xenophobia is common to almost all Spaniards, as was ironically demonstrated during the civil war, when the propaganda workers on both sides spent much time accusing the other of trying to import such a foreign novelty as Communism or Fascism. Among the Carlists, however, the hatred of anything either foreign or new reached fantastic proportions. Strangely enough, it has provided the principal link, almost the only link, between the Carlists and the fascists, the third important group of Franco supporters.

It was no accident that the founder of the Phalanx party was a son of General Miguel Primo de Rivera, dictator of Spain from 1923 to 1930. The general's *coup d'état* was inspired as much by Catalan industrialists, who wished to copy Mussolini's new technique of breaking up strikes, as by the recurrent tendency of Spanish generals to chase out the politicians. His public works program, to which Spain owes her remarkable highway system, was copied from the Fascist regime in Italy, and so was the much less successful attempt to create a Primo de Rivera party. When Alfonso and his dictator went on a pilgrimage to Rome, the King presented Primo de Rivera to Victor Emmanuel with the words: "This is my Mussolini."

The old general, however, was neither clever nor cruel enough to live up to the description, and early in 1930 he was unfeelingly dismissed by Alfonso, who mistakenly thought that he could thereby save his throne. The help that fascist support could provide in strengthening the hold of a dictatorship was duly noted by General Sanjurjo, Primo de Rivera's commander of the Civil Guard, and General Mola, later chief of police, and they did not forget it when the time came to overthrow the Republic. They realized that times had changed, and that an old-fashioned military uprising was no longer adequate to establish a lasting regime in Spain; something more than a return to the old regime was needed and fascism was part of the answer.

But the actual beginning of the Spanish fascist movement was left to three young men of humble origins who could not expect to move in the exalted circles frequented by generals. On March 14, 1931, exactly a month before the Republic was proclaimed, there appeared in Madrid the first number of a little magazine entitled *La Conquista del Estado* (*The Conquest of the State*), published by Ramira Ledesma Ramos, a postal clerk, and Ernesto Giménez Caballero, of whom little is known except that somehow he had found the means to spend several years in Germany and had been greatly impressed by the Nazi movement. At almost the same time another pro-fascist movement was being started in Valladolid by Onésimo Redondo, who had recently been an instructor in Spanish at the University of Mannheim. Redondo's weekly, *Libertad,* was the first to introduce *Mein Kampf* to Spanish readers. The two groups merged in the following November, adopting the name of "Committees of National-Syndicalist Action" (*Juntas de Ofensiva Nacional-Sindicalista*), a title which was so cumbersome that the organization was always referred to by its initials as the *JONS*. The *Jonsistas,* handicapped by lack of money, made little progress in the years that followed.

Meanwhile José Antonio Primo de Rivera had entered politics to defend the memory of his father against attacks by Republicans, who were attempting to saddle the former regime with responsibility for all the things that had gone wrong in Spain. It appeared to the young Primo de Rivera, as it had to Sanjurjo and Mola, that the failure of his father's regime had been due primarily to its lack of popular support. By March 16, 1933, when he published the first and only number of his magazine, *El Fascio,* he was as complete a fascist as the name indicated. Only, in accordance with the spirit of the Requetés who had fought for Don Carlos, he announced that it must be Spanish fascism: "We are Fascists, because we find our origins in Mussolinian principles; we are Nazis, because in National Socialist doctrines vibrate our faith and doctrine. But we are, above all, Spaniards. The National-Syndicalist State, corporative and totalitarian, is of Spanish type. It is not a block from the Italian or German quarry. It is a Spanish creation." [1]

[1] Apart from the fact that it was bad propaganda during the civil war, the Spanish fascists object to being called fascists because of their belief that the local brand is much superior to Mussolini's. Nevertheless I use "fascist" in re-

Ledesma Ramos and Giménez Caballero had both collaborated with Primo de Rivera in publishing *El Fascio,* but the dictator's son decided to go his own way and not affiliate with their group. On October 29, 1933 he founded the Spanish Phalanx in collaboration with Ruiz de Alda, a tough aviator who had flown with Ramón Franco to South America, and Alfonso García Valdecasas, who later became the director of the Institute of Political Studies. Primo de Rivera, who was only thirty at this time, from the outset took a leading role in the new party. The attraction of the Primo de Rivera name, along with his private fortune, which enabled him to finance the new party, under any circumstances would have made this inevitable. But Primo de Rivera was a remarkable leader in his own right. Except for his capacity for grandiloquent phrases, his speeches and editorials did not, it is true, reveal any marked ability as a thinker. Ledesma Ramos, Giménez Caballero, and Onésimo Redondo, the three young men who had preceded him in spreading the fascist gospel, were clearly his intellectual superiors. The level of his attainments was illustrated by the fact that Kipling's "If" was his favourite poem, which he used to recite to his followers before going out in the street to lead pistol affrays with the Communists.

Such a choice of literature, however, was an indication of qualities which admirably fitted him for leadership of the struggling fascist movement. Primo de Rivera was endowed with remarkable physical strength and unsurpassable courage. No matter where he was, in a bar or a drawing-room, any slighting remark about his father would make him pounce upon the offender and pommel him until he retracted. Claude G. Bowers, our Ambassador to the Spanish Republic, detests

---

ferring to the Spanish type chiefly because there is no other convenient way in English to describe members or aims of the Phalanx. *Falangista* is the Spanish for a member of the Phalanx but "Phalanxist" does not exist in English.

fascism but he admired young Primo de Rivera for his devotion to his father's memory and his unquestioned bravery. For a time he was on the legal staff of the Spanish Telephone Company, and the Americans who worked with him shared Bowers's opinion.

Even more remarkable was the passion with which Primo de Rivera demanded the return of Spain's great days. The earlier fascists had shared this dream of regaining the lost glory, but theirs was the bitterness of poverty and frustrated hopes. Primo de Rivera, however, had an enthusiasm that was little contaminated by bitterness; with his battle cry: "I love Spain because it does not please me," he almost revived the burst of nationalistic fervour that had sent Spaniards to the farthest corners of the earth in the great days of the Catholic sovereigns.

Lofty motives and personal antipathies combined to make him a fascist. He hated Alfonso because he symbolized the comfortable acceptance of an inferior position for Spain in the world—and also because the King had treated his father shabbily. Although he was one of the gilded youth of Madrid, he disliked the aristocracy. They, too, were the negation of his dreams for Spain. Not only had they turned on General Primo de Rivera once the dictatorship began to go badly, but the chief of a great house had refused to allow his daughter to marry Primo de Rivera—who was a parvenu in comparison with families that traced their lineage back to the paladins who placed the Cross on the heights of Granada.

For this reason Primo de Rivera never used the title of Marquis de Estella, which he had inherited from his father, and his views on the Church and the landowners, the age-long problems of Spain, were decidedly Left-wing. Even after making allowance for the fact that such radical views are a customary part of fascist tactics, the similarity of his views to those of the more extreme Leftists was remarkable. In the spring of 1936, for example, when he was contesting a by-election at Cuenca against a Socialist candidate, he professed complete agreement with the views of the opposition on all except one point—autonomy for Catalonia and the Basque provinces.

It was, of course, impossible for anyone with the Primo de Rivera name to be accepted by the Republican parties. They were wise, for just as Sir Oswald Mosley was an extreme Socialist before he founded the British fascist party, this rich young man ended by turning to fascism as a solution. His father's dictatorship, as we have seen, had displayed a distinct fascist tendency, and this decision was made the more inevitable by the fact that Germany and Italy, the two nations upon whose help Spain would have to rely in order to realize young Primo de Rivera's burning ambition, were both under fascist control.

Despite the mixed motives that led him to take up fascism, Primo de Rivera threw himself into the battle with full and characteristic enthusiasm. It was literally a battle because the strong Communist, Anarchist, and Socialist parties in Spain all were alive to the fascist danger; street fighting was frequent. I obtained a glimpse of what Spain must have been like then during a visit to Seville, where I struck up with a young Spaniard of rather effete appearance who had been an ardent fascist "worker" from the earliest days. When I asked him what he had done, he replied in a matter-of-fact way that he had been a gunman (*pistolero*) and proudly exhibited his original membership card, signed by Primo de Rivera.

The older *JONS* could not match such aggressive leadership, and when the two fascist groups merged on March 4, 1934, as the *Falange Española y de las J.O.N.S.*, the greater vigour of the Phalanx was reflected in the fact that Primo de Rivera and Ruiz de Alda both were placed on the triumvirate which was to direct the united party; ever since then the common name for it has been the Phalanx. Even this, however, did not satisfy the imperious Primo de Rivera, and in a few months he had become sole *Jefe* and most of the leading *Jonsistas* withdrew to nurse their wounded feelings. Such was the sense of discipline in the party that was to confer this sadly needed virtue upon Spain.

Even under Primo de Rivera's undisputed leadership the fascist movement in Spain did not make much progress until 1936. He was elected meanwhile to the Cortes, but he owed his seat more to the family name than to the party, and no other fascist got in. Primo de Rivera himself lost his seat in the Popular Front land-slide, and after the long years of struggle the victory of fascism in Spain seemed further away than ever.

But the constant disorders that ensued—which were partly the result of the brawls that the fascists provoked with the Communists—then began to give the Rightists a real scare. What with peasants taking over some of the great estates in Estremadura, continual strikes, and the danger that at last the Republic would carry out some reforms, they did not know what Spain was coming to. These fears were played upon by the fascists, who constantly repeated the alleged prediction by Lenin that Spain would be the first country after Russia to go Communist, and insisted that the Communists were at that very moment plotting to overthrow the relatively harmless Republic.

This technique, which was copied straight from Rome and Berlin, produced results. Thousands of Rightists who had scoffed at Primo de Rivera now joined the party in the belief that Spain "must choose" between Communism and Fascism. And Casares Quiroga, a prominent member of the Popular Front government, further aided the Phalanx by announcing that "Fascism is the enemy." The government was so alarmed by the growing strength of Spanish fascism that Primo de Rivera and the entire high command of the Phalanx were arrested in March; the *Jefe* remained in prison until his execution at Alicante the following November.

Until the outbreak of the civil war, however, Primo de

Rivera was allowed to keep active control of the party through his brother, Fernando, who meanwhile was negotiating with General Mola and other leaders of the uprising that was being planned by the Army. At just what stage the Army decided to bring the Phalanx into the movement is still not clear, but Sanjurjo, who was in exile in Portugal, and Mola certainly wanted to let the son of their old chief have a part in it. According to Alvarez del Vayo, José Antonio Primo de Rivera and Sanjurjo went to Berlin together in February, before the elections, to solicit the aid of Hitler. The negotiations with the Army, however, did not go smoothly, and late in June an urgent message was sent to the Phalanx provincial leaders directing them to have no part in the rebellion. Several days later, however, new orders were sent out giving the password and directing full co-operation.

The failure of the uprising in Madrid and Barcelona saved the life of the Republic for the time being and brought the death of most of the Phalanx leaders; Fernando Primo de Rivera and Ruiz de Alda, for example, were killed when the Model Prison in Madrid was stormed. Raimúndo Fernandez Cuesta, who was imprisoned but later managed to get out, and Manuel Hedilla, a leader who had left Madrid to help organize co-operation with the Army, were almost the only members of the party high command who survived. Meanwhile Sanjurjo had been killed, and on October 1, 1936 Franco, who had been in the Canary Islands in the months before the uprising and apparently had had nothing to do with the negotiations with the Phalanx, was named generalissimo. This change of command threatened to prevent the fascists from winning a prominent position in the uprising, for Franco was not bound by a sense of obligation to the Primo de Rivera family, and since he was a devout Catholic, there was likewise no reason for him to approve of the Left-wing tendencies of the Phalanx. If the war had ended quickly enough to save young Primo de Rivera from a firing squad, there are few things on earth more certain than that he and Franco would have parted company very quickly. Franco, the military dictator of Spain, would not have been the one who lost the contest.

For, despite the phenomenal growth of the Phalanx between February and July, it probably had less than 100,000 members when the war broke out. Most of the fascists preferred to remain a considerable distance from the front, and if it had been merely a question of mobilizing the fighting strength of the Nationalist zone, the Carlists, who hated the fascists, and whose courage was beyond question, would have been much more useful to Franco. For a time Franco wavered between the fascists, the Requetés, and several other youth movements sponsored by various Rightist parties.

On April 19, 1937 Franco issued a decree "unifying" the Phalanx and the Carlists and adopting the Twenty-Six Points of the Phalanx as the official program of his regime. The word Traditionalist was added to the name of the Phalanx, which thereafter was referred to as the F.E.T. de las J.O.N.S., and as a further sign of this "union" of incompatible elements the Carlist red beret and the fascist blue shirt were combined to make the official party uniform. Thereafter the news reels of the world were seldom without views of Franco holding up his hand in a passable imitation of Hitler or Mussolini.

Pressure from the Führer and the Duce was the principal reason why Franco took this lamentable decision. It was now clear that the war would last a considerable time, and, in contrast to the large quantities of gold from the Bank of Spain which were available to the Republic, Franco had very little money. If Germany and Italy would not send him matériel, and troops as well, he had no chance to win. And Hitler and Mussolini were unwilling to provide sufficient help unless he proved his loyalty by adopting their type of regime.

Adoption of the Phalanx program also was urged upon Franco on the ground that it would give his supporters something more to fight for than merely another military dictatorship without even a king to help rally support. For reasons which are still obscure, Franco from the very first made clear his opposition to the restoration of Alfonso, and Don Juan's application to join Franco's army was refused. If no restoration of the monarchy was promised, the average Spaniard had a right to ask whether the Nationalists had any program whatever beyond the overthrow of the Republic.

Finally, there were the not unrelated facts that Serrano Suñer, then known merely as Franco's brother-in-law, escaped into the Nationalist zone in March 1937, and that soon afterwards the disputes among the surviving Phalanx leaders, and between the fascists and the Carlists, passed all previous bounds. Fascist writers have revealed, in fact, that the internal Phalanx disputes were brought to a head by the arrival of Serrano Suñer, who, although not until now a member of the party, had been a close friend of Primo de Rivera and had designs on the leadership. At about the same time Cuesta also arrived in Nationalist territory, and Franco, who had to decide whether he would adopt fascism, also had to choose between the two contestants.

It may be assumed that Franco realized he could not hope to conduct the war and govern the home front as well, and that Serrano Suñer seemed an ideal choice to take over most of the job. Like Jew Süss in Feuchtwanger's novel, Serrano Suñer had no strength of his own and it was easy to believe that he would not dare to create trouble.

Cuesta, therefore, was given the position of secretary general of the party, which on the surface was the most important post, and was made Minister of Agriculture as well. Serrano Suñer was content with the Ministry of Interior (later renamed Ministry of Government) and the title of president of the Political Committee of the Phalanx. But by this means he won control over both the police and the Auxilio Social, the Nationalist relief agency, and with these weapons in his hand he began his rapid rise.

That he was destined to be master of the Phalanx was obvious from the start, and Manuel Hedilla, the only member of the fascist high command besides Cuesta who had reached the Franco zone, promptly tried a Captain Röhm type of putsch to forestall it. He swaggered over to Franco's headquarters to demand a show-down, but the generalissimo's Moorish bodyguard disarmed his escort, and Franco's answer after hearing him out was to order his imprisonment, from which he was only released in 1941, over four years afterwards.

Bickerings between the old guard of the Phalanx and Serrano Suñer's group have continued ever since, but the brother-in-law steadily increased his hold. Both Spaniards and the outside world came to regard Serrano Suñer as the entire Phalanx, and his dismissal in September 1942 from both the Foreign Ministry and the presidency of the Political Committee produced premature rejoicing. Thus far, however, there has been no sign that the fall of Serrano Suñer portends the liquidation of fascism in Spain though the fascist party is detested by the generals, the aristocracy, and all except the fascist wing of the Catholic Church. And, of course, by an overwhelming majority of the Spanish people, although they have nothing to do with the march of events.

But these forces seem powerless as long as the Germans are at Hendaye, ready to march in should Franco make a move to rid himself of the Phalanx. From the very nature of the case, Hitler must do everything to keep Spain under his control. The Spanish fascist party is his agent, although it is not, of course—for this is Spain, which yields its fealty to no outsider—quite so completely dominated by him as the fascist movements in Norway and other conquered nations. The overthrowal of Hitler, and probably Franco as well, may be necessary in order to cleanse Spain of this blight.

# Chapter IV

## THE FASCIST EL DORADO

The Spanish fascist movement which fought the foreign influence of Soviet Russia so bitterly was itself an imported product. The entire principle of a rigidly disciplined nation, with one order of chieftains rising upon another, and all commanded by the Leader, came jointly from Italian and German fascism. So, of course, did the fascist salute, even though the Spanish fascists insisted upon referring to it merely as "the raised arm" (*brazo en alto*). The symbolism was a little muddled with regard to the yoke and arrows, emblem of Ferdinand and Isabella, which was adopted as the sign of the Phalanx. This was supposed to recall the great Imperial days of Spain, but the bundle of arrows was at the same time the equivalent of the bundle of rods which symbolized the Mussolinian dispensation.

There is no question of the fact that Italy was the original inspiration of the Spanish fascists. Mussolini had taken a Latin, Catholic nation, which in its softer way is as individualistic as Spain itself, and cured it of parliamentary government, strikes, and other annoyances. He had done more: he had taken a weak nation and given it the appearance of such a formidable military power that the British turned tail in 1935 when Mussolini sent his troops into Ethiopia. What the Italians had done the Spaniards could do much better, the early fascists believed, and this confidence was strengthened by the underlying contempt which Spaniards held for Italians even before Guadalajara.

Italian Fascism nevertheless was a very useful source of both ritual and doctrine. The continuous chant of "Franco, Franco, Franco" with which the Spanish air resounds was an adaptation of the Roman *"Duce, Duce, Duce."* Etiquette among the several fascist movements compelled Primo de Rivera to select the *camisa azul,* but this navy blue was so near the pure black shirts of Italy that Mussolini had grounds for charging plagiarism. The officials of the Phalanx, in their tunics, riding breeches, and boots, all black, were not distinguishable at all. The custom of stencilling portraits of Franco (very fat-jowled, and with a helmet clearly Made in Germany) and Primo de Rivera in public places was another importation. So was the reiteration of pat phrases from the writings and speeches of the Fascist Founders.

More important still was the ideological basis of Spanish fascism, almost all of which came from Rome. The Spanish fascists borrowed the notion that Spain (*cum* Italy) was the successor of the Roman Empire. Stripped of its elegant verbiage, this boiled down to the idea that Europe once was united in the Catholic Church, and that it was the pernicious work of the Protestant Reformation, aided by Voltaire and Jean Jacques Rousseau, that destroyed this unity. It was to be the task of Spain, whose Most Catholic Kings had been the most powerful sovereigns of Europe, to restore it to the world. These aspirations were not, however, incompatible with the claim that Spain (*cum* Italy) also was fated to be the Protector of Islam [1] and the aid and comfort of the Mohammedans in Morocco, Algiers, and elsewhere. The Mussolinian interpre-

[1] Santiago, the patron of Spain, as is well known, was of the greatest service in expelling the Moors. But no fascist saw anything incongruous in the fact that Franco made a special point of taking his Moorish bodyguard with him to Santiago de Compostella when he went there in the summer of 1939 to render thanks to the saint.

tation of Pope Leo XIII's encyclical *De rerum novarum,* and of Pope Pius XI's later *Quadragesimo anno,* also was grist for the Phalanx mill.

Nevertheless, there was always an underlying preference among the Spanish fascists for Germany; and the poor showing of the Italian expeditionary force which fought during the Spanish civil war confirmed it. Long before that, in fact, Spanish nationalists had looked to Germany for inspiration. Ideological considerations apart, this was inevitable. For Germany, despite her defeat in the World War, remained the embodiment of order, discipline, efficiency, and the capacity to subordinate individual interests to the interests of the Reich, the very model of everything that Spain was not but must become in order to regain her position as a great power.

The Germans had started with few of the great advantages —natural frontiers, a position dominating the principal trade routes, rich colonies, and unrivalled mineral resources—which were Spain's. Yet an industrious, intelligent people, ably directed by an authoritarian government (the Spanish fascists, despite their lip-service to the Catholic Church, ignored the fact that the Hohenzollerns were Protestants, as well as Hitler's enmity for Christianity), had twice in twenty-five years felt bold enough to challenge the combined strength of Britain and France. And anyone who has noticed the difference between the neat efficiency of a German post office and then tried to send or receive mail in Spain must concede that Spain could learn much from beyond the Rhine.

Moreover, as good friends should, Spain and Germany did not live too close together and had not had too much to do with each other. England, France, and the United States had had dealings with Spain that roused nationalist Spaniards to indignation at the very mention of Gibraltar or Cuba. On the other hand, Spain had had the best of it in her relations with Germany in the past. While the Reich was still divided into hundreds of petty states, Spain had already achieved her national unity. Spaniards could glory in the memory that their Charles V had been Holy Roman Emperor, and until the fall of the monarchy Spain retained the German double-headed eagle in her coat of arms even though her German possessions had been lost with everything else.

Moreover, once Germany emerged as the greatest land power of Europe, her interests led her to support Spain against the other great powers. At Manila Bay the German squadron threatened to take a hand in behalf of the Spaniards; in the long-drawn-out wrangles over Morocco which followed, Germany supported Spain against England and France. Always fulfilment of Spain's imperialist ambitions was clearly dependent upon German help against the democracies. For England and France, the age-old enemies, had gradually whittled down the power of Spain in the centuries since the Invincible Armada, and the United States finished it off. Meanwhile Britain and France made it their business to prevent a revival of Spain's strength, or so the Spanish fascists were convinced, and they used their military and industrial strength to reduce Spain to the status of a colony. Spain's railroads and mines, for example, were almost all developed by British and French capitalists.

These had no desire to see a strong, aggressive government in Madrid, and in earlier and more clear-sighted days London and Paris never hesitated to give effective help to maintain a friendly regime in power. A moment's reflection would have shown the Spanish fascists that by exchanging German domination for that of England and France they were jumping from the frying-pan into the fire. But Hitler's propaganda had cast its spell upon them as it had upon the British and French. Spanish zealots were intoxicated by the sense of partnership with the Nazis, who so clearly were to be the masters of the world; *Arriba,* the Madrid organ of the Phalanx, after the collapse of France hailed the Goth and Vandal invaders of Spain as proof that the nation's martial prowess was derived from this antique Teutonic strain.

The ideology of the Phalanx was, to be sure, little affected by this scramble to get on the Nazi band wagon. In one important respect the Franco regime was, in fact, entirely at variance with the gospel of *Mein Kampf*. Spain was almost as much the melting-pot of peoples as the Balkans, and the Spanish fascists did not attempt to create the mythos of a super-race. Anti-semitism, along with other hateful things, was revived under Franco despite the fact that the Jews in Spain long since have been assimilated and only a handful practice their religion. But the pretext, at least, was on the same religious grounds that first impelled Ferdinand and Isabella to expel the Jews from Spain, and the Phalanx doctrine called for a truly catholic disregard of race.

On the other hand, German influence was apparent in the Left-wing program of the Phalanx, which found expression in its red and black banner, and the near deification of Primo de Rivera. (The cult of the Founder, however, seemed to owe more to the Soviet glorification of Lenin than to the Nazi heart-throbs over Horst Wessel.) From the Nazis came Spanish fascism's claim that the series of disasters which finally had isolated Spain behind the Pyrenees was due to a league of treacherous foes both abroad and within Spain. Above all, the might of Germany, which subsequently crumpled the vaunted French Army at the first blow and swept over all Europe with lightning speed, fired the imagination of the Phalanx. The influence of Italy steadily waned, and officials of the Phalanx, the Auxilio Social, the police, the learned professions, and in fact everyone who mattered in Franco Spain went continually on pilgrimages to Berlin.

The best statement of the aims of the Franco regime is contained in the Twenty-Six Points of the Phalanx. (Originally there were twenty-seven, but the last point, demanding that young men under forty be given leading positions in the government, was not accepted by Franco, who was then forty-five.) The domestic part of this program envisaged the conversion of Spain into "one gigantic syndicate of producers," and a mass of reforms including the nationalization of banks, breaking up large neglected estates, more irrigation works, and so on.

Thanks to the inefficiency of the regime and the opposition of the privileged classes, little has been done in this direction. To all intents and purposes, Spanish fascism consists of three points: the renewed subjugation of all Spain to Castile (it will be noted that the party was organized in Madrid and Valladolid, the latter being the place where Castilian is said to be spoken with a purer accent than anywhere else in Spain); the Empire; and cutting loose the bonds which connected Spain to England and France and, in general, to the main currents of European civilization. It was this program that inspired the *gritos de ritual* with which all public gatherings in Spain were ended: The speaker, arm raised in the fascist salute, would shout: *"Spain!"* and the crowd would shout back in unison: *"One." "Spain!"* he would repeat. *"Great!"* was the response. *"Spain!"* again, then: *"Free!"* And all together: *"Up Spain, viva Franco!"* It will be useful to examine these aims as stated in the official declaration.

### ESPAÑA UNA

1. We believe in the supreme reality of Spain. To strengthen it, elevate it, and improve it, is the urgent collective task of all Spaniards. In order to achieve this end, the interests of individuals, groups and classes will have to be remorsely waived.

2. Spain is a destined unity in the universe.[1] Any conspiracy against this unity is abhorrent. Any form of separatism is an unpardonable crime. The existing constitution [of the Republic], in so far as it encourages any disunity, commits a crime against the

[1] I am using the official translation, as published in Arthur F. Loveday's *World War in Spain* (London, 1939), despite its occasional clumsiness.

destiny of Spain. For this reason, we demand its immediate abrogation. . . .

25. Our movement will incorporate the Catholic spirit—of glorious tradition and predominant in Spain—in the national reconstruction. The Church and the State will arrange a Concordat defining their respective spheres. But the State will not permit any interference or activity which might lower its dignity or the National integrity.

*From the Twenty-Six Points.*

This oneness included Portugal, of course, although the Franco government naturally disclaimed any such intentions whenever the Portuguese government protested against an over-explicit threat by *Arriba*. For the time being, however, the fascists were limited to Spain, which was not one but several nations despite over four centuries of unified government. The continuance of this exaggerated regionalism was due in part to the mountain barriers, which made internal communication difficult and permitted local customs to remain almost unchanged; also Spain's poverty prevented her from developing an adequate system of state schools, which would have gradually broken down these differences. As a result, Catalonia still retains its own language, which is perhaps as close to Provençal as to Castilian. The Catalans certainly have as much in common with the French of the *Midi* as with Castilians, and the poems of Mistral, the Provençal poet, helped produce an important revival of Catalan literature in the late nineteenth century.

The Basques, too, had their own language, which did not bear any resemblance whatever to Castilian; although Basque literature did not attain the literary distinction of Catalan, the Basques had had a considerable cultural and political awakening. The home-rule movement had even spread to faraway and backward Galicia, Franco's birthplace. The *Gallegos*, who talked and acted like the Portuguese, hoped that home rule would give them the railroads which Castile had failed to provide. Aragon and Valencia, following suit, also developed home-rule movements, and the fascists contended, with some justification, that unless the movement was checked there would eventually be nothing left except Castile, Andalucia, and Estremadura, the most backward and poverty-stricken areas.

General Primo de Rivera had helped bring down his regime by destroying Catalonia's home rule, and the party which his son founded advocated even sterner measures. All power must be centralized in Madrid, and the use of any other language than Castilian was to be forbidden. Also marked for destruction were the ancient *fueros* or special rights which Navarre and the Basque provinces had received centuries before. Unquestionably this intransigent attitude of the Phalanx had something to do with the decision of Catalonia and of the two maritime Basque provinces, Guipúzcoa and Vizcaya, to side with the Republic when the war broke out. The third Basque province, Álava (in which Vitoria is located), and Navarre supported Franco.

The statement concerning the fascist policy toward the Church needs little comment. It was adopted, according to the official Phalanx historians, over the strenuous opposition of many of the fascist extremists, who considered it much too friendly. At that, it was a clear warning to the Church that in a fascist regime it would cease to be a dominating influence.

### ESPAÑA GRANDE

3. We have a will to empire. We affirm that the full history of Spain implies an empire. We demand for Spain a pre-eminent place in Europe. We will not put up with international isolation or with foreign interference. With regard to the Hispano-American countries, we will aim at unification of culture, of economic interests and of power. Spain claims a pre-eminent place in all common

tasks because of her position as the spiritual cradle of the Spanish world.

*From the Twenty-Six Points.*

It was the belief of the Spanish fascists that imperialistic adventure would unify a divided people. They contended that Spain's decadence was hastened, at least, by the gradual loss of the Empire, which caused Spaniards to confine their energy to affairs at home, breeding disunity. A good war was their solution for these difficulties. This ambition was held mainly by the Phalanx. The Carlists hated England and France, which was a start, but it was impossible for a clique which turned its back upon the outside world to build an empire.

As for the moderates, they had no interest in "a pre-eminent place" for Spain in Europe or Latin America. Some would have been glad enough if England one day had handed back Gibraltar, but they saw only too well that the Rock would be useless without a navy to keep it up in the style to which it was accustomed, and such a navy meant higher taxes. Some Army officers dreamed dreams of adding the rich African colonies of France to the barren strip along the Mediterranean that is Spanish Morocco. These putative gains, along with Gibraltar, would give Spain control of the Strait, and from there it was easy to imagine the course of empire. But the terrible disaster of Anual in 1921, in which Spain lost 10,000 men in a battle with the Riffi, was not very encouraging. Even though French help later enabled Spain to finish the conquest of Morocco, the more competent officers saw that Spain still did not have the industrial production required to wage modern war.

The strength of the nations who stood in Spain's path was a further deterrent to imperialist adventure. The British were determined to hold Gibraltar and to keep other nations from interfering with Portugal, a semi-protectorate. France would hold to her African possessions with equal determination, and the fascists expected the United States to invoke the hated "Monroeism" against their ambitions in Latin America. Therefore the only hope of attaining these conquests was by joining the Axis band wagon, which commended itself on fraternal lines in any case. It was obvious that Germany sooner or later would crush the arrogant "pluto-democracies," the fascists believed, and Spain had only to wait for her moment. When it came, as *Reivindicaciones de España* revealed, Spain would take all of French Morocco, and part of Algeria, including Oran, giving an unbroken stretch of territory sweeping north and northeast from below the southern boundary of Río de Oro, already a Spanish colony, to a point about halfway between Oran and Algiers. This would give Spain the vital stretch of coast on the northwest corner of Africa, and would permit her to dominate sea and air communications leading from Europe to the Western Hemisphere and the Far East as well.

These aspirations were supported by the usual claims of prior discovery, large Spanish elements in the population, and other arguments which are customary when one nation wants territory owned by another. In addition, there was the unusual contention that Spain had been specially designated by both Providence and the Nazi science of geopolitics to unify Europe and Africa. In other days Spaniards had resented the French taunt that Africa begins at the Pyrenees, but now the fascist school of expansion gloried in the idea as justification for its dreams of empire. The fascists pointed out that there was little difference in the people or the land on either side of the Strait,[1] and they claimed that Spain was destined to be a sort of half-way house to interpret Europe to Africa by ruling as much of it as could be obtained.

1 The long Moorish occupation undoubtedly had a strong effect upon Spanish customs and temperament, apart from the considerable amount of Moorish blood to be found in inhabitants of Valencia and other regions of southern Spain. In moments of anger Spaniards sometimes call one another Moors, with perhaps some justification.

The fascist aims, however, ranged much farther than the Gates of Hercules. The authors of the *Reivindicaciones* were particularly disturbed lest someone should "stupidly or maliciously" assume that this was all they wanted for Spain. "In this work," they declared, "it was intended to proclaim above all else *the necessity of a foreign policy for the motherland* [fascist italics]. And Africa, although it is one of the indisputable bases of that policy, is not the only one or even the most important: Spain lives in a peninsular symbiosis with Portugal, the flesh of her flesh and the original key of her existence. At one and the same time Spain looks out upon the Atlantic and the Mediterranean. Finally, Spain is the head and spinal column of the Hispanic world scattered over the globe. For our generation has nothing to do with doors half-opened. One by one it wishes to open all, destroying at the same time the wall of lack of understanding and fear with which a certain door, once open, has been sealed up. Our uneasiness must watch all horizons and slopes. Spain cannot limit her new foreign policy to the circumscribed space of a parallel or a meridian."

Exactly what these veiled references meant in detail is not worth puzzling out, but the general implication is clear.

Such statements were repeated so often that even such a hard-bitten soldier as General Varela, Serrano Suñer's bitter enemy, finally was converted. In the dark September days of 1940, when it seemed that Britain would be crushed by Nazi air raids and the Nazis would be masters of Europe, General Varela remarked to a friend of mine that although he welcomed a German victory, it was fortunate for the world that there would be one great power left to check Hitler. Asked whether he meant the United States or Russia, Varela replied that he meant neither. Spain, he said, was destined to organize the twenty nations of Latin America into a powerful bloc which would counterbalance Nazi might.

ESPANA LIBRE. ¡ARRIBA ESPAÑA!

4. Our armed forces on land, on sea and in the air, must be as efficient and numerous as may be necessary to assure Spain's complete independence at all times and that world leadership which is her due. We shall restore to the armies on land and sea, and in the air, all the dignity which they deserve and, following their ideal, we shall see to it that a military view of life shall shape Spanish existence.

5. Spain will seek again her glory and her riches by means of the sea. Spain must aspire to become a great maritime power for her defence and for her commerce. We demand for our Motherland an equally high standing for our Navy and our Air Force.

*From the Twenty-Six Points of the Phalanx*

This program is so completely a copy of the usual fascist aims that it requires no extended comment. Spain's war potential does not permit the attainment of these ambitions, and she must depend upon the might of Germany. This was virtually admitted by Serrano Suñer in the course of the interview with the *Völkischer Beobachter* referred to at the beginning of this book. Spain, he declared, was now "enjoying complete and absolute independence" for the first time in two centuries—presumably a reference to the accession of the Bourbons in 1700. But in the same breath he announced that the *Imperio* "is not in these days the work of one alone, but the enterprise of several wills agreed upon the proposition to give a certain norm and order to the world." Germany and Italy had suffered from the same unjust treatment, and he emphasized the solidarity with them of Franco, who "at the right time" would decide Spain's policy. Spain's understanding with Germany and Italy, he said, was perfect because "not one of their rights conflicts with ours."

Explaining Spain's claim to Gibraltar, Serrano Suñer emphasized that this was not incompatible with his statement that Spain had no territorial claims in Europe. For "it is not correct to call a territorial claim the restoration of what is owed to us out of elementary justice and constitutes a part of the living and torn flesh of the motherland." As for French Morocco, "the geographical position of Spain, and her tradition as the projection of one continent toward another, contain natural demands which only a decadent policy could abandon. . . ."

"We have no other claim," Serrano Suñer went on. "But one should not fail to recognize our will to project a moral influence into Hispano-America and restore the prestige of Spanish culture in opposition to the attempted usurpation of another culture, putting the same generous spirit in this task that Spain placed when she gave her blood, her force, and the best of her spirit in the work of discovery, conquest, and evangelization. In this sense, our claims are also for America [as used in Spanish, this refers solely to the portion of North and South America discovered by the Spaniards] in order to defend the rights of these sister nations."

The fascists realized, however, that even though the Germans would provide the airplanes and tanks needed, and probably do most of the fighting, Spain would have to provide one foundation for her empire—the will to conquer it. There is a limit, of course, to the height to which a nation can raise itself by its own bootstraps. If the difficulties are insuperable, unlimited amounts of chauvinism cannot make it a great power. But Spaniards are a brave and enduring race, and despite the centuries of military disasters, the hard fighting of their civil wars showed what they were still capable of when they had a cause in which they believed. And Spain's geographical advantages, which had given her a head start in the early days of colonization, were still there. The difficulty was that Spain did not have the "will to empire," the determination to obtain "world leadership" which the Phalanx demanded, rightly enough, as a prerequisite.

When the fascists looked into this matter they discovered that the Spanish-American War was a turning-point in the history of both countries. Our victories at Santiago and Manila Bay had brought the tardy recognition, by ourselves and other nations, that we were one of the great powers of the world. Either Schley or Sampson—it was a nice problem to decide which deserved most credit—had annihilated Cervera's fleet, and our word was law in the Western Hemisphere and even in a remote archipelago in the Pacific. In the burst of jingoism which followed we ignored the reaction of Spain, which had provided us with the occasion for these triumphs.

When the war was over, the Spaniards learned, as Salvador de Madariaga writes in his study of Spain, that Admiral Cervera had been ordered to his doom off Santiago "knowing that he would have neither base, nor coaling station, nor transport ships, nor any of the most elementary requisites for a fleet to exist, let alone fight." Not even the bravery of their ill-equipped soldiers and sailors was sufficient to avert the loss of Cuba, Puerto Rico, and the Philippines, and the power which had discovered and colonized most of the New World no longer owned a foot of territory beyond the seas. It was the end of a long road.

The reaction was all the greater because Spain's defeat was no isolated phenomenon. For centuries her power had been declining, and it was only surprising that she had held on to the remains until 1898. Now, however, she had definitely lost her position in the world, and there ensued a period of self-examination which perhaps hurt even more than defeat. Ángel Ganivet and Joaquin Costa, later joined by Miguel de Unamuno and José Ortega y Gasset, stood out among the writers who sought to determine what had brought Spain down. Detailed examination of the findings of this "Generation of '98" lies outside the scope of this book. Costa, for example, insisted that Spain must Europeanize herself, and coined the slogan "School and Larder" to emphasize the practical aims which he considered necessary for a national revival. Ganivet, on the other hand, insisted upon the permanent and eternal virtues of Spain and contended that the disasters resulted from the introduction of foreign "novelties" in thought and customs.

The diverse lessons that they drew, however, agreed upon one point: Spain must abandon thoughts of empire and develop her own neglected resources.

The ensuing period of material development was separated by an immeasurable gap from the tragic and heroic days of Philip II, but it undoubtedly was the only policy open to Spain at the time. The coming of age of Alfonso XIII in 1902, after the long and disastrous Regency, inaugurated a period of relative peace and internal order during which Spain made considerable material progress and began to establish some approach to efficient and orderly government.

It was small consolation, but at least Spain was now relieved of the excessive burden of maintaining a fleet and army to defend the Empire. Both her capital and her ablest young men, most of which had automatically gone out to the Indies in the old days, now began to stay at home and grow up with the country. The result was an unprecedented increase in Spanish manufacturing, particularly in textiles, chemicals, and machinery. Ironically enough, Spain, having had few ships while she had an empire to trade with, acquired quite a respectable merchant marine after she lost it.

Yet another beneficial result was the development of better relations with Latin America. While Spain still owned even one colony, her administrators were a definite liability and her former subjects always feared she might try to reconquer them. After 1898, however, it was obvious that she was too weak to do any harm and that the United States was much more of a threat. As a result, relations with the mother country began to be more friendly. Paris continued the intellectual capital of every Latin-American country, and they traded mostly with England, Germany, and the United States. But they did begin to feel more kindly disposed toward Spain, and there were many banquets at which Spaniards and Latin Americans spoke of the Castilian equivalent of hands across the sea. October 12, which we in the United States call Columbus Day, came to be celebrated in Spain and many Latin-American countries as the "Day of the Race."

This, however, was a long way from regaining the lost Empire. A practical spirit, the opposite of the fierce ambition that had sent out Cortes and Pizarro, de Soto and Valdivia, now dominated Spain. Rivalries between England and France gave her an opportunity to strengthen her foot-hold in Morocco, but the opposition to the resulting war, which dragged on continuously from 1909, demonstrated that Spaniards had at last interested themselves in the prosaic task of making a living instead of winning and losing empires.

It was precisely this practical and realistic attitude that the Phalanx had to eliminate in order to develop the will to empire. To inspire the Spanish people with the will to start fighting the heretics again was the great problem. For many reasons this was a difficult task, but perhaps the greatest obstacle was what the fascists claimed was the "black legend," allegedly invented by foes of Spain to discredit the achievements of Spanish explorers and administrators. This had produced a belief among the more advanced Spaniards, at least, that the loss of the Empire had been due to the cruelty, unsound economics, and general undesirability of Spanish rule—that, in other words, Spain had deserved to lose it. The history of Spanish conquest and colonization in Latin America has been mostly written by American or English historians, such as Prescott, or by Creoles filled with local patriotism who condemned Spain at the same time that they exalted the achievements of their own people. Neither group had been notable for its friendship toward Spain, and both had cited the complaints of Father Las Casas and other critics of Spanish cruelty and inefficiency with telling effect. It was necessary above all to counteract this "black legend," whose most harmful influence was found among the Spaniards themselves.

In 1934 Ramiro de Maeztu, an able newspaperman who had worked his way through intellectual anarchism, English-model liberalism, Nietzschian doctrines of the superman, and Guild Socialism before ending up as a fervent Catholic, published an important book, *Defensa de Hispanidad,* exalting the contribution of the Spanish Empire to Catholic civilization. By *Hispanidad,* a coined word which has only been admitted to the Spanish language since Franco took Madrid, Maeztu meant the qualities that are the essence of things Spanish, the Spanish race, the Spanish language, the Catholic religion, a whole way of life. Under his influence Spanish historians began to look more kindly upon Spanish rule, to point out the wise and humane laws of the "Council of the Indies" which governed Latin America, and to emphasize the gulf that separated North America, with its Protestant, English-speaking, Anglo-Saxon civilization, from *Spanish America* or *Ibero-America.*

Maeztu's teachings were taken up immediately by the Phalanx, which at the same time was exalting the greatness of Spanish achievements in Europe back in the days when Spain ruled Portugal and the Low Countries, Sardinia and Sicily, Franche-Comté and Roussillon. Soon, however, a logical objection developed: if Spain's rule had been so perfect, why had she lost her Empire in Europe, why had her colonies in the New World revolted?

This problem was very much the same which confronted Hitler when he sought to explain the defeat of Germany in the World War. The answer was exactly the same that the Führer offered: Spain had been defeated by the alliance of perfidious Albion (the grand old phrase is used in Franco Spain in utmost seriousness) with the despicable French and the barbarian Yankees. Yet even this, Spaniards were assured, would not have been enough to bring her to ruin but for the treason of un-Spanish elements which had stabbed the motherland in the back. This point of view found its best expression in Giménez Caballero's *Genio de España,* (fourth edition, Barcelona, 1939); according to Caballero, Spain had had no fewer than thirteen " '98's," or crushing defeats, beginning with the Treaty of Westphalia in 1648 and culminating not in the Spanish-American War—though of course that was included—but the 1930 agreement among Republican leaders to overthrow the monarchy. With the inauguration of the Republic, Giménez Caballero said, "Napoleon entered Spain again to the sound of the *Marseillaise,* the hymn of the French Empire."

The following passage from Caballero, who took part in Franco's successful offensive against Catalonia in the early months of 1939, gives an indication of a good fascist's state of mind when his regiment reached the French frontier:

> On February 10, 1939 God gave me the glory of raising the Spanish flag at Port-Bou, on the last peak of the Pyrenees. And there, kissing the flag, I shouted to my comrades of the Fourth Navarre Regiment: "At last there are Pyrenees." [1] Because the history of Spain can be told in one phrase: There are Pyrenees or there are not. . . . When we were friends of England and France, our age-old enemies, Spain ceased to be Spain, to have frontiers (the path from 1700 to 1936). We have barely begun to recover the old and fecund Romano-Germanic contacts.

This theory was elastic enough to account for almost any conceivable disaster. According to it, whenever England or France, or both, were not fighting Spain, they were weakening her with "foreign novelties" which corrupted Spain's pure customs. Carlists and fascists could unite upon this theory, if nothing else. It was applied with remarkable ingenuity, par-

[1] Fascist Spain often twists around Louis XIV's famous boast, made in 1700, after the imbecile Charles II, last of the Spanish Hapsburgs, had willed the throne to the grandson of the Sun King. This action was expected to bring Spain under the rule of France—as it would have but for the intervention of England.

ticularly to the loss of Latin America. Until its invention it had been very hard to explain the promptness with which the colonies, ignoring the ineffable blessings of *Hispanidad,* had revolted the moment that Spain's grip was weakened. Bolívar and San Martín had seemed to care very little about the fact that they were of the same race and religion and spoke the same language as Ferdinand VII. France could be blamed indirectly, since the Napoleonic Wars had weakened Spain; the British warned off the Holy Alliance when it attempted to recognize the revolted colonies. It was still not enough.

With Maeztu's aid it was now discovered that the American colonies had revolted, not against the reactionary government of the Bourbons, but against the un-Spanish liberties brought in by Napoleon's armies. According to the new interpretation, the better elements in the colonies could not tolerate such abominations in the motherland as constitutions, manhood suffrage, and Freemasonry, all of which gained a hold in Spain as a result of the invasion. Therefore the Creoles had revolted, not against Spain, but against the un-Spanish regime which, as all right-thinking people know, had been imported against the wishes of His Most Catholic Majesty.

According to this explanation, by the time the correct absolutist principles were restored in Spain it was too late and the independence movement had got out of hand. The patricians in the revolted colonies wished to return to the bosom of the motherland, but the local Freemasons and their friends blocked such a wise decision, while the Freemasons and Republicans in Spain aided and abetted. There is a fractional amount of truth in the new revelation: like the American Revolution, the revolt of Latin America was partly a civil war. The amount of objective truth in it, however, matters little. The important thing is that the fascists believed it and have now imposed the doctrine upon Franco and the other ruling forces in Spain. It forms the basis of the Hispanidad program in Latin America, which exists mainly to fight the United States, although it is equally useful as a means of whipping up feeling against England and France. More than any other doctrine of the Phalanx, it proves the utter uselessness of any attempt by the United States to appease Franco.

# *Part* II

# AWAKENING TO REALITY

## *Chapter* V

## CONFLICT WITHIN THE NEW ORDER

Fortunately for Spain and ourselves, Spanish fascism carries the seeds of destruction within itself. Anyone who doubts it has only to study the continuous wrangling within the Phalanx and the violent disputes between the party, on one hand, and the Monarchists (both the moderates and the Carlists), the Church, the Army, and conservative influences in general, which have continued from the beginning of the civil war to the present day. Only the steady nerve of Franco, and, since June 1940, the presence of German troops on the frontier, have prevented these conflicts from breaking into open revolt. His method has been to remain in the background until one side or the other went too far, suddenly intervene to right the balance, and as suddenly withdraw again to the comparative quiet of his country residence. This technique, which was not unknown in New Deal Washington, is probably the only course open to Franco, but it is a long way from settling the fundamental problems of Spain. It has been equally ineffective in winning any solid base of support for his regime. Because of the Phalanx and its foreign allies, each of the strangely divergent forces that combined to support the uprising has failed to get its way on one important point or another, and his government, despite its iron suppression of opposition, probably has less popular support than any other in the world today.

It is not possible yet to give a unified account of Franco's government since the end of the civil war. Fundamental issues of domestic or foreign policy have been inextricably intermingled with personal ambitions and quarrels among generals and party leaders who, because of the black curtain of the Spanish censorship, are little known to the American public. Franco's supporters were and are united on only two things: their enmity to parliamentary government and their determination to prevent a comeback by the "Reds"—an inclusive term which would include the Spanish equivalents of Herbert Hoover and Wendell Willkie as well as Norman Thomas and Earl Browder. Spanish individualism, moreover, is carried to such lengths that it is seldom possible to say that the "Army" or the "Phalanx" wants to do this or that. A majority may be found in favour of a certain program, but others, disliking its sponsor, will be bitterly opposed. Here an attempt will be made to summarize Franco's policies with regard to some of the most difficult domestic problems which he has had to face.

Foremost among them was the treatment of the defeated Republicans. The sufferings and slaughter which the civil war inflicted upon Spain had left an inevitable bitterness among both victors and vanquished. All the different groups supporting Franco had their dead to mourn, and it was probably inevitable that thousands of Republicans were executed and hundreds of thousands imprisoned in the months that followed the end of the civil war. Typical of this attitude was the thirty-year term meted out to Julian Besteiro, a moderate Socialist whose only part in the war had been to join in the eleventh hour *coup d'état* which made possible the occupation of Madrid without bloodshed.

This rough justice was imposed by Army courts martial, and as time went by the Army leaders grew sick of these killings and began to urge clemency upon Franco. Perhaps they realized that after all there was not so very much difference between the *miliciano* and their own soldiers. In any case, common sense dictated the release of the prisoners if only because the barracks in which many were held were needed to accommodate troops.

The fury with which the Phalanx demanded the blood of the "Reds" was almost unbelievable in view of the fact that at the same time it was endeavouring to win over the working classes. A vast program of cheap vacations at the seashore, Sunday joy rides in airplanes, visits to art galleries, and so on was projected by "Education and Rest," a party activity which was modelled directly upon the Nazi "Strength through Joy." Little of this program materialized, but the party relief agency, the Auxilio Social, which was copied from the Nazis' "Winter Help," did an admirable work in providing food and clothing for penniless Republicans. Thousands and tens of thousands of families whose wage-earners were dead, in prison, or in exile would have died of hunger but for the Auxilio Social. So would the dependents of workmen who were at liberty but were disqualified from holding jobs. Auxilio Social officials even claimed that they refused to inform the police of the whereabouts of hunted "Reds." Whether they carried their impartiality so far I cannot say, but in the course of inquiries from one end of Spain to the other I never heard a complaint that the Auxilio Social refused its pitifully small rations to anybody because of his political views.

The conflict over the policy to be followed in making good the material damage done by the civil war was similar in some respects to that which raged during the early years of the New Deal in the United States. President Roosevelt's objective was recovery from the depression and reform of the abuses which had helped produce it, but critics insisted that over-emphasis on reform was holding up recovery. In Spain the business men, who were intent upon patching up the economic machinery and getting it started somehow, complained that the Phalanx was so intent upon its dreams of future military and industrial greatness that it delayed recovery.

The fascist influence also was responsible for the formulation of an elaborate autarchy program, which, although it has accomplished some good, on the whole has been a mistake. Still more important was the elaborate system of exchange-control and regulation of all forms of business life which was set up in order to bring about a planned economy along fascist lines. In view of the governmental inefficiency, this in itself was deplorable. But it was not all. In order to punish the Catalans and Basques for having sided with the Republic, a sustained effort was made to favour the industrial development of other areas despite the fact that Catalonia and the Basque provinces are more progressive and better equipped to continue as the workshops of Spain. Enraged by the endless red tape and favouritism with which they have to contend, many of Spain's business men have been growling ever since 1940, at least, that "this gang is redder than the Reds."

The incorrigible inefficiency of the Franco regime also has delayed recovery. Three years have gone by since the civil war ended, but the poor are still living in the shell-torn huts adjacent to University City. It would have been possible to patch up many of them and make them reasonably comfortable, and one day I asked a young official of the *Direccíon General de Regiones Devastadas* why this had not been done. He looked at me with the smile of compassion that zealots reserve for those of an alien faith, then proceeded to show me the plans to rebuild this section to the heart's desire.

Instead of a collection of small one- and two-room houses there was to be a huge modern apartment building, and the extra land thus made available would provide playing fields, flower gardens, and countless other amenities denied until now to the poor of Spain. The planning of this project was excellent, and the design for the complete rebuilding of Guernica, with architecture of a type well suited to the rainy climate, was even better. But in the desire to make these plans even more perfect, work had not yet been started on either.

When I left Spain, a beginning, at least, had been made on Guernica and I suppose it is now well along toward completion. But Guernica was destroyed in the spring of 1937, and during the five years that they were waiting for a super-Guernica to be rebuilt, its inhabitants had to crowd into the homes of near-by peasants or sleep on the ground. It was a heavy price to pay for perfection. Latest reports say that the Madrid project is still on the draughting board.

Nowhere has the influence of the Phalanx upon Franco's policy had more disastrous effects than in the ruthless measures taken against Catalonia and the Basque provinces which sided with the Republic. Apart from economic discrimination, publications in either Catalan or Basque have been forbidden. Neither language is taught in the schools or used in the courts; priests are even forbidden to conduct services in the local language. Most of the Basque Republicans were conservative and devout Catholics, and so were some of the Catalans despite the strength of the Anarchists in Barcelona. But all, without exception, have been lumped under the term "Red Separatist." For months Franco's *Official Bulletin* every day recorded sentences imposed upon Basques who had taken no active part in the war.

A typical "crime" had been committed by a husband and wife who had given their children Basque names and talked Basque with them. They were condemned *in absentia* to the loss of half their property. Pious Basque peasants who spoke no Spanish, had no interest in the war, and had stayed on their farms were denied interpreters at their trials and were sometimes given jail sentences for having once belonged to the Basque Nationalist party. I was never able to obtain direct confirmation of reports that Nationalist forces shot some of the Basque priests who had supported the Basque Republic. Trustworthy Basques insisted to me, however, that Franco had imprisoned a number of priests after the capture of Bilbao and Santander and that some of them, at least, were still in jail years after the war. In any case, it is a fact that Cardinal Vidal, Archbishop of Tarragona, and the Bishop of Vitoria were not allowed to return to Spain after the civil war because of their respective "Red Separatist" views on home-rule for Catalonia and the Basque provinces.[1] This dispute was patched up to some extent during the Concordat negotiations, but the intransigent attitude of the Phalanx toward the Basques and Catalans has had disastrous effects upon the regime's relations with the Church, with the Carlists, and above all with its supporters in the two most progressive industrial areas in Spain.

Phalanx influence was powerless, however, to prevent the complete restoration of the Church to all the power that it had held under the monarchy and more besides. Divorce was abolished, and so was civil marriage (unless both parties could prove that they had not been baptized Catholics). Either party to a divorce obtained under the Republic was permitted to have the case reopened. The Jesuits, who had been expelled by the Republic, were allowed to return and were given back their huge property holdings. The annual State payment to the Church, which had been considerably reduced by the Republic, was restored to 62,000,000 pesetas (about $5,400,000). The Church schools which had been closed by the Republic were reopened. Religious instruction became compulsory in the State schools, and pupils, as in the sixteenth century, began the day with a salutation to the Virgin recognizing the Immaculate Conception.

An extremely severe *ex post facto* law, punishing anyone who had ever been a Freemason unless he recanted and revealed the secrets and membership of the order, was decreed. Church dignitaries, headed by Cardinal Gomá, Archbishop of

[1] In December 1941 the Vatican finally succeeded in obtaining permission for Cardinal Vidal to return to Spain.

Toledo and Primate of Spain, were assigned the most prominent positions at all public functions. One or two Protestant churches still managed to keep open in Madrid and Barcelona, but the British and Foreign Bible Society's stock of Testaments and of booklets of excerpts from the Scriptures was destroyed on the excuse that the paper was needed to help make more paper for essential publications. To the casual observer, Spain was as completely back in the fold as in the days of the Counter-Reformation.

The Phalanx was considerably less enthusiastic about the Church, however, than this indicated. From the Nazis it had absorbed a hostile attitude toward any kind of international organization—of which the Church was obviously the most powerful. Although the struggle was quieter than it has been in Germany, it was no less determined; the party leaders realized only too well that they would have to drive the firmly entrenched Church from its position before they could make a true fascist state.

Only the weakness of the regime and the influence of Madame Franco, who is a devout Catholic, has kept the quarrel from breaking out into the open. And fascist influence was at least strong enough to carry on a rear-guard action. Serrano Suñer's censors did not allow the Vatican newspaper, *Osservatore Romano,* to circulate in Catholic Spain, and when he visited Rome in the fall of 1940 he violated all the rules of conduct laid down for a Catholic statesman by refusing to ask for an audience with the Pope. Franco even established a fascist Youth Front, copied from Hitler's, which was intended to bring up Spanish boys and girls within the party rather than in Catholic youth organizations.

The Church, however, was alive to the danger that the Youth Front represented, and at the start virtually made the decree a dead letter. Its strength was demonstrated impressively in the dispute between the Phalanx and Cardinal Segura, Archbishop of Seville, over the erection of memorials to the dead on the Nationalist side. Elsewhere throughout Spain the list of names was painted upon the outside wall of the parish church, with a cross and an inscription honouring Primo de Rivera above it. Cardinal Segura, however, who had been expelled by the Republic for his monarchist views, was not a prelate to change them; he did not believe that the cult of a dead fascist had any place on the walls or anywhere else connected with churches, and he did not permit the inscription to be placed on a church in his archdiocese. *Arriba* attacked him openly, but he did not give way, and attempts by the fascists to obtain his dismissal got nowhere.

The triumph of the Church was completed in the summer of 1941 by an agreement over appointment of bishops, which had been one of the most bitterly contested issues between the Vatican and mediæval kings and was still hotly disputed in Spain. Under Alfonso, the crown had nominated three candidates, from whom the Pope made his selection. The anticlerical Republic, however, did not care to exercise its right of "presentation," and the Vatican, although it had supported Franco, refused to hand it back to him. The champion of the Catholic world was informed that the right of presentation belonged to the King of Spain, and that as Spain now had no king, the situation was just as it had been under the Republic. Members of the Phalanx complained bitterly that the Church, having gained back every privilege which it had enjoyed under the monarchy, also was attempting to keep the additional power which it had obtained from the Republic. They pointed out, accurately enough, that Franco had thrown away his bargaining power by doing everything the Church wanted without exacting anything in return.

By that time, however, such reflections were too late, and some settlement had to be reached. No bishop had been appointed since the first days of the Civil War, and nearly half the bishops had died since 1936; the vacant sees were being administered by apostolic delegates. The death of Cardinal

Gomá brought matters to a head. Franco was too weak to hold out, but signing of the agreement was delayed until the summer of 1941 by the search for a formula that would spare the regime unnecessary humiliation. As finally arrived at, it provided that Franco would present candidates for bishoprics, the Vatican would select those acceptable to it, and Franco would then make the appointment. But the Vatican was not bound in the slightest by his nominations, and it could put anybody it wanted on the list of candidates to be submitted to Franco. Obviously (it was an old mediæval practice) there was nothing to prevent the Vatican from naming the one candidate it desired and filling up the list with others who were completely unacceptable to Franco. The blow was softened by the Vatican's acceptance of the Bishop of Salamanca, a Franco adherent, to succeed Cardinal Gomá as Primate, but there was no question of the fact that Franco lost the battle.

The Spanish aristocracy, which is extremely Catholic, bitterly resented the attitude of the Phalanx to the Church. But unlike the business men of Barcelona and Bilbao, the landed aristocrats of Spain otherwise had little real cause for complaint against the Franco regime, which addressed itself to the work of undoing any damage to their interests that they had suffered from the Republic. This was not large. The grandees had been frightened by talk of breaking up the great estates, but they had managed to sabotage the Republic's first Agrarian Reform Law and the second was just getting into operation when the civil war began. Only a few hundred thousand acres had actually been taken over, either in accordance with law or as a result of the movement among the peasants in the spring of 1936 to seize the land without waiting for the slow operations of the government.

The test of any Spanish regime was its attitude toward this fundamental question, and it may be supposed that some of the grandees had anxious moments when Franco adopted the

Phalanx program with its demand for land reform. Carlists and moderate royalists together, however, proved more than strong enough to prevent the regime from harming the interests of the landowners. All land which had been occupied by the peasants, legally or otherwise, was returned to the owners, and soon there was no longer even any mention of breaking up the great estates. Instead emphasis was shifted to private irrigation and drainage projects, under government sponsorship. Until the end of 1942, at least, there was no indication that anything whatever had been accomplished by these, although no doubt there were as many elaborate plans as there were for the rebuilding of the devastated towns and cities of Spain.

Although the price of agricultural products fixed by the government did not always please the landowners, their only serious complaint was the new tax schedules drawn up by José Larraz, Franco's able Minister of Finance (now out of office). With a few exceptions the great estates were paying the same taxes that they had in 1885, when the price of farm products was much lower, and Larraz proposed that all the land in Spain should be re-assessed so that it would come nearer meeting its share of the cost of running the government. The revaluation scheme was so elaborate, however, and the opportunities to hold it up were so numerous, that there seemed no prospect that it would take effect for several years if ever.

In general, the old nobility, fighting very much the same type of fight that it had under the Republic, managed to keep the Phalanx from hitting its pocketbook, but otherwise had little or no say in the government of Spain. A few of the more energetic noblemen were in the Army, but only a handful were members of the plebeian Phalanx, and very few held positions of importance in the civilian government. The principal exception was the Duke of Alba, who is Franco's Ambassador in London. Like Cardinal Segura, he was constantly under attack from the fascists and has escaped dismissal only because of his high prestige with the British aristocrats, who could not forget even if they wanted to that he is a descendant of an illegitimate son of James II and holds the British dukedom of Berwick.

Franco's refusal thus far to restore the monarchy is the most convincing proof that the aristocracy, despite its expectations, did not control the regime. Alfonso got back his estates, as the nobility had, but not his throne. There was dispute over both the monarch and the type of monarchy which were to be restored, but it was obvious that fascist influence would be weakened by any sort of restoration. The moderates and some of the more enlightened Carlists were too realistic to envisage an absolute monarchy. Certain concessions to modern times were inevitable, and they desired an amnesty, a free press, and the ultimate restoration of parliamentary government. Naturally, they expected to deal themselves a winning hand; under a restored monarchy a large number of Leftists would be disqualified, and they intended to give the king the right to collect taxes and run the government without parliament if the opposition forces became unruly.

Primarily, however, the monarchists wanted to eliminate fascism, enabling Spain to adopt a policy which would permit her to obtain the food and other necessities that she needed from the democracies. The restoration would be the next step, but it was necessary to unite on a candidate. For years after the establishment of the Republic the monarchist movement had been handicapped by the objections of both Carlists and some moderates to Alfonso. Early in 1941, therefore, Alfonso sent a representative to Madrid with a letter offering to stand aside in favour of his son, Don Juan, if there was no other way to effect a restoration. For a time ducal visages in the Ritz Bar were more cheerful than at any time in the past ten years. Some of the more fervent monarchists, in fact, seemed to really believe that they would be bowing low to an anointed king in a few weeks.

Their hopes were dashed when Franco received the royal representative and told him that no restoration could be expected at that time. Whatever reasons Franco may have had, it was obvious to anybody but a grandee that Germany would not tolerate such an action and that the troops at Hendaye would swiftly stop it if it were attempted.

The death of Alfonso a few weeks afterwards, however, not only gave Don Juan an undisputed claim to the throne—uniting moderates and Carlists—but provided the opportunity for an informal plebiscite on the fascist regime which gained in impressiveness from the fact that, unlike the Hitler type, it was genuine. Within an hour after the death of the King became known the members of the nobility were hastening to the Ritz Hotel, residence of Don Fernando of Bavaria, the ranking member of the royal house in Spain, to express their sympathy by signing the visitors' book in the lobby. For two days the line of callers stretched out on the sidewalk. Mourning banners, bearing the escutcheons of Spain's great families, were displayed from the town houses of Madrid, and although a mysterious order of the government held up the sailing of the ship which was to take hundreds of royalist sympathizers to Rome for the funeral services, others got there by plane.

Far more important were the home-made banners which were displayed by the working people of Madrid and other cities throughout Spain. National mourning was decreed by Franco, but this time no warnings from the police, which were customary and necessary to evoke the proper air of rejoicing on fascist holidays, were needed to induce the humble Spaniards to show their feelings. Even the poorest hung out the national flag or a sheet with Alfonso's portrait pinned to it if they had nothing else with which to show their feelings.

These banners did not, of course, indicate any grief for Alfonso. The poor were still Republicans, but they saw that unless they received help from outside, the monarchy was the only hope of ridding Spain of the Phalanx and regaining some limited form of free government. It was remarkable what accurate information shopkeepers, taxi-drivers, and the miscellaneous citizenry of Madrid had concerning Alfonso's letter—which of course was not published—and other moves of the royalist leaders. This indicated that the underground Republican organization was in touch with the royalist group. Supporting this supposition was the fact that the working people—with an understanding of realities beyond most of the nobility—insisted that nothing must be done now. The least disorder, as they said, would bring in the Germans.

In subsequent months there have been frequent negotiations between royalist leaders and Don Juan, but the Germans are still at Hendaye and nothing happened. In the summer of 1942 it was reported that Franco might at last accept his restoration, but as the reports came from Berlin it is possible that this was some subtle move of Nazi propaganda. It is difficult to believe that the Nazis would consent to the return of Don Juan, even if he agreed to accept a role similar to that of Victor Emmanuel. And the uncompromising opposition of the Phalanx to any restoration was demonstrated by numerous clashes with the Carlists both during the civil war and afterwards. Serrano Suñer's police were kept busy painting out the signs of *Viva el Rey* which appeared every week or so on the monument around the corner from our apartment.

A year before his death a special church service arranged by the monarchists on Alfonso's name day produced a vivid scene illustrating this still unsettled conflict between fascist and aristocratic Spain. After the service the courtyard of the church was crowded with members of the nobility bowing and curtsying as they took their leave of the Infantas. Suddenly three tough young *Falangistas* appeared from nowhere, elbowed their way into the centre of the dignified gathering, and gave the fascist battle cry: "*¡Viva Franco! ¡Arriba España!*"

Except for a few faint hisses of disapproval, the bluebloods of Spain contented themselves with staring. But if looks could kill, the trio would most certainly have been candidates for a fascist funeral.

Parallel with these conflicts over policy were the continuous jurisdictional disputes between the different branches of the government striving for supremacy in amorphous Spain. Of these there were at least four and in addition, even bureaucrats within the same ministry fought continuous paper wars. Frequently questions of policy also were involved, and the result was a formless and limping government whose inefficiency had to be seen to be believed. A detailed description of the numberless cases of overlapping jurisdiction would leave the reader as confused as the Spaniards were themselves, but it will be useful to examine the principal divisions of the government over which Franco nominally exerted control:

1. The Army was the foundation of the regime. Eight captains general exercise the supreme authority in as many military regions, which are comparable to the corps areas of the United States Army. They are supreme commanders of the armed forces in their districts, and their activities are unchallenged, theoretically at least, by the civil authority. Also members of this military hierarchy are the military governors of the provinces contained in their zones. Its control over the daily life of the people is considerable because of the fact that Spain is still under martial law. Not only political prisoners but ordinary murderers and highway robbers are tried by court martial. The principal responsibility for keeping order rests upon the Army, and for this reason, the Civil Guard, or national police of Spain, has been transferred from the Ministry of Government to the jurisdiction of the Army. As time has passed, Franco has depended more rather than less upon military courts. When extraordinary efforts, for example, had to be taken in 1941 to repress sabotage on the railways, they were given authority to have saboteurs executed on the spot.

A few months later, when the civil authorities proved powerless to suppress the black markets, the military courts were given jurisdiction, with authority to impose the death penalty for violations of the rationing laws.

2. Next came the civilian government, which is one of the most highly centralized in the world today. Harking back to Philip II, who felt it necessary to regulate in minutest detail the operations of his officials in far-away Peru, the Minister of Government names mayors and other officials in the most obscure villages throughout Spain. Franco consistently supported this policy of centralization, which was responsible for many of the complaints by Basques and Catalans against Madrid in the old days. As we shall see, it produces much more dissatisfaction now because of the accompanying attempt to set up a controlled economy, for which both speed and knowledge of local conditions—both lacking—are required.

The Ministry of Government, which is an expanded version of the old-time Ministry of Interior, has almost a monopoly of regular government activities that come in contact with the ordinary citizen. Under it are the police (with the exception of the Civil Guard), administrative agencies, the posts and telegraphs, the public health service, and the bureau in charge of reconstructing devastated areas, to name only a few. Each of the fifty provincial governors (including one for the Balearics and two for the Canary Islands) is appointed by the Ministry of Government, and they are shifted about frequently to prevent them from developing excessive attachment to any province. In the old days they exercised a considerable amount of authority, but in present-day Spain most of their functions have been taken over by the Army and the Phalanx. They devote most of their attention to the operation of the food-rationing system.

3. Independent commissions, loosely connected with the regular government departments, or completely autonomous, are numerous. Prominent among them are: the commission

in charge of returning to Spain the child refugees who had been sent by the Republic to France, England, Mexico, Russia, and other countries; the agency which distributes food and other rationed articles (the Spanish OPA); the special courts to enforce the rationing laws (which as we have seen were partly superseded by the Army in 1941); and the "Tribunals of Political Responsibilities," to try disloyal citizens whose offences are not grave enough for a court martial.

4. The Phalanx, following the Nazi precedent, is almost a government within itself, with its own militia, rationing system, police, foreign service, and so forth, and with provincial chiefs whose duties merge with those of the civil governors. Serrano Suñer, as president of its Political Committee, or supreme council, was entitled to a seat in the cabinet independent of his position as Minister of Government and subsequently Foreign Minister.

The Secretary General of the party also held an ex-officio seat in the cabinet. On the other hand, the Minister of Labour is in charge of the organization of vertical syndicates under direction of the Phalanx.[1] This overlapping was increased by the fact that the party undertook responsibilities which in other countries would have been entrusted to regular government departments. For example, the Auxilio Social, which is a semi-autonomous unit of the Phalanx, was placed in charge of relief and of orphanages. To the Feminine Section of the party, which, being headed by Pilar Primo de Rivera, a sister of the Founder, was more closely under party direction, was assigned the campaign to reduce infant mortality and to provide visiting nurses for the poor. Even more important was

[1] By a decree of June 23, 1941, the entire economic life of Spain was to be organized into "national syndicates" of the Phalanx, grouped in the following classifications: cereals; fruits and horticultural products; olives; wine; beer and beverages; sugar; wood; cattle; fish; leather; textiles; confectionery; metal trades; chemical industries; fuel; water and electricity; paper, printing, and the graphic arts; transportation and communications; hotel-keeping and catering; insurance; banks and markets; entertainments; colonial products.

the decree of May 1941 by which control over censorship and propaganda activities of all kinds was entrusted to the party's Vice-Secretariat of Popular Education.

In the beginning these various activities were financed from party dues, tag days, sales taxes, one-dish days, and so on, and the national treasury made up the difference. Later, however, as more and more government activities were undertaken, the collection system was changed. All receipts except from party dues were ordered paid into the national treasury, and the State subsidy was increased accordingly.

A basic weakness was the fact that Franco was the only means by which these varied and overlapping agencies could be co-ordinated. As commander-in-chief of the armed forces he had supreme jurisdiction over the Army and the captains general. As chief of state and his own Prime Minister he directed the regular departments. The independent agencies reported directly to him. Finally, as national *Jefe* or chief of the Phalanx he was theoretically in charge of all its various activities. But only the ruthless efficiency of a Göring could have brought order out of this chaos.

A certain amount of confusion is inevitable in any fascist state, as is demonstrated by the fact that even in Germany there have been frequent conflicts between the Army leaders and the Nazis. In individualistic Spain, however, these quarrels raged with unique violence. Within the Phalanx, for example, there was a particularly bitter feud between the Feminine Section and the Auxilio Social, because the latter, which provided special food for pregnant women and nursing mothers, also wanted to assume responsibility for the delivery of babies, which was supposed to be a monopoly of the Feminine Section.

Equally widespread were the disputes between the Phalanx and the other governments of Spain. These persisted even in instances where Serrano Suñer's dual position as master of the

Phalanx and Minister of Government—prior to his taking over the Foreign Ministry—might have been expected to eliminate duplication. The Public Health Service was in his own Ministry and was doing excellent work with the small amount of money it received, but Serrano Suñer nevertheless proceeded to give the Feminine Section of the party authority and much larger funds to do the same thing. With more justification, in view of the slowness of his agency for reconstructing devastated regions, he also empowered the Phalanx to set up its own housing agency. Temporary barracks were thrown up by the Phalanx in a surprisingly short time, and although they were far removed from the perfection sought by the old-line agency, at least they were realities and not mere gleams in the designer's eye.

As Serrano Suñer's control over home government gradually increased, he was enabled to iron out most jurisdictional disputes with comparative ease. The Phalanx and the Army, however, did not get along, and as independent forces have fought ever since the end of the war. With the exception of a few officers, such as the swaggering General Juan Yaguë, the Army detested the Phalanx. Soon after the end of the civil war General Queipo de Llano made a speech denouncing the Phalanx and Serrano Suñer, and although it did not appear in Serrano Suñer's newspapers, the speech caused such a scandal that Queipo de Llano was exiled to Rome—under the guise of making him head of a Spanish military mission to study the Italian Army, for which the general held the most complete contempt. The still undestroyed influence of the Army over Franco was demonstrated by the fact that after Serrano Suñer replaced Beigbeder at the Foreign Ministry, the protection of General Varela saved Beigbeder from arrest by Serrano Suñer. And the Army's unyielding opposition was principally responsible for the dismissal of Serrano Suñer from the Foreign Ministry in September 1942, though Varela had to go too.

# Chapter VI

## FRANCO AND THE SPANISH LAVAL

Vichy France and Franco Spain offer obvious points of resemblance, and nowhere are they more pronounced than in the close parallel between Laval and Serrano Suñer. It is difficult to decide which has done more to injure his country; although, because of the vast consequences of France's surrender, Laval has been a more useful agent for Hitler, Serrano Suñer has made the most of his less extensive opportunities to harm the cause of freedom. Both seek to bring their countries into the war on Germany's side, both are likely choices as Gauleiters when Hitler finally takes over these vassal states. And just as the fall of Laval in December 1940 produced premature rejoicing among those Americans who still favour appeasement, the fall of Serrano Suñer in September 1942 was interpreted by the same people as a triumph of Anglo-American diplomacy. But Laval re-emerged when Hitler decided that circumstances required it, and so will Serrano Suñer—or a more effective partisan of the Axis—when the Führer believes that it is time.

That Laval was imposed upon Pétain by Hitler seems clear, but at the beginning family ties were mainly responsible for the even stranger association of Franco and Serrano Suñer—and they played a part in their separation. The soldier and the politician married sisters, and the lives of millions of Spaniards have been made still more miserable in consequence. Seldom in history have two men of such opposite temperaments been thrown together, but the affection which the sisters felt for each other somehow bridged the gap between the corpulent, smug Franco and the thin, nervous brother-in-law. The sufferings of present-day Spain are a family achievement.

Franco was born in El Ferrol, Spain's great naval base in isolated and rain-swept Galicia, in 1892. He came of an old Navy family, and although his elder brother Nicholas (now his Ambassador to Portugal) became an engineer, while the youngest son, Ramón, later won fame as an aviator, "Paquito" was destined for the Navy. The examinations for the naval academy were cancelled, however, as a result of the destruction of the Spanish fleet in the war with the United States, and Franco went into the Army instead. His record at the Toledo Academy was good, though not brilliant, but he soon distinguished himself in the war with the Moors, and when he won his stars at the age of thirty-two he became the youngest general in Europe.

During this period of his career, according to his official biographers, he had distinguished himself for daring courage, he was twice wounded, and he became the idol of Spain's Moorish "Regulars." At the same time, however, his careful study of the terrain and painstaking staff work had marked him as an authentic son of Galicia. For the *Gallegos* are renowned in Spain for their calmness and slow deliberateness, which make them the butt of numerous jokes by the quick-witted Castilians. As second-in-command and organizer of the Spanish Foreign Legion, founder and first superintendent of a new military academy at Saragossa, and later as chief of staff of the Spanish Army, he apparently was a good organizer and executive.

Although official accounts of his career seek to give the impression that for years he took no part in politics, and only assumed the leadership of the revolt as a result of the "anti-Spain" attitude of the Republic, it is inherently impossible for a Spanish general not to be a politician and an orator as well. At first his interests were entirely in Morocco, where he dreamed great dreams of Spain's future domain, and he almost mutinied when General Primo de Rivera, convinced that Spain's resources were inadequate to deal with Abdel-Krim, ordered the abandonment of everything except the fringe of the coast which Spain had held when she began the conquest of Morocco in 1909. The Saragossa Academy was dissolved, and Franco, though still not a national figure, was left without a command for over a year after the Republic took charge. His part in the suppression of the Asturian revolt, however, made him only too well known, and when the Popular Front came in he was made military governor of the far-away Canary Islands.

It was from there that he wrote to the Popular Front's Minister of War protesting against the government's measures to reduce the size and trouble-making capacity of the Army. The tone of the letter was clear warning of his intentions, but the Popular Front leaders seem to have thought that he was too far away to make trouble. They had forgotten the airplane, and thanks to the enterprise of an Englishman with fascist sympathies who chartered a special plane, Franco reached Morocco and rallied both the Spanish and the Moorish troops there to the Nationalist uprising.

His success in landing his forces in Spain was of the greatest service to the Nationalist cause, but Franco would not have reached his present position but for Sanjurjo's accidental death. In October 1939 Franco assumed the supreme command, and thereafter the Nationalist campaigns bore the imprint of his phlegmatic temperament. According to military authorities, the strategy of his campaigns was excellent, though some have criticized him for not taking chances that might have brought the war to a close months or perhaps years sooner. On the other hand, his refusal to make a move until each detail had been worked out with the utmost thoroughness was responsible for the almost unbroken success of his offensives. And readers of Hemingway's *For Whom the Bell Tolls* will realize that the failure of the Republic's generals to cultivate this meticulousness was disastrous.

When Franco at last captured Madrid, therefore, it seemed that he would make an excellent chief of state. The caution that he had shown during the war seemed to make him all the more fortunate a choice when peace finally came. The exhaustion of the country called for hard working, careful administration rather than brilliance. There was every reason to expect that he would give Spain an efficient dictatorial government which would soon extricate her from her worst difficulties. It would be years, to be sure, before Spain regained strength enough even to discuss the fascist visions of restoring the Empire. But the resources and vitality of the country were so enormous that the outlook was definitely favourable.

Instead, the situation in Spain has steadily gone from bad to worse since the end of the civil war. Both material conditions and the morale of the people were worse in 1940 than they had been in 1939, worse in 1941 than they had been in 1940, are worse now than they were a year ago. It must be conceded that his regime has had bad luck. In both 1940 and 1941 the weather was very bad for crops, and there has been a succession of floods, fires, and other calamities to add to the burden of reconstruction. Above all, the outbreak of the European war, following so soon the end of the war in Spain, greatly complicated the task of reconstruction. At the same time the new war made it much more difficult to bring order out of the confusion resulting from the conflicting policies and personal ambitions of his divided followers.

Nevertheless, an able general has unquestionably made a bad dictator. He has not, it is true, committed the one fatal error which would destroy his regime and bring untold suffering to his people: despite heavy pressure from the Spanish fascists and alternating cajolery and threats by the Nazis, he has so far refused to bring Spain into the war. But more positive virtues have been lacking, and although a do-little policy has its merits, the failure of his regime to make an approach to decent administration is in remarkable contrast to his record as a soldier.

Lack of self-confidence certainly was not responsible for his poor record. His whole manner radiates the most absolute faith in himself, and some of the Spaniards used to enjoy making fun of his obvious complacency. An eyewitness gave me a magnificent account of how Franco kept Der Führer of all Europe waiting for more than half an hour when they held their transcendental first meeting at Hendaye. Franco had spent the night at San Sebastián, less than thirty minutes' drive from the frontier, and this tardiness meant that he had not even set out until after the time fixed for the interview. Hitler, who until then had had presidents, chancellors, and pocket dictators waiting on *him,* was pacing up and down the railroad platform. But Franco, complete with embonpoint and a broad smile, walked up as leisurely as though the Führer had nothing better in the world to do than wait.

My own belief is that the failure of Franco as a dictator has been due partly to the personal reaction that followed his long-deferred victory. An Army officer who hitherto had been known mainly as the brother of a famous aviator was now the master of Spain. Now, after the hardships of a soldier's life, royal palaces and all the consideration due the chief of state were his to command, and he wanted to enjoy calm, relief from strain, and the good things of this life. He had the opportunity to relax for the first time since he had entered the Toledo military academy as a boy, and he has apparently been unwilling to perform the drudgery which is necessary if anyone, whether a dictator or a democratic statesman, is to keep his grip upon a nation's affairs.

More important were the signs that Franco also was incapable of the constant effort of will which was required to impose a united policy upon the intractable and mutually hostile groups that constituted his supporters. Some of these, as we have seen, were precisely the same blocs that had prevented the Republic from accomplishing anything, and until they were smashed Spain could never expect to have an orderly and coherent government. Since Franco was partly dependent upon them to maintain his regime, it would have been difficult for him to take effective action against them, even—which is doubtful in view of his conservative background—if he had had the desire. To govern Spain under such conditions was extremely difficult, and if ever a truly horrible punishment is desired for a detested Nazi, I can propose nothing better than to give him Franco's task of handling stubborn and unyielding Spain.

As though this were not enough, Franco made his task more difficult by shutting himself up in the country, out of contact with the people and their problems. By comparison with Serrano Suñer, at least, he seems rather human, and I do not believe that he would have tolerated the cruelty and inefficiency of the regime if he had been acquainted with the true situation. His original intention had been to live in Madrid, and he had selected for his residence the ducal palace, on the corner of Fortuny and Cisne, which the United States has had for many years to house its Madrid Embassy. Mrs. Alexander W. Weddell, wife of our Ambassador, was on her way to Madrid to look over the less desirable building which he had offered in exchange when it was discovered at the last minute that our palace was unsuitable.

This was because the adjoining apartment buildings looked down upon the Embassy and its gardens and he would have been, so it was thought, in constant danger of being picked off by a sharpshooter. At last Franco chose to live in the Pardo, a former royal palace a few miles outside Madrid on the road to the Escorial, using Alfonso's former palace in the capital for audiences with miscellaneous military, civilian, and party officials.

Even during the relative calm of Alfonso's regime assassinations had been prevalent in Spain, and great precautions were taken to guard Franco every time he left the security of the Pardo. Civil Guards, Assault Guards, and soldiers, all armed with rifles and facing the crowds, lined the entire route when he drove into Madrid. These made sure that everyone held up his right hand in the fascist salute—the longevity of fascist rulers partly results from the fact that it is very difficult to throw a bomb or fire a pistol while doing so—until Franco went by. In addition he was always escorted by motorcycle troops and several automobiles full of policemen.

Ordinarily no advance notice was given of Franco's public appearances. On great occasions, such as the anniversaries of the beginning and the end of the civil war, when it was obvious that he would have to show himself, even larger numbers of police and soldiers lined the route, and machine-guns and riflemen were mounted upon the buildings overlooking the scene. His most effective protection, however, was his personal bodyguard of Moorish cavalry. These magnificent horsemen, in their white, blue, and red burnooses, surrounded his car with such skill that it was impossible for any person standing at street level to see him as the procession whizzed by. Nevertheless the absence of attempts on his life must have been due more to the feeling among Republicans that, bad as things were, his death would make them even worse.

Certainly the police at times displayed remarkable carelessness. For example, at the opening of an exposition of the work accomplished in reconstructing the devastated regions (consisting mostly of architectural drawings), another American newspaperman and I gained admission by calling out continually, "Foreign press, foreign press," and walking resolutely past the innumerable guards. However, we did have to show our invitations, which had been issued by the hundreds, in order to enter the room where Franco was presiding over the speech-making. Then we returned to the exhibition hall, which we had entered without showing any credentials whatever, and started to look at the drawings. After a time I happened to glance around and there was Franco, less than two feet away, also having a look at the exhibits. He was alone except for Baroness von Stohrer, the German Ambassador's wife, to whom he was pointing out one plan that interested him particularly. I remember being impressed by his stockiness —he has very broad, powerful shoulders—but above all by the fact that it would have been extremely easy for an assassin to slip in.

Perhaps because of the danger of assassination Franco has withdrawn himself more and more from public view as the years have gone by. At first he used to go into Madrid once a week to hold audiences, but gradually he has held them less often. The weekly cabinet meetings are held at the Pardo, and he leaves it mainly to receive new ambassadors. The pomp and circumstance of the monarchy was revived for these occasions. The ambassador usually arrived escorted by a detachment of Franco's Moorish bodyguard, and the palace was a brilliant scene with the Moors, khaki-clad household troops wearing white gloves, and lancers in their bright blue uniforms and spiked helmets drawn up in the courtyard.

Every year on January 6, the Feast of the Epiphany, Franco has followed Alfonso's custom of giving a resplendent dinner to his cabinet and the diplomatic chiefs of mission.[1] He also gives a garden party at the royal palace at La Granja, near

[1] In some respects Franco outdid kings in his insistence upon etiquette. On their arrival at these dinners the diplomats merely filed past a dais where Franco stood with uplifted arm, and he did not mingle with them. The Duke of Alba, whose pride in his Spanish and English royal blood is probably unexcelled by any other grandee, once made the mistake of calling on Franco wearing a lounge suit instead of morning clothes or diplomatic uniform. He was told to go away and come back suitably dressed for an audience with His Excellency the Chief of State.

Segovia, on July 18, the anniversary of the beginning of the civil war. Madame Franco has occasionally made public appearances, and for a time their teen-age daughter, Carmencita, presided at functions for poor children, and so on, very much in the way that Princess Elizabeth, as heir to the throne of England, has been trained for her future duties.

But this phase is over, and more and more Franco and his family have remained within the grounds of the Pardo. His isolation there approaches that of the Grand Lama. Little or nothing has become known of the way he passes his time; I did learn that he played tennis frequently, but that was about all. The aristocracy felt itself too superior to associate with a couple of middle-class origin, even if Franco and Madame Franco had wanted to have anything to do with them, and for the most part he invited his old friends from the Army days, particularly General Juan Vigon, his deputy chief of Staff during the war, now Minister for Air and one of his principal advisers. And, of course, the Serrano Suñers.

Ramón Serrano Suñer, who was born in Saragossa in 1901 of a middle-class family, owed his remarkable rise to two fortunate chances: the first was his friendship with José Antonio Primo de Rivera, whom he came to know when they were attending the University of Madrid; the second was the fact that he and Franco married two beautiful sisters of an upper middle-class Asturian family—and Señora Carmen Polo de Franco and Señora Zita Polo de Suñer, who are devoted to each other, wanted their husbands to govern Spain together.

Little in his early career had given any indication that Serrano Suñer would rise to high position. After leaving the University of Madrid he went to study law in Rome and at the University of Bologna. It was in the early days of Fascism, and he became a fervent admirer of Mussolini. Upon his return to Spain he obtained employment in various minor government posts in Saragossa. He was elected to parliament in 1933 as a member of the CEDA, the leading Catholic party. In

Madrid he renewed his friendship with Primo de Rivera, who meanwhile was busy organizing the Phalanx, but did not leave the CEDA. He was imprisoned when the civil war began, but managed to escape from the Republican zone disguised as an Argentine sailor.

Soon after his arrival in Nationalist territory Franco adopted the fascist program, the Phalanx became the official party of the State, and Serrano Suñer, as Minister of Interior and president of the party's Political Committee, began his rise to power. From the beginning he was an enthusiastic champion of Italy and Germany, and his success in organizing the Auxilio Social gave him more and more influence. His visit to Rome after the conclusion of the war was a great success [1] and his prestige was enhanced when Ciano returned the visit and concentrated his attention upon Serrano Suñer rather than Count Jordana, then Franco's Foreign Minister.

Nevertheless, when Franco reorganized his cabinet in August 1939, the opposition of the Army to Serrano Suñer was still too powerful, and the Foreign Ministry went to Colonel Juan Beigbeder. But Serrano Suñer did succeed at that time in ridding himself of his most powerful rival within the party, Raimúndo Fernandez Cuesta, the Secretary General. Cuesta had been one of the original high command of the Phalanx and a closer friend of Primo de Rivera, and it was necessary to dispose of him. The solution was honourable exile as ambassador to Rio de Janeiro, where Fernandez Cuesta still is. Serrano Suñer was now master of the Phalanx except for Franco's nominal control, while his position as Minister of Government, with control of the press and police and numberless other activities, made him the dominant figure in the Franco regime.

1 Serrano Suñer, who is not afflicted with false modesty, was chairman of the committee which selected a panegyric upon this event, bearing the title *The Marriage of Spain with Glory,* as the best piece of writing that appeared in the Spanish press during the year 1939.

Whether the two men have any real regard for each other I could never discover. In the beginning there is no doubt that Franco selected Serrano Suñer for high position primarily because of his obscurity, which seemed to guarantee that he would be loyal to the creator of his greatness. As time went on, and Serrano Suñer's influence steadily grew, Franco seemed content to allow him to conduct internal affairs more or less as he chose, and to take as strong a pro-Axis line in his newspapers as he chose—provided only he did not get Spain into the war.

I sometimes suspected that in holding on to Serrano Suñer, despite his manifest unpopularity, Franco was playing a subtle game, and was deliberately setting up his brother-in-law as the whipping-boy of the regime. Except to the extent that Franco may have believed this unpopularity was a pledge of Serrano Suñer's loyalty, I do not think, however, he was so Machiavellian. Even in the solitude of the Pardo Franco must have heard of some of the jokes that the Madrid wits were always making about this strange relationship. They insisted, for example, that the reason El Ferrol had been renamed El Ferrol del Caudillo was that it was the only town in Spain which Serrano Suñer had not taken away from him. Only a half length of Franco was shown on most posters, and they used to say this was because Serrano Suñer had stolen his trousers.

Their favourite was the alleged occasion upon which Madame Serrano Suñer ran across a girlhood friend who, having spent many years in the jungle of South America, knew nothing of recent happenings in Spain. Madame Serrano Suñer proceeded to explain with natural pride that her husband was Foreign Minister of Spain, chief of the Phalanx party, the friend of Hitler and Mussolini. And what had become of her sister Carmen, the friend asked. "Oh," she replied, "she just married an Army man." By this time, of course, Serrano Suñer's nickname of "Cuñadissimo" (Brother-in-law-in-chief, by analogy with *generalísimo,* general-in-chief) was too trite for use except for one variant: you asked who was the most famous brother-in-law in Spain, and the answer was: Franco.

These stories only reflected the remarkable ascendancy which this frail and handsome man, with his grey hair brushed straight back in a pompadour, had gained over Franco. His bitterness, which was increased by such diverse misfortunes as the execution of two of his brothers by the Republicans, and a bad stomach, was shown in his every action and word. Yet with friends, or with opponents worthy of his steel, such as Sir Samuel Hoare, or Colonel Sosthenes Behn, the head of the International Telephone & Telegraph Corporation, Serrano Suñer could be charming.

From all appearances he was devoted to his wife and their four handsome children, and the little homey touches his household gave the Ministry of Government building, in which they had a large but by no means luxurious apartment, were in ironic contrast to the unceasing care with which he was guarded against assassination. A bell rang whenever he was about to enter or leave the building, and his bodyguard quickly lined the corridors, forcing all employees and visitors to shut themselves in their offices. He got in and out of his car in the building garage, which he could reach without going out into the street.

Yet with all this grim activity the informal life of a Spanish family went on as usual. From the censor's office you saw children's clothes hanging out to dry from the windows of the Serrano Suñer apartment across the courtyard. Every now and then you met a nurse pushing a smart baby carriage through the halls of the grimy building—it was the youngest Serrano Suñer being brought in from his morning walk. And it was rather touching to see one of the most bitterly hated men in Europe get in his car on a Sunday afternoon to take the children to play on Uncle Francisco's estate; always there was an escort car of heavily armed Phalanx militiamen to protect the little excursion.

These precautions demonstrated that Serrano Suñer was fully aware of his supreme unpopularity. But his ambitions were so lofty that this did not deter him from carrying on a cool and well-directed campaign to win control of the government. As his first step it was necessary to exalt the Phalanx and its contribution to winning the war. The means lay ready to hand in the career of Primo de Rivera, the Founder and, as Spain must never forget, the close friend of Serrano Suñer. Already there was a definite tendency toward a José Antonio cult (the full name is never used in Franco Spain). Although the Founder was executed early in the civil war, the fascists for years referred to him merely as "The Absent One" (*El Ausente*), or capitalized the pronoun "He" as though he were a divinity. The recovery of his body after the war removed any doubt that Primo de Rivera was really dead, but November 20, the date of his execution, became a holiday in the fascist calendar,[1] and with great skill Serrano Suñer directed a flood of newspaper publicity upon the Founder of the Phalanx, con-

[1] Adding fascist to the existing national and Catholic holidays, Spain is now almost as well supplied with *fiestas* as in the Middle Ages. Not counting Easter Sunday, twelve religious holidays are celebrated, of which two, the feast day of Spain's patron, St. James (Santiago in Spanish), and the anniversary of the proclamation of the dogma of the Immaculate Conception are also national holidays. In addition there are seven national holidays, although three are *meramente oficiales,* on which only government offices are closed. The combined list is as follows: January 1, Circumcision of Jesus; January 6, Epiphany; March 19, San José; April 1, end of the civil war; Holy Thursday; Good Friday; April 19, unification of the Phalanx and Traditionalist parties; May 2, uprising against the French in 1808; May 22, Ascension Day; June 12, Corpus Christi; June 29, Sts. Peter and Paul; July 18, Feast of Labour (beginning of the civil war); July 29, Santiago; August 15, Assumption Day; October 1, Day of the *Caudillo* (anniversary of Franco's assumption of the supreme command); October 12, Day of the Race (Columbus Day in the United States); November 20, anniversary of Primo de Rivera's execution; December 8, Dogma of the Immaculate Conception; and Christmas. In addition, each town has its own patron saint, and each trade or profession its own patron, adding two more *fiestas* to the list.

veniently ignoring the contributions of everyone else.

Borrowing a term usually reserved for St. Stephen, the first Christian martyr, the Spanish press christened José Antonio the protomartyr of the movement. Every detail of the Founder's career was glorified, and soon an opportune quotation from his most casual utterance brought all arguments to an end in Spain, just as quotations from Lenin did in Soviet Russia. It was Serrano Suñer who proposed and directed the exhumation of the remains in the autumn of 1939, and their interment—with the honours paid to a captain general—before the high altar of Philip II's Escorial, resting-place of the kings and queens of Spain. From Alicante, where Primo de Rivera was executed, the coffin was carried to the Escorial on the shoulders of picked groups of fascists. Not once was it allowed to touch the earth during the three-hundred-mile journey. Only two words, "José Antonio," were placed on the huge granite slab that marked the burial place. This was considered enough to identify him as long as the Escorial lasts; thereafter a pilgrimage to his tomb was the first business to be done by distinguished German and Italian visitors.

Primo de Rivera's cell at Alicante also was made into a shrine, but at the time I left Spain plans for the supreme memento of his martyrdom had not yet been carried out. This was nothing less than the preservation for all time of the indentation which his face had made in the earth during the two and a half years that the coffinless body was buried at Alicante. The corpse had been buried with those of other executed prisoners in a common grave. But fortunately, Serrano Suñer's press explained, the Founder's body had landed at one side of the ditch, and the impression of the face was said to be easily recognizable. Even more fortunate, it was said, was the fact that a new process had been found by which the *moulage* could be preserved for centuries. Once the plaster of Paris solution was injected into the earth, the impression could be moved anywhere. But the general opinion was that it would be most fitting to place it in the prison cell. . . .

Serrano Suñer had reasoned, correctly enough, that the Phalanx needed a hero, and that José Antonio, being irrefutably dead, would not be any competition. Curiously enough, however, his extreme measures to establish the cult nearly cost him his place in the government. For some of the generals the Escorial burial was the last straw. Already hating Serrano Suñer and the Phalanx, they were enraged that Primo de Rivera received greater honours than those paid Sanjurjo, Mola, and even the greatest kings. A committee of the generals, including General Varela and General Aranda, took advantage of Serrano Suñer's absence in Andalusia in January 1940 to demand his dismissal. Otherwise, they said, they would withdraw from the government and would not be responsible for the consequences.

Franco met this difficulty with his usual calm. He told them that he had great confidence in Serrano Suñer, but that he would certainly dismiss him if they insisted. Only, he said, Serrano Suñer should be allowed to save face by coming back and resuming his duties for a week or so. Then, when the situation calmed down, it would be easy to announce that he had to retire because of ill health, or send him off somewhere as ambassador. The generals reluctantly agreed, but when Serrano Suñer came back he and the two wives were able to persuade Franco that he was irreplaceable and that after all there were other generals in the Army. He stayed on, and although the generals blustered they did nothing.

But the incident taught Serrano Suñer a lesson, and he began quietly to stalk enemies—meaning everyone of independent mind in the party, or the civilian branch of the government, or the armed forces. The first victim was General Muñoz Grande, Secretary General of the party, and later commander of the Blue Division of "volunteers" serving on the Russian front, who was dismissed the following March. General Yagüe, Minister for Air, was ousted in June. Rafael Sánchez Mazas, one of the two or three best minds in the Phalanx, was dismissed from his party post in August.

All this time Serrano Suñer's own prestige was mounting with the German victories, and by October 1940, after his visit to the Axis countries to discuss Spain's entry into the war, he was ready to move against Colonel Beigbeder. Serrano Suñer took the Foreign Ministry, at the same time retaining control of the Ministry of Government. For although the post remained vacant, with Franco nominally in charge, actually the Ministry was run by Serrano Suñer's own henchmen. Elated by his long-deferred victory, Serrano Suñer was confident that now he could bring Spain into the war at once. His Phalanx guards quickly appeared in the sedate corridors of the Foreign Ministry, and he exultantly told the permanent officials that "there is not a moment to lose," and that they must be alert "every second" for the decisive days ahead.

Serrano Suñer, however, was soon undeceived by the interview between Hitler and Franco at Hendaye which took place a few days later; on his subsequent visit to Germany and Italy he failed to obtain sufficiently tempting promises of booty to overcome Franco's fear of entering the war. He then embarked upon a new campaign to eliminate the last of his foes from the government and to induce Franco to retire completely to the upper clouds as merely chief of state, corresponding to Marshal Pétain's position later, while he, as Prime Minister and the real head of the government, became the exact equivalent of Laval. In the course of this campaign he eliminated a few more fascists who had been talking too independently, including José María Alfaro [1] and others of less note.

Meanwhile he succeeded in imparting a definitely hostile

1 Alfaro, who had been a friend of Primo de Rivera and was a former editor of the fascist paper in Madrid, *Arriba,* was then Serrano Suñer's Undersecretary of Press and Propaganda. The story went that with magnificent naïveté he believed the official announcement a short time before that letters within Spain were no longer censored and wrote to a friend what he thought of Serrano Suñer.

tone to relations with England and particularly with the United States. To this period belong such related actions as the creation of the Council of Hispanidad, to fight the United States in Latin America, and the abolition of the last remains of international control in Tangier, constituting annexation instead of the temporary occupation which was the basis on which the British sanctioned the entrance of Franco's troops.

Meanwhile the influence of the favourite was steadily growing in every branch of the government, except, of course, the armed forces, and there was no hint of the approaching quarrel between the brothers-in-law which finally brought Serrano Suñer's downfall.

The campaign went so well that Serrano Suñer at last embarked on a far-reaching effort to integrate the sorely divided Spanish State by giving the Phalanx complete control. One of the principal means was the appointment of provincial chiefs of the Phalanx as civil governors of their provinces; for example, Miguel Primo de Rivera, a brother of the Founder, whom Serrano Suñer had already made chief of the Madrid Phalanx, became civil governor of Madrid. Everywhere Serrano Suñer was busy eliminating the last vestiges of the fascist old guard and installing men whom he could fully trust.

In the late spring of 1941 it was generally expected that the Germans would come through Spain within a few weeks at the latest, and Serrano Suñer's speech on May 2, the Spanish Fourth of July, was so venomous against "pluto-democratic meddling" —that is, offers of economic help upon condition that Spain remain neutral—that it seemed he and the Germans had at last persuaded Franco to take the plunge.

On the same day that Serrano Suñer spoke, I learned of an order by Antonio Tovar, a protégé of his who had succeeded Alfaro as Undersecretary of Press and Propaganda, exempting Phalanx publications from the government censorship. I could not understand the purpose of the order, since *Arriba* and the provincial Phalanx newspapers already were using the utmost violence in attacking England and the United States. I supposed that it was simply another sign, like the simultaneous exemption of high-ranking officials of the Phalanx from arrest, except on the personal orders of Franco or Serrano Suñer, of the party's constantly growing dominance over the regular government.

I soon discovered that this interpretation was wrong. On the contrary, both Serrano Suñer's speech and the censorship order were prompted by a bitter dispute with Franco which is still one of the mysteries of contemporary Spain. All sorts of reasons were suggested, from a quarrel between the two sisters to Franco's fear that Serrano Suñer was about to attempt a putsch, but nobody really knew. For months it had been generally believed in Madrid (although naturally nobody could prove it) that the Germans were so displeased with Franco's obstinacy that they intended to remove him after they marched in and set up Serrano Suñer as the Spanish Quisling.

If this talk was the reason for the quarrel it certainly took Franco a long time to act; possibly Serrano Suñer's old foes in the Army still had difficulty convincing Franco that his brother-in-law was dangerous. But whatever may have been the reasons, the quarrel became public when Franco suddenly appointed Colonel Valentín Galarza, a devoted personal follower, to the key position of Minister of Government—thus taking away Serrano Suñer's control of both press and police and virtually making him a prisoner in the Foreign Ministry.

This threw an entirely different light upon the May 2 speech, which was now seen to have been a despairing final fling at the democracies rather than a menacing attack. The Phalanx press had obviously been exempted from censorship in the hope that it would be allowed to express Serrano Suñer's policy even after Colonel Galarza had muzzled the other newspapers.

Meanwhile, however, the exemption order remained in effect, and incoherent but unmistakably snarling editorials, some of which were written by Serrano Suñer himself, appeared in *Arriba* every morning until the order was annulled by Galarza. As a sign of the new era, the twenty or more fascist militiamen who were always lounging around Serrano Suñer's garage in the Ministry of Government building were withdrawn and it was supposed that his family would next be ordered to move out.[1] Serrano Suñer's anger after a visit to Franco—the building grapevine said that he had fired his faithful chauffeur—seemed to prove that he was done. Government officials began to disclose their real sentiments toward the falling colossus.

Nothing, not even the entreaties of Madame Serrano Suñer to her sister, seemed capable of stopping the enraged Franco. As though to show the significance of Galarza's appointment, the Undersecretary of Government, who had been running the Ministry under Serrano Suñer's orders, was dismissed. So was Count Mayalde, Serrano Suñer's chief of police. So were many of the provincial Phalanx chiefs who had been named civil governors, including Miguel Primo de Rivera. The dismissal of both Tovar and his Directors of Press and Propaganda followed and it seemed certain that Serrano Suñer himself would be forced out of the government, and possibly out of the party as well. Meanwhile Franco brought back to Spain three of his best generals, who had been stationed in Morocco and the Balearic Islands, apparently to make sure of help in the event of trouble with the Phalanx or the Germans.

The Nazis had viewed this family squabble with mixed feelings and for a while took no action. They were not greatly pleased with Serrano Suñer, who had so often given overconfident assurances that he would bring Spain into the war; they were inclined thereafter to concentrate their attention upon the Army, which, as events had shown, retained enough influence to keep Franco from declaring war. Nevertheless, Serrano Suñer was a valuable ally and his foes, after all, were

[1] The crisis was so acute that Madame Serrano Suñer went house-hunting; among those she visited was an apartment belonging to some friends of mine.

Germany's. At last, some time in the middle of May, von Stohrer, the German Ambassador, went to see Franco and told him he had gone far enough. It was time, von Stohrer made very clear, to stop.

Franco stopped, and although Galarza remained at his post, Serrano Suñer promptly regained much of the ground he had lost. As peace offerings, two of Serrano Suñer's remaining rivals, José Larraz, Minister of Finance, and Gamero del Castillo, Vice-Secretary of the Phalanx and Minister Without Portfolio, were dismissed and Miguel Primo de Rivera entered the cabinet as Minister of Agriculture. Finally the wheel swung almost full circle when Press and Propaganda were taken out of the Ministry of Government and placed under Serrano Suñer's Phalanx. But not entirely, for as long as Galarza remained Minister of Government, Franco could be sure that someone on whom he could rely was in charge of the police, while General Varela, as Minister of War, guaranteed the loyalty of the Army.

Serrano Suñer, in fact, never recovered his lost supremacy, and in September 1942 a new offensive by the generals drove him from both the Foreign Ministry and his position as head of the Phalanx. Opposition from the party's Secretary General, José Luis de Arrese, who after his appointment a year before had developed unsuspected qualities of independence, was partly responsible. The Vatican, which held Serrano Suñer responsible for the anti-clerical tone of the Phalanx and was not appeased by his last-minute effort to support the restoration of the monarchy under Don Juan, also brought its powerful influence into play.

It would seem that Franco's desire to obtain essential economic help from the United States also played its part. Whether we had offered him anything directly in exchange for Serrano Suñer's dismissal has not, of course, been revealed. The week before, however, President Roosevelt had made his remarkable announcement of our desire to help Franco Spain to preserve her artistic treasures and encourage her tourist industry. What this portended is still not clear, but it was obviously an effort to weaken German influence. Franco's action, on the other hand, appears to have been made with the knowledge of the Nazis and perhaps, to judge from their newspaper comment, with their grudging consent. Serrano Suñer had been a loyal servant, but during the previous crisis in the spring of 1941 a neutral diplomat who had friends among the top officials of the German Embassy told me that already they questioned the desirability of intervening to save him.

The long-standing feud between Serrano Suñer and the generals had taken on new bitterness since the summer of 1942, when a bomb was thrown at Varela while he was leaving a church service in Bilbao, killing several people in the crowd. Nevertheless, one of the principal reasons why the generals succeeded in 1942 when they had failed before was the result of an old-fashioned family row produced by Serrano Suñer's love affairs. Never while I was in Spain did I hear any suggestion that Franco had a mistress, and until Serrano Suñer took over the Foreign Ministry his faithfulness to his wife also was unquestioned. But although he condemned unmercifully the foreign policy of his predecessor, Colonel Beigbeder, Serrano Suñer approved of the latter's mistress, the blonde wife of a prominent diplomat stationed in Madrid. With Beigbeder lying low at his home near Ronda in order to escape arrest, Serrano Suñer succeeded him in the lady's affections.

How much disturbance this created in the two households is still not clear, but in view of the fact that many Spanish husbands keep mistresses, perhaps it was not excessive. Another misstep, this time with a Seville woman, appears to have been disastrous. Several months before Serrano Suñer's dismissal the *New Republic* revealed the disturbance created by this liaison, and it added that Serrano Suñer, having contracted a venereal disease, then infected his wife. I have no evidence to support the latter assertion, but from sources within Spain

I have confirmed the fact that he did take a mistress from Seville and that both Madame Serrano Suñer and Madame Franco were indignant. His position as brother-in-law this time was a handicap, and Serrano Suñer, no longer with friends at court, was overthrown.

In his fall, however, he brought down with him both Varela and Galarza, whose appointment as Minister of Government a year and a half before had opened the drive against him. And he was succeeded as Foreign Minister by Count Jordana, who, although reputedly a monarchist, seemed able to get along with the Axis well enough during the civil war, when he was in charge of foreign affairs. Unless our strength in North Africa becomes overwhelming, there is reason to suppose that just as Pétain dismissed Laval, then took him back on orders from the Nazis, Serrano Suñer also will return to power. Already, in fact, he has been restored to a position on the Council of the Phalanx, an unimportant matter in itself, but an indication that he is trying to come back. Should Franco balk when Hitler makes his demand—which may not come until the moment is exactly right for Spain's long-deferred entrance into the war—it is highly possible that the Nazis will try to install Serrano Suñer as the chief of government. His notorious unpopularity of course is a drawback, but he has one quality that makes him as useful a pawn as Laval. Both know that they are doomed men if the forces of Fighting France and a free Spain regain control, and their very lives are thus bound up with the fascist cause. Later the Nazis will have no time for him, but in the decisive months ahead we may depend upon it that they will find a use for his talents.

It must be emphasized that some parts of Franco's economic policy were well conceived. High on the list was his attempt to hold wages and prices at the July 1936 level. The wisdom of this policy will become more apparent to Americans as we go farther and farther along the road to inflation; no one can say that Franco's effort has succeeded, but he has done his best. Certainly his monetary and fiscal policies have been well directed toward this goal. At the end of the civil war Franco was confronted with the problem created by the billions of Republican pesetas in circulation in addition to his own. There was no gold backing for either, and he adopted the harsh but unavoidable method of repudiating all Republican pesetas, even those which had been issued before the civil war. At the same time he froze the two billion pesetas on deposit in the banks of the Republican zone; later a graduated scale of redemption was imposed, ranging from 100 per cent on deposits which had been made before the civil war, to 10 per cent or nothing on those made in the last few months before the end of the conflict.

Moreover, by assuming the entire national debt incurred before the civil war—including postal savings—Franco bound both the moneyed and the lower middle classes to his regime. José Larraz, as Minister of Finance, took advantage of the resulting feeling of confidence to convert billions of securities at lower rates of interest, thus reducing heavy carrying charges and further strengthening confidence in the regime. Under his able administration it seemed for a time that Spain was definitely on the road to recovery. One sign was the reappearance of ten- and five-centime pieces, worth roughly one cent or half a cent, which had been hoarded for the value of the copper they contained. Merchants who had hidden their fine watches and English cloth throughout the war now put them on display. And the consumers' goods industries, although still handicapped by the shortage of raw materials, dies, and machinery, began to produce all sorts of things which Spain had gone without ever since the beginning of the civil war.

This recovery would have been greater but for uncertainty resulting from the avowed imperialist aims of the new regime. These were reflected in its extensive war preparations, which kept the budget unbalanced despite the crushing burden of the new sales taxes. Under the Republic, annual expenditures had averaged four and a half billion pesetas, against receipts of about four billion. Because of reduced economic activity, Franco's heavier taxes have produced considerably less than four billion pesetas a year, and meanwhile he has been spending about seven billion—expenditures on the armed forces accounting for much of the increase.

Aided by the absence of other investment opportunities, Larraz was highly successful for a time both in his refunding operations and in floating the new securities necessary to meet current expenditures. By the end of 1941, however, these new borrowings had raised the national debt to around thirty billion, say two and three quarter billion dollars. This is a small sum compared with our federal debt, which unprecedented war expenditures have brought to ninety billions.[1] But we have 130,000,000 people, compared with Spain's 25,000,000. The per capita debt load of the United States is $692 compared with the $110 of Spain, but there is an enormous difference in the wealth of the two countries, and confidence in the survival of the Franco regime has declined steadily from the day that Hitler's troops reached the Spanish frontier.

Subsequent borrowings therefore have been made with increasing difficulty, and more and more wealthy Spaniards are attempting to send their money abroad. The others are steadily investing in real estate or anything which they think will outlast the Franco regime.

This of course is only a symbol of the more important signs of economic deterioration, idle factories, steadily more ineffi-

[1] I have not taken into account either debts of local governments in the two countries, or Spain's debts to foreign countries.

cient transportation, and actual famine, which now afflict Spain. The Spaniards have a saying that "Mr. Money" (*Don Dinero*) never makes a mistake, and there was a similar flight from the peseta in the last days of the Primo de Rivera regime. Even before I left Spain, the government propaganda authorities had had to withdraw the posters showing Franco in a heroic pose, with arms crossed over his chest, which for a time were displayed on every street corner, in the lobby of every apartment house. To stand with arms folded is the symbol of unemployment in Spain, and too many disillusioned Spaniards had scrawled over the poster: "And so are we all."

Totalitarian control of the nation's business life was as complete as the long-standing vested interests would permit. Not a bottle of sherry could be exported, or a ton of coal imported, without a permit from the Ministry of Industry and Commerce. The necessary wangling often required months, and, in the case of imports, it was then necessary to persuade a separate agency, the Foreign Money Institute, to provide the pounds, dollars, or pesos. Nor was this all. No factory could be established, nor could an existing one be enlarged or even repaired, without a permit from the all-powerful Ministry. All wages and prices were fixed by the government, and as scarcely a single enterprise of any importance in Spain could operate without imported articles, the government's control was complete. Furthermore, it had the authority, and sometimes exercised it—principally against British firms—to compel a mine or factory to keep operating at a loss when its owners wished to close down.

In agriculture it was the same. A government agency had a monopoly over all dealings in wheat, Spain's most important crop. Dealings in other products were left in private hands, but prices were fixed by the Ministry of Agriculture. Distribution of rationed foods (which now include virtually all foods) to retailers is handled by the Rationing Office. As for transportation, a system of priorities for railroad freight was imposed as early as 1940, and in the following year the government took over the railroads entirely. Trucks and buses are almost as effectively under control since the government is in charge of issuing import licences for new vehicles; rationing of gasoline and tires is a further means of enforcing compliance with its orders. Ocean and coastal shipping are completely under a bureau of the Ministry of the Marine, which operates several lines and controls the itineraries and cargoes of the remainder.

By chance I had obtained an insight into the aims and methods of this totalitarian economy before leaving England. Soon after the end of the civil war one of the London financial papers carried a brief notice announcing the formation of "J. March & Co., Ltd.," which was to have a monopoly of all Spain's trade with England in the future. This was interesting news, because already Franco was being sounded out by the Foreign Office and the Quai d'Orsay on the possibility that, if he behaved himself and resumed trade with the non-Axis world, he could have half a billion dollars or so from a syndicate of Dutch, Belgian, French, and British banks. Deep within the financial district I found the new company's modest office, which did not approach the luxury of the Dorchester House suite where Franco's diplomatic representatives had their headquarters during the civil war. March, a peasant's son who by means of smuggling and less edifying activities had become the richest man in Spain, was not in London. The manager, however, was more than willing to explain his chief's aims.

The new company intended to take over Spain's trade with the entire world, he told me proudly. I agreed that this was a tremendous undertaking, but inquired if this meant that the Germans and Italians also would have to handle their dealings through the company, abandoning their profitable separate arrangements with Spain. A little embarrassed, my informant admitted that Germany and Italy were excluded. But he quickly recovered as he started telling me how Spain would apply the system of economic pressure so well developed by the celebrated Dr. Schacht of the Reichsbank.

J. March & Co. intended to keep separate accounts for each country, collecting the foreign-exchange proceeds of Spanish exports and reimbursing the producer in pesetas. In the same way it would pay for all imports. Naturally, he declared, the aim was to make Spain as self-sufficient as possible, at the same time developing her exports. He pointed out that by concentrating the nation's buying and selling power in one agency, Spain would be able to obtain much better terms than she had before. Take the case of the United States, he told me. We had been selling Spain about twice as much as we had bought from her, but this would not continue. We had huge stocks of cotton, gasoline, and other raw materials that we must dispose of, and we needed to sell Spain our electrical supplies, typewriters, and so forth as well. But we would soon learn that in order to do so we must buy more Spanish products and thus balance the accounts between the two countries.

In that case, I suggested, Spain must intend to restore close relations with France, since her trade with Spain was already about even, and particularly with England, because the British normally bought twice as much from Spain as they sold. The manager shook his finger at me in protest. England, he said, had been in the habit of buying goods from Spain, such as cork, which she could obtain nowhere else. On the other hand, Spain had been buying coal and other British products for which there was a limited market. Therefore England also must toe the line. For Spain intended to use her monopoly goods to force the purchase of her competitive products, and if England could not be made to accept the new order, so much the worse for England.

This was the tested method of Nazi economic domination, and although the difference between the economic strength of Germany and her Spanish protégé was extraordinary, nothing could convince the manager that the economic blackmail which had worked for one would not work for the other. If ever it falls to me to produce *The Gondoliers,* I shall know where to look for the Duke of Plaza Toro.

Straight out of Gilbert and Sullivan, too, was the one serious attempt that had been made until then to utilize the inestimable advantages of government control of Spain's foreign trade. This resulted from the inspiration of someone in the Ministry of Industry and Commerce, who recalled that Spain used to make a very good profit supplying England with new potatoes in the middle of winter. The only difficulty was that if she exported these potatoes Spain would not have enough for herself. Finally an ingenious solution was developed, based on the fact that England at this season had plenty of old potatoes, which were of course much cheaper than the *primeurs.* Spain would ship the new potatoes to England, sell them at high prices, buy an equivalent amount of old ones, and make a neat profit in sterling.

The idea seemed foolproof, but was not. For the special emissary who came to carry out the transaction had unfortunately been directed to sell the potatoes in the fruit instead of the vegetable market. His London agents immediately pointed out the mistake and proposed that he cable back to the Ministry for amended instructions. No, said the official, that would take weeks, and by that time it would be too late. He was then urged to go ahead on his own authority and straighten out the matter when he got home. No, he said, that would mean a firing squad. He proceeded to carry out his orders to the letter. As he had been warned, there was nobody to buy new potatoes except some dealers of Jewish descent who saw their opportunity to do something against a Hitler ally. Their ring offered an absurdly low price, but the representative of the great principle of State economy had no alternative and had to take it. So Spaniards ate old potatoes instead of new potatoes, and Franco lost several hundred thousand dollars on the transaction.

Several months later, when I went to see officials of the Ministry of Industry and Commerce at Bilbao, I found the distance between aim and performance just as great as I had expected. Business men and manufacturers were gathered there from all parts of Spain, pleading for the raw materials, machinery, and other imports without which they could not stay in business. The Minister, an estimable Army officer named Alarcón who knew nothing of business matters, was incapable of determining which of their applications were justified by national necessity and which were for non-essential articles that would yield the importer a fabulous profit but would not help Spain's recovery in the slightest. The clever young men around him had their eyes fixed far in the distance upon all the glories that were to be, but there was a total failure to realize that the first necessity was to get going again the factories that Spain already had.

The hard-headed Basque and Catalan business men who were there pleading for help were not at all interested in the Hitlerian El Dorado. Their dislike for these young zealots, which was extreme, was fully justified. One of the leading manufacturers of Bilbao took me over his plant and showed me a small machine. If it should break down, he told me, his factory, with 5,000 employees, would be out of action for months until another could be imported. A stand-by machine would cost only three hundred dollars, which was nothing by comparison with the importance of his product in maintaining the economy of Spain. But the young officials of the Ministry were too busy planning for the autarchy of the future to pay attention to present needs and had refused him the three-hundred-dollar permit despite all his arguments.

The fascist dreams had not caused too much damage during the civil war, when ineluctable necessity compelled utilization of all existing resources to produce matériel. Besides, Catalonia remained in the hands of the Republic almost to the end, and the clever young men had therefore had little scope for their more ambitious schemes. When peace came, however, these visionaries had their inning. In view of Spain's magnificent mineral and hydroelectric resources, and her excellent geographical position, there was some excuse for such visions. And it must be conceded that in its emphasis upon increasing production of paper, coal, and other goods, most of which hitherto had been imported despite Spain's capacity to produce them at home, even the autarchy program had some merits.

But until Spain could begin to provide herself with basic necessities, an all-out attempt to make her self-sufficient was useless. In any case, Spain could never free herself from dependence upon the outside world for gasoline, rubber, and other raw materials. Even if she could do so, the autarchy program was no less a mistake, for it was sacrificing the well-being of millions of Spaniards to build up Franco's war machine. It was the Nazi policy of guns instead of butter all over again, except that, as only a handful of Spaniards had ever been able to afford butter, these imperialist ambitions had to be paid for out of the bare necessities of life.

The Nazi influence upon Spain had evil results in another direction. For high up on the list of the Franco regime's mistakes was the determination with which it insisted upon paying off its debt to Germany with products necessary for Spain's very existence. Few nations in history have ever gone without in order to pay foreign debts, but Spain was an exception. Mussolini gave Franco an extremely favourable settlement of the five-billion-lire war debt, but Hitler had different ideas. Exactly how much fascist Spain owed the Nazis has not been revealed, but Larraz once intimated that it was between 200,000,000 and 300,000,000 marks (between $80,000,000 and $120,000,000). By comparison with lend-lease transactions this is an insignificant sum, but it was important for Spain, amounting probably to the average proceeds of an entire year's exports since the end of the war. In view of the fact that Hitler's principal aim had been to train his aviators and tank crews, Franco had every reason to demand a moratorium. His failure to do so, and the determination with which the Spanish fascists sought to pay off the last pfennig of this debt, was one of the principal causes of the misery from which the Spanish people are suffering.

Germany, which had accounted for half the foreign trade from Franco's zone during the civil war, was determined not to lose her grip. But for the outbreak of the European war, there is no question that by now the Nazis would have been in complete charge of Spain's principal industries. One of the reasons why Franco was so long in handing back control of the Spanish telephone system to American interests was the fact that the Germans had marked it as their special prey; they were busy buying up iron mines, factories, and shares in Spanish concerns when the Polish campaign began.

Franco's best chance to free himself came between September 1939 and the collapse of France. German influence on Spanish business life declined during this period. A trickle of Spanish goods did get to the Nazis through Italy, but the Nazis in return could only supply Franco with inadequate amounts of dies and other chemical products by airplane. For the most part, in fact, the Nazis had to confine themselves to blocking trade agreements with England and France; although they ultimately failed, they did manage to prevent the pact with France from being put into application until they themselves had reached the Pyrenees.

Once land communications with Germany were established by the collapse of France, the exploitation of Spain's resources was resumed with even greater determination. By this time Belgium and Sweden were supplying all the iron ore the Nazis wanted, and the Nazis are still allowing England to buy the high-grade ore from the Bilbao mines. Apart from food, the

Nazis did need Spanish oranges, olive oil, cork, mercury, wolfram, hides, wool, and other products, and the fascist zealots proceeded to let them have them. But Germany no longer was in a position to spare the products that Spain needed, and except for small quantities of chemicals and machinery she paid nothing for products which would have produced invaluable free exchange for the *Devisen*-poor regime.

But more disastrous than the exports to Germany was the Nazi economic machine that Franco was trying to copy. A few examples of how the Spaniards worked their borrowed system will show how completely it was unsuited to Spain. One day when I was leaving the Puerta de Hierro country club after a game of tennis with a European diplomat, a Spaniard walked up to him and asked him if "my shipment of tennis balls" had come yet. Obviously my friend's diplomatic pouch was being used, thus avoiding payment of duty, and the necessity of obtaining an import permit, a grant of foreign exchange, and many other difficulties. I knew that the diplomat had only a speaking acquaintance with the Spaniard, and as we drove back I asked him what was the arrangement. The answer, it turned out, was simple. A syndicate of some of the more prominent players had gone to see Colonel Beigbeder, then Foreign Minister, about the shortage of tennis balls. Beigbeder had told them that by "regular channels" this would be difficult, and himself proposed that they get some tennis-playing diplomat to bring them in. As my friend said, "If Beigbeder doesn't mind the violation of his own laws I am sure I don't."

There were innumerable instances of the governmental inefficiency which made such methods not merely necessary but accepted practice. For example, there was the case of a sunken ship at Valencia which had been raised by the Spanish government's salvage agency. These salvaged ships almost made up for the losses incurred by the Spanish merchant marine during the civil war, but this particular merchantman had been hit too hard by a Franco bomb to be repaired. She had therefore merely been patched up enough to take her around to Bilbao to be broken up for scrap. But although the need for scrap was pressing, and the ship was the property of the Spanish government, the Director General of Customs refused to allow her to be broken up until duties had been paid. It was in vain that officials protested that the Spanish government could not be forced to pay duty to itself on its own property; the Director General had his book of regulations, and so far as I know, the bureaucratic battle is raging yet.

This sort of thing was not, of course, the invention of the Franco regime. An English newspaperman who was in Barcelona during the civil war told me of acting as intermediary between an American relief agency and a Republican collector of customs who insisted upon collecting duty on a relief shipment of food to the population, which was starving then as it is starving now. It was pointed out to the collector that only a certain amount of American money was available with which to buy the food, and that if he required payment of the duty, the next shipment would be reduced by that amount. But for him, as for the Franco official, regulations were regulations, and the dispute was settled only when the city government of Barcelona paid the duty.

Under Franco it seemed that there was no limit to this superb inefficiency. There was, for example, the shipment of several hundred copies of *The Spanish Arena,* by William Foss and Cecil Gerahty, which was held up at Irún for at least two years after the civil war. The books are probably there still, despite the fact that they contain a foreword by the Duke of Alba, were published by the Right Book Club of London, and are the best Franco propaganda that has appeared in English. Orders had been issued to the frontier authorities to stop any books concerning Spain, and all the efforts of Serrano Suñer's Press and Propaganda officials never budged them.

A personal experience gave me a further insight into the

strange operations of the Franco regime. My mother and my wife's parents, who were concerned over the shortage of food for our baby, conceived the idea of sending us a shipment. Immediately we wrote back informing them of the difficulties we would have in obtaining an import permit, and insisting that they do nothing of the kind. Naturally enough, however, they could not believe that any government would refuse to allow food to be imported into a starving country, and they sent a few dollars' worth of special baby food anyway. Immediately I went to the leading customs broker of Madrid, explained the situation, and asked him to do the necessary. He flatly refused, saying that all efforts would be useless because it was impossible to obtain the import permit.

My next move was to ask the help of Merry del Val, chief of the Foreign Press. He wrote to the authorities explaining that the shipment was for a foreign correspondent, that any special consideration would be appreciated, and so on, but was so obviously sincere when he told me that it would do me no good that I decided to give it up and have the food sent back to the United States. The customs broker, however, said this could not be done. Once any merchandise had reached a Spanish customs house, duty would have to be paid or it would be confiscated. I explained that I was perfectly willing, even anxious, to pay the duty if I were allowed to import the food. But this, it appeared, made no difference.

At this point I remembered an acquaintance in the Ministry of Industry and Commerce and told the story to him. He said that although it was against the regulations, he thought he could fix it. First, however, I would have to file my application for an import permit, making seven copies, not counting the one I kept for reference. I had to make three trips to the other end of town to file the application; once I walked in just as the clock was striking the office closing hour, the next time I was given a temporary receipt, and it was only on the third trip that I obtained a receipt with the docket number.

My friend had told me to wait two or three weeks before getting in contact with him, since it would require that long for the processing of my application to go far enough to make possible his intervention. I waited a month, then asked him to swing into action. He did his best, but at the end of another month he informed me that my application could not be found. I waited another two months, and still it had not turned up. My ally was apologetic but said that, after all, such papers were always being lost. When I finally goaded him into action, he simply telegraphed the collector of customs to admit the shipment without a permit, which was done. As there was no railroad priority obtainable, the small case was delayed another week or so until there was a truck available. Apart from several packages of Cream of Wheat, which had been slit open at the bottom and emptied, the shipment was in as good condition as when it left New Orleans nine months before.

Except for the happy ending, this was by no means an unusual experience. A Spanish friend of ours who had bought a car in France just before the collapse and brought it in on a triptyque wished to pay the duty and matriculate it in Spain. Three times he made out an application for an import permit, and three times the papers were lost. Finally the Spaniard told his friend in the Ministry that he would be damned if he would make out any more papers, and that unless the matter was settled without more complications he would simply keep the car on a triptyque and the government would lose the customs duty. Somehow or other, the car in the end was imported, with the same informality as our food.

Without a powerful friend somewhere it was difficult to live in Spain and certainly impossible to carry on business. As a result, every company of any importance had a fixer, whose sole duty was to maintain contacts with officials of the Ministry of Industry and Commerce, the rationing authorities, the police, and other agencies which could be useful, or create trouble, as they were minded. Individuals usually depended upon brokers, who were employed for the most routine tasks. It was possible, I suppose, to obtain your own ration card if you did not mind waiting in line for hours day after day. But even with the help of a fixer from one of the big companies, it was two weeks after we moved into our apartment before we obtained ours. Ordinarily, however, the fixers could and did do almost anything, and I have yet to see a Spanish law that they could not get around.

All of this was by no means plain bribery. Bribery existed, as I knew from friends who sold articles to the Army: after paying off the captain and subordinate officers they were called on to pay the colonel as well. In big business deals, when it was a question of millions of pesetas' profit if an official would grant the necessary permit, there certainly was bribery. But minor matters could usually be handled with a pleasant manner and perhaps a package or a carton of cigarettes. And whisky, being expensive and a sign of the cosmopolitan, was perhaps even more prized. But there was no doubt of the fact that *simpatía* had to accompany these little tokens of good feeling.

Sheer don't-give-a-damn was another reason for the failure of Franco's Spain to approach the ideal of equal justice under law. A little incident at Vigo, where my wife and baby took a Spanish boat for home in May 1941, was a typical example. We arrived only the evening before the sailing, and in the rush to comply with the various formalities it was discovered at the last minute that both would have to be vaccinated in order to get on the boat. The baby was asleep at the hotel, but my wife and I rushed around to the port medical officer to see what could be done. Without so much as feeling her pulse, the doctor proceeded to make out a certificate stating not only that he had vaccinated her that day but that she was free from contagious disease. The fee was four pesetas (about thirty-five cents), which went to the government, so there was no question of this negligence benefiting the doctor himself. Seeing how matters were going, I asked him to make out a certificate for the baby as well, which he did for another four pesetas, despite the fact that she might have been laid up in the hotel with all the diseases a baby can have.

For anyone whom the Spanish officials remembered by sight and had nothing particularly against, it was still easier to evade regulations. While I was spending Christmas of 1939 with my wife and baby in Saint-Jean-de-Luz I was called back to Madrid. The day train left at nine o'clock, and it seemed impossible to make it, since the frontier did not open until nine. But I presented myself anyway, explained my difficulties, and was permitted to cross over without having my baggage examined, making a money declaration, or doing any of the thousand and one things connected with entering or leaving Spain.

If a Spanish official's interest coincided with your own, you were in an even stronger position. It is for this reason that I am one of the few Americans who managed to get a driving licence under Franco. I knew that to obtain it I would have to present innumerable documents and go to vast trouble, but I wanted to see just how long the business would take. There were about thirty of us, mostly truck-drivers, waiting one afternoon in the licence section of the Ministry of Public Works to take the "theoretical" test, to be followed a few days later by the "practical." Most of them had been there several days without being called, but luckily, because of my membership in the Royal Spanish Automobile Club, which of course had a fixer for members, I was one of the first called. The examiner quickly passed me, then inquired if by any chance I wanted to take the driving test that afternoon as well. Naturally I jumped at the opportunity to finish with the long process.

In a few minutes another official joined me and directed me to drive down the Castellana Avenue. The regulations provided for all manner of stopping and backing and fancy turns, but we kept straight on, almost to the Atocha railroad station, before he told me to pull over. Getting out of the car, he asked if I would mind waiting a minute. Finally I realized what was up: the poor man had to do some shopping, and as he could not afford a taxi, was using me for the purpose. His visits to numerous stores lasted over an hour, and at the end he congratulated me upon being as fine a driver as ever touched a wheel.

Amid all such goings-on, however, these officials retained that magnificent self-respect which is one of the most engaging qualities of a Spaniard. It was the custom for foreigners coming back from Portugal to present a bottle of whisky to the chief customs official, and a flat fifty of American cigarettes to each of the small fry, thus reducing to a minimum embarrassing questions about the amount of food we were bringing in without a permit. On one of these trips I ran into the *Jefe* standing outside the customs house and gave him the usual present. He accepted it, but quickly led me inside and explained that he must return it, for he had just been relieved of his duties and another *Jefe* was in charge. When he saw that he could not induce me to take it back, he proceeded to have a talk with his successor, and with this help I went through with the usual ease.

An American who landed at the Madrid airport with a large quantity of cigarettes had an even more revealing experience. For some reason it was against the law for travellers by airplane to bring in cigarettes, and they were all taken away from him. A day or so later he happened to go back to the airport, where he encountered the official responsible and jokingly told him that he hoped he was enjoying the cigarettes, which were selling on the Madrid bootleg market at $1.60 a package. Though obviously enraged, the official said nothing. But the next day the cigarettes appeared at the American's office, with law, regulations, customs duty, everything waived. The now well-known story of the parachute troops also illustrated this point: Ordered to jump, the German soldier barked: *"Heil Hitler!"* and was gone; the Italian refused and finally had to be pushed out; the Spaniard also objected to obeying orders, but when the commanding officer told him it was because he was a coward, he shouted: "Nobody can call me a coward," ripped off his parachute, and plunged down.[1]

The taint of inefficiency extended to every conceivable form of government activity. Sometimes this produced high comedy: In the middle of the night the police raided a Madrid job-printing establishment which was running off hundreds of copies of a mysterious document containing the floor plan of the Escorial. They decided that they had discovered a widespread plot against the regime, for they knew that Franco and the entire high command would assemble in the Escorial basilica on the following day for the burial of José Antonio; they locked up the printer with a complete feeling of satisfaction at duty well done. It was many hours later before the fascist committee in charge of arrangements could convince them that it had commissioned the printer to do a rush job on the programs for the funeral services, and that the floor plan was included in order to show the great men of the regime where they were placed.

It was not funny, however, when even the relief work of the Auxilio Social, the most successful of all the Nazi-model innovations of Franco, was seriously handicapped by his regime's inability to get things done. The Auxilio Social seems to have been administered fairly honestly, although its first director, Mercedes Sanz Bachiller, was ousted abruptly by Serrano Suñer at the end of 1939 on charges that she had embezzled several million pesetas. But as she was allowed to remain at liberty, there was presumably insufficient evidence to convict even in Franco's courts.

In some things, such as its refusal to discriminate against the families of "Reds" and its generally humane attitude to-

[1] Perhaps it was Nazi agents who thought up a different climax: the next soldier was British, and when he was ordered to jump he threw the Frenchman out of the plane.

ward its beneficiaries, the Auxilio Social did an admirable work. Its children's dining-rooms were painted in cheerful bright blue and yellow, and there were always flowers on the tables where the little ragamuffins ate the two meals a day which kept them alive. Instead of the prison-style numbers which are used in orphanages elsewhere to identify a child's clothes, the Auxilio Social embroidered them with flowers. The children were intensively drilled in the fascist song, ritual, and so on, but this could be overlooked when the officials were so obviously trying to instill in them good table manners, habits of cleanliness, and other accompaniments of a decent life which had been denied the great submerged mass of the Spanish people.

But the effect of these attractive qualities was diminished by the appalling waste of money and energy resulting from the inability of Auxilio Social officials to draw the line between boondoggling and legitimate activities. No figures on its administrative costs were made public, but from the amount of money spent building its luxurious headquarters in Madrid, on its expensive publicity service, and on innumerable conferences, congresses, and gatherings of all kinds, they must have been large. Soon after the dismissal of Mercedes Bachiller, in fact, a friend of mine in the diplomatic corps gave me figures from the Ministry of Finance showing that only twenty-five per cent of the Auxilio Social's total expenditures actually went toward buying and cooking food. (As the poor had no money with which to buy fuel to cook at home, the Auxilio Social prepared everything in its own kitchens.)

It was perhaps true, as its apologists claimed, that only so much food could be obtained at legal prices no matter how much money was available.[1] But in view of the misery of the

[1] The Madrid Auxilio Social report for July 1941 listed 139,329 beneficiaries and a total expenditure of 2,390,697 pesetas, an average per person of slightly more than 17 pesetas ($1.53) per month! This was all that was spent to provide the food necessary for them, whether it was a child, a nursing mother, a

Spanish poor, who could not afford to buy clothes, medicines, or the other things needed to raise their standard of life above that of animals, certainly more productive ways to spend the money could have been found.

Unintentionally, no doubt, the Auxilio Social widened the gulf between the haves and the have-nots. The flowers for the children's dining-rooms were bought in season and out, regardless of cost, but the parents were not so fortunate. A few of these older people had the very attractive porcelain lunch pails which you saw in the Auxilio Social propaganda booklets, but the majority collected their daily ration of thin soup and a little bread in rusty tin cans. They were supposed to take it home to eat, but most were too hungry to wait. I never managed to harden myself to the spectacle of these poor wretches, who sat down on the sidewalk outside the soup kitchen and gulped down the food in the full view of passers-by.

Serrano Suñer was entirely justified when he suppressed some of the more showy manifestations of the Auxilio Social's humanitarian activities. One of these, which I thought was the invention of some enemy of the regime until an Auxilio Social official boasted of it, consisted in providing nursemaids for the children of middle-class families who had come down in the world. The propaganda booklets contained winsome photographs of a beautiful recruit in the women's *Arbeitsdienst* [1] dressed in a spotless white Auxilio Social uniform, and pushing a smart baby-carriage while three or four other well-mannered children walked sedately alongside. My informant, who seemed to lack any understanding that millions of

---

beggar rounded up from the streets and placed in work camps, or any other unfortunate in the capital.

[1] The theory was that all young girls should give six months' service to the party, meanwhile living at home. Actually, however, this was required only of those who wanted jobs in the government or in government monopolies. A decree requiring that able-bodied men should give two weeks' work every year to the State, or the equivalent in salary, was issued soon after the end of the civil war, but this met with so much opposition that it was annulled a few months later.

Spanish children were starving, told me with satisfaction that this special nursemaid service was of inestimable benefit in maintaining the "morale" of the people.

Some of these practices were corrected when Carmen de Icaza, an energetic woman who has found time meanwhile to write several plays and novels, succeeded Mercedes Bachiller as head of the organization. But not all, as was demonstrated by the trials which the American community in Madrid underwent before it succeeded in outfitting an orphanage to be administered by the Auxilio Social. The plan was sponsored by Mrs. Weddell, wife of our Ambassador, and it was at first agreed that the Americans would take over some large house in Madrid to renovate. The official who was to co-operate with the Americans insisted, for reasons best known to himself, upon one particular house, which was completely unsuitable. It was rented none the less, and the Auxilio Social for months paid a very high rent on an empty building until the Americans decided to spend their money improving an existing orphanage in Vallecas, a village just outside the capital where many Madrid factory workers live.

The orphanage was located in the former village almshouse. With its fine ironwork and a wooded balcony overlooking a small patio, it was a charming example of Castilian baroque architecture; by an arrangement similar to that which Philip II instituted at the Escorial, one side of the chapel could be opened out so that the bedridden could see the elevation of the Host.

The almshouse had been abandoned for many years before the civil war, and according to the story told by Auxilio Social officials, it had been commandeered by a woman who felt sorry for the orphans of slain Republicans despite the fact that her husband had been killed by the "Reds" of Vallecas. Now that the war was over, the Auxilio Social was taking over the orphanage, and it suggested that the American community remodel the building and install the necessary furnishings.

The American committee accepted the new proposal with alacrity. Thereupon ensued a tremendous struggle on the part of the Auxilio Social to induce the Americans to equip the almshouse with comforts which were unknown to all except the wealthiest and most Europeanized Spaniards. This would have been a laudable aim but for the fact that as the committee had only a definite sum of money, such expenditures decreased the amount available for essentials. Some of the plans would actually have diminished the usefulness of the building for the purposes for which it was intended.[1]

One of its attractive points was the tile pavement of the patio, which was in perfect condition and made the patio an excellent refuge for the children against the burning heat of summer and the icy blasts of the Castilian winter. I shall never forget Mrs. Weddell's expression when she went out to the orphanage one day and discovered that this pavement had been ripped out without a word being said to the Americans who were paying the bills. The Auxilio Social authorities explained that they thought a hard flint pavement, with sharp pebbles sticking out, would be more "typical" and was needed to restore ye olde time atmosphere. They seemed genuinely disappointed over the materialistic spirit of Americans who put more emphasis upon the comfort of the barefooted children than the "typical." Thanks to American control of these fancies, the orphanage turned out to be both typical and comfortable. Later it was hailed by Serrano Suñer as a model of what an Auxilio Social orphanage should be, although of course he did not make any reference to the fact that Americans had paid for the improvements.

Such incidents reflected a fecklessness which was charming in individuals but did not produce the remorseless common

[1] A garbled version of these discussions leaked out to the United States and is responsible for the frequently made assertion that Mrs. Weddell donated a clubhouse to the Spanish fascists. There is no truth in this statement. The building would, it is true, make an excellent clubhouse or private home. But I saw the children installed in it after the remodelling was done.

sense necessary to operate a totalitarian economy. For it was, after all, mainly lack of common sense that permitted bands of German soldiers to roam through the northern provinces—a friend of mine watched the operations of one gang that penetrated as far south as Salamanca—buying up potatoes, meat, eggs, and dairy products to take out of a starving country. Despite numerous other difficulties, the inherent cause of Spain's misery lies within the Franco regime itself. The economic problem that confronted Franco was complicated, but the basic principle on which he should have operated was quite simple: there was just so much foreign exchange available from exports and it was the duty of the regime to sell these products in the most advantageous market, then jealously guard the proceeds for basic necessities.

Regrettable though it was to hold down imports of food to a minimum, it was obvious that if all the slender pile of *Devisen* went for this purpose, the result in the end would be economic collapse. It was better for Spaniards to go hungry while the government bought seed, fertilizer, and farm machinery for the new crop. Unless raw materials could be obtained from somewhere, the factories would be shut. Without Diesel oil for the fishing boats, coal for the railroads and factories, gasoline and tires for highway transportation, even a predominantly agricultural country must collapse sooner or later.

But there was no one in the government with the ability, the inflexible will, and the authority to determine a well-rounded program and stick to it. Demetrio Carceller, who was named Minister of Industry and Commerce after it became apparent that the Army could not run the economic machinery, is an able man whose rise from humble beginnings to the position of one of Spain's leading textile engineers is similar to the typical American success story. But Carceller was an ardent fascist, and his conduct of affairs has been twisted and unrealistic for that reason. Moreover, as questions of foreign policy and the special interests of pressure groups were interwoven, only the direct participation of Franco in the government—or the out-and-out dominance of Serrano Suñer—could make possible a unified and coherent policy.

The pressure of special interests, joined with plain blundering, wasted Spain's resources in countless ways. It was absurd for a war-exhausted country to spend a million dollars a month on gasoline and petroleum products, much of which were used merely for joy-riding. Yet it was not until a year after the end of the civil war that the first attempt was made to ration gasoline, and this step was taken only as a result of an acute shortage of both foreign exchange and shipping, aggravated by pressure from the British, who finally suspected that some of the gasoline must be leaking through to Germany.

As a corollary, restrictions were then placed upon the importation of passenger cars. But big new American models, shiny with the brightwork so beloved in Detroit, continually were being registered as gifts to Spaniards from non-existent relatives in Portugal or the United States. Not until the autumn of 1941, when large automobiles, starting with the smallest-size standard American car, were barred from the road, did these relatives stop making their "gifts." And meanwhile the young men in the Ministry were busy with plans to establish a Spanish automobile factory, which they intended to locate in Madrid, far from every possible source of raw materials, accessories, and skilled labour, rather than provide jobs for the "Red Separatists" of Bilboa or Barcelona.

On the other hand, there was an inexplicable desire to stop imports of food even though no loss of foreign exchange was involved. The sole exception was that the government did permit both foreigners and Spaniards to have small packages of food sent to them from Portugal, even though it was obvious that the Spaniards could pay for them only with money which they had smuggled out of the country at one time or another or refused to hand over in exchange for pesetas. Only the wealthy, however, had the money and the contacts in Portugal with which to take advantage of this system. But then only the wealthy benefited from one of the strangest purchases ever made by a starving country. This was Ovaltine, and at first I thought I was dreaming when I passed a grocery store where the packages were on display. Then I decided that this must be from some pre-war stock, since it seemed impossible that any official would permit the use of foreign exchange for such a luxury product when that amount would have provided so much more plain dried milk for Spain's starving children. But the wrapping showed that it was freshly imported from Switzerland, and the price of seventy cents for a small package—nearly as much as a labourer received for an entire day's work—indicated that the importer had made a very nice profit.

On the other hand, the government was very zealous of its prerogatives when it was a question of food brought back by the seven or eight thousand Spaniards who crossed over to Gibraltar every day to work as day labourers or domestic servants. The English money that they received had to be turned over to the exchange-control at once, and the authorities were very strict regarding the small amounts of bread, sugar, rice, and other food which the Gibraltar officials, despite the fact that England was at war, humanely permitted these workmen to take back with them every night. La Linea, the frontier station, and the entire neighbouring region was thus fed from Gibraltar. High authorities on the staff of the general commanding the Campo de Gibraltar used to make frequent visits, returning with their automobiles piled high with food. These officers of course did not pay duty on their purchases, but the lot of any workingman caught trying to bring in more than the prescribed amount was hard.

I shall never forget the scene which took place when I was returning to Spain after a visit to Gibraltar in November 1939. At first I was the centre of attention, for I was bringing in a small quantity of food, cigarettes, tennis balls, stationery, and other articles non-existent in Spain. The customs supervisor, glorying in his opportunity to show an *Inglés* the might of Spain, was noisily assessing each article, whether it was a can of cigarettes or a can of tennis balls, upon its weight. He seemed to sense his triumph when he ended up with a total amount of duty that was double the cost of my purchases.

The bystanders were still exclaiming over the figure he had announced when there was a sudden outburst of sobbing from an old woman standing at a customs table near by. A glance disclosed the reason. Scattered on the table was perhaps a quarter of a pound of rice, and the torn lining of her coat was evidence that she had been caught trying to smuggle it in. A Civil Guard, with the strange lack of pity which Spanish officials often display toward the humble, told me with relish that the old woman would pay dearly for her crime. The standard penalty, he said, was cancellation of the permit to work in Gibraltar, and there was neither food nor work to be had in La Linea.

Along with this harshness there was a Micawber-like belief that food would turn up from somewhere and save the government from the disagreeable consequences of its own mistakes. By the end of August 1939, when the last of the wheat crop was in, a few easy calculations were enough to show that there would not be enough to last until the next crop. A bread-rationing system was finally imposed, but a few more calculations would have demonstrated that even with reduced consumption, there would still not be enough. Whether it wanted to do so or not, Spain very clearly must either accept credit from the democracies to obtain this wheat, or draw upon its small stock of foreign exchange to buy it. But amid much talk of the Empire and Spain's past and future glories, nothing was done.

In January, 1940, when the Franco government was still haggling with France over a commercial agreement, the situation was desperate. Marshal Pétain, who was then French Ambassador, therefore arranged for France to send several shiploads of wheat from Marseille before the agreement was even signed. Exactly the same procedure was followed after the still worse harvest of 1940; again the Franco government waited until January before arranging the importation of wheat and corn from Argentina, and the emergency this time was so pressing that every seaworthy vessel in the Spanish merchant marine was taken off its usual run and rushed to Buenos Aires and other wheat ports.

The same incompetence was shown in administering all phases of the totalitarian economy. Frequently the Ministry of Industry and Commerce, after months of delay, would at last approve an application for the importation of essential raw materials or machinery. Then the foreign exchange, after more delay, would be granted by the Money Institute. But meanwhile prices or freight charges had gone up, and the whole process had to be repeated, or it would be discovered that the article could no longer be obtained at all. Occasionally the Ministry would authorize the importation of something or other but deny funds with which to pay transportation or other necessary charges.

Sherry was and is an extremely important export, and casks made of imported wood are necessary for its production. Their cost was small, and afterwards they could be sold to Scottish distillers, who use them to age whisky, for a good profit in foreign exchange. But it was only with the greatest difficulty that the Jerez *bodegas* obtained even a minimum of their requirements. It was the same with the pit props necessary in mining coal, despite the fact that coal was perhaps the most important of all the commodities that Spain must have in order to keep going; there were no reserves, and sometimes the Seville-Madrid express was delayed while coal was being taken on from a collier that had just tied up at the dock.

This incompetence was equally apparent in the management of Spain's farm production, which, after making all allowances for the lack of fertilizer, and so on, should have been sufficient to meet minimum needs. In the old days Spain had produced enough sugar to meet her own requirements. But the prices fixed by the government for sugar beets were too low, and farmers preferred to raise other crops which were more remunerative but less needed by the nation. Mutton also was made too cheap, and farmers held their sheep off the market.

More disastrous still was the low price fixed for wheat, the basis of the ordinary Spaniard's existence. It was this, more than the lack of fertilizer or the bad growing seasons—although these of course played their part—that accounted for the shortage of bread. According to the United States Agriculture Department's figures, Spain's average pre-war wheat crop was 160,338,000 bushels compared with 105,448,000 bushels in 1939, 79,412,000 in 1940, rising—thanks to the improved crop season—to 108,944,000 bushels in 1941. But the significant fact was that wheat acreage in 1941 was less than in 1939, when planting in the Madrid area was disrupted by the activities of Franco's troops around the doomed capital. That the price of wheat rather than post-war conditions was responsible was demonstrated by the fact that although acreage planted in rye, barley, and oats remained at the 1939 level, the rice crop was only half a million bushels short of normal and corn acreage even returned to the pre-war average.

The effect of such mistakes was aggravated by the inability of the Franco regime to distribute efficiently the food that it did have. I first became aware of this failure while driving from Madrid to Seville in the fall of 1939. My car broke down in a small *pueblo* where, I discovered, there had been no bread for three weeks. But at the next village, a few miles farther along, on the same excellent highway, there was all the bread one could eat. As late as the spring of 1941, when Spain was starving, we stopped at a café on the road from Madrid to Saragossa, in a sugar-beet area, and were served real coffee, with unlimited quantities of sugar and white bread.

With variations depending upon local conditions, these contrasts were to be found throughout Spain. They were partly the result of the inadequate transportation system, but clumsiness in working the machinery of distribution was mainly responsible. In the winter of 1940, for example, the excellent Galicia potato crop came on the market. My wife and I, who were sick of chick-peas and rice, were delighted with the ration of one kilo (2.2 pounds) per week per person. This was ample for us and we decided that things were looking up. Suddenly, however, the government in a burst of optimism removed all rationing restrictions on potatoes. Immediately the hungry *Madrileños,* with a hoarding instinct that was only too warranted, bought up every potato in the shops. Again we had none, and for two months we were unable to buy another potato at any price. For by this time the transportation crisis had become acute, and no priorities were obtainable to move them by rail. It should have been possible to ship them by truck, but this was more expensive, and as the rationing authorities refused to raise prices to meet this higher cost, the potatoes rotted in the fields in Galicia while the rest of the country went without.

As though this were not enough, each of the forty-seven provinces of Spain was permitted to act with regard to food almost as a separate nation. Municipal customs duties were collected upon food "imported" into Madrid and other large cities, and in addition special permits were necessary to move it from one province to another. The fascist aim, as we have seen, was to unify Spain, but the fascist regime revived these mediæval restrictions nevertheless.

A well-intentioned effort to protect the more poverty-stricken areas from being drained of their food supplies also aggravated the problem of distribution: each civil governor had the right to forbid shipment of any type of food from his province until he was sure that its needs were provided for. This was a socially desirable aim, for otherwise producing areas might go hungry while Madrid's higher prices siphoned off their food. But like so many well-intentioned Franco policies, this worked out badly. The hoarding mentality was universal, and civil governors proved very reluctant to permit any kind of food to go out until they were sure beyond any doubt that there were ample reserves in their respective provinces. It is scarcely necessary to emphasize the disastrous effects of this particularism upon the food supplies of a nation that already was living upon a hand-to-mouth basis.

# *Chapter* VIII

## SPECIAL PRIVILEGES AND THE BLACK MARKET

The blundering attempt to impose a totalitarian economy was all the worse because Spain was traditionally the land of special privilege. Franco's success in restoring these privileges therefore produced a singularly vicious combination: the rich stayed rich, if they did not get richer, and the poor were even hungrier than they had been in the worst days of the civil war.

This misery is in sorry contrast to the cry of social justice raised by the early Spanish fascists. It was all the more deplorable when contrasted with the fine idealism of a few of Franco's supporters, who believed he would win them a better Spain. These hopes have been bitterly disappointed. In few countries of the world is there such grinding, soul-destroying hunger and such luxury for the favoured of fortune.

Even with equal rights for all and special privileges for none—a principle which does not exist in the bright lexicon of "young" and fascist nations—some hardships would have been inevitable as a result of the civil war and the mistaken economic policy which followed it. But the suffering was increased immeasurably by the restoration of the old privileges; despite the steadily increasing misery of the poor, the wealthy managed to obtain virtually everything that they needed. And a new class of parvenus, who had made their money by special "favours" obtained from the government officials in charge of operating the faltering economic machine, spent their profits with an abandon which was one failing that could not be charged against the old families.

The Franco regime had, in fact, loaded still more privileged classes upon a suffering country. In order to hold its two most valuable supporters, the Army and the Phalanx, special arrangements were made for officers of both to obtain food from government commissaries. Even the common soldier ate far better than the ordinary citizen, while the food supplied to officers of the Army and the Phalanx, and to the more important officials of the government, more than compensated them for their comparatively low salaries. By 1941 the Phalanx had instituted its own separate rationing system for the rank-and-file members of the party, thus setting any kind of fascist above the general population.

An excuse for this practice was found in the special arrangements that were made to enable members of the diplomatic corps to live just as comfortably as though neither the civil war nor the greater war which followed had taken place. Despite the general misery, each embassy and legation was given a special monthly quota of sugar, potatoes, coffee, rice, lentils, and other staples which was far in excess of the amounts that the diplomats were able to obtain through the usual ration cards —although they were allowed to use these as well.

The object, presumably, was to prevent the diplomatic observers from realizing just how badly off Spain was, and it succeeded to some extent. When the American community was raising funds to equip the Vallecas orphanage, the wife of a member of our Embassy proposed a benefit party. She suggested that each American family donate eight dozen sandwiches for refreshments, just as at home. The wives of American private citizens were astonished, for they were finding it difficult to obtain even the one small roll a day per person to which they were entitled under the rationing scheme. Finally they realized that although bread had been rationed for some time, the fact was not known generally among diplomats, who had ample flour with which to make their own white bread.

The weight of circumstance finally compelled the Franco regime to reduce these quotas of the diplomatic corps, but during the first two years after the civil war many diplomats had more of the staple goods, at least, than they could eat. This was particularly true in the case of those who had foreign exchange with which to buy still more food, imported duty-free, from Gibraltar, Portugal, Argentina, and the United States. I knew several diplomats who had storerooms crowded with between five hundred and a thousand dollars' worth of food—enough, as they boasted, to enable them to live a year or more even if they were besieged in their apartments and could not obtain a single loaf of bread or after-dinner mint from hungry Spain.

Diplomats also were permitted to purchase meat, the most difficult of all foods to obtain, from the same government butcher shop which supplied Franco, Serrano Suñer, and other chiefs of the realm. I knew one chargé d'affaires who complained bitterly because he received only 132 pounds (60 kilos) a month for himself, his wife, and the persons whom they entertained. Criticisms of the regime by American and British diplomats did not omit their claim that the Axis representatives not only obtained the best cuts of meat, but received a special ten-per-cent discount besides. There was general regret early in 1941 when a dispute between the government butcher and the Serrano Suñer cook, who complained that he had been given beef instead of veal, resulted in the closing of the butcher store. It reopened after a time, but has never regained its old free and easy style of operating.

The wealthy classes of Spain did not have such official privileges, but as they had recovered their lands and their factories intact, they were able to buy what they needed. Apart from food obtainable on the black market, there was a considerable supply of non-rationed articles available, of course at extremely high prices. Until 1941 there were no restrictions except the size of one's pocketbook upon purchases of fish, chicken, game, ham, sausage, liver, tripe, kidney, and similar foods. Visitors passing through from France, Holland, and other occupied countries used to walk past the butcher shops marvelling that such abundance still existed in the world.

For inexplicable reasons, comparable to our own failure to convert the automobile industry to war production until months after Pearl Harbor, it was years before the Franco regime could bring itself to restrict consumption of other foods that were even more essential to the health of the Spanish working classes than meat. Until early in 1941, for example, pastry shops were allowed to operate just as usual, and while the poor stood in line for their pitiful daily ration of uneatable bread, the wealthy continued their pleasant custom of stopping off on their way home from Mass to consume some of the admirable Spanish éclairs or *mille-feuilles;* it was not until the famine had long since reached its acute stage that the government finally ordered pastry shops to use wheat flour on only one day a week. On other days almond paste had to be used instead of flour, but consumption of sugar, chocolate, and shortening was still not checked. And until I left Spain you were still free to buy all the candy you liked despite the shortage of the materials used in making it. I can remember only two occasions during our residence in Madrid when chocolate was distributed on the ration cards, and although an American could not use the dark, greasy stuff, the Spanish poor considered it a great treat. It was the same with ice cream, soft drinks (Coca-Cola was hard to get because of the shortage of bottles, not for lack of sugar), sandwiches in Madrid's numberless cafés, and other luxury articles.

Any kind of food that was adjudged *de lujo,* in fact, was not subject to rationing or price-fixing regulations; therefore we were able occasionally to buy sweet potatoes, which sold for two or three times the price of Irish potatoes, and sometimes eggs. Butter, being as clearly *de lujo* as it was rancid, was not rationed though it was always scarce; the usual practice was to give Leonese's or some other fancy grocery store a large order for sherry, almonds, and so forth, then threaten to cancel it if the clerk made any difficulties about sending along half a pound or so of butter. Almost always there were ample supplies of green peas, tomatoes, and various kinds of fruit, which were not rationed until the winter of 1941. Except for bread, wealthy families could get along quite satisfactorily with the help of purchases in the black market.

Eternal vigilance, however, was the price that all had to pay for keeping sufficient supplies of food in the larder. In Madrid and Barcelona, therefore, many wealthy families did not think it worth while to reopen their town houses, took suites in the big hotels, and let the restaurant-keepers do the worrying. This was, to be sure, practicable only in the two great cities. Elsewhere it was difficult to obtain eatable food even in the most expensive restaurants; in the government-operated tourist inn at Merida, for example, dinner sometimes consisted of fish cooked in rank olive oil, and fruit. The bad and insufficient food available in luxurious hotels, where there were lackeys to anticipate one's every desire, was as ironic a contrast as one could find even in Spain.

In Madrid and Barcelona, however, the restaurants were much better supplied. Not only were the wealthy concentrated there, but most of the foreigners travelling through Spain passed through one or both of these cities. Following Nazi practice, the Franco regime apparently was determined to show that there was plenty of food in Spain despite everything you read in the "pluto-democratic" press. The government therefore winked at the methods which the restaurant-operators used to obtain their supplies, and the business was so profitable that new establishments, each more sumptuous and more expensive than the last, continually sprang up. At the Rex, Scelto's, Paul's, Roncesvalles, the Ritz, the Palace Grill, to name only a few of those in Madrid, the well-to-do could dine with as much pleasure as in New York—perhaps better than in New York today, for there were also unlimited quantities of the finest sherry, wines, brandies, and liqueurs. It was almost impossible to get a good dry Martini, but the excellent sidecars and Bacardi cocktails, although made of home products, were some compensation for this hardship.

The American correspondents met occasionally to entertain an ambassador or some other distinguished personage, and our luncheons were a fair sample of the food that was obtainable in Madrid in the black months of 1941. We usually started off with some twenty varieties of hors d'œuvres, including various kinds of sardines, anchovies, herring, artichokes, potato salad, and so forth, and then went on to an excellent grilled sole. Afterwards there was as fine a *châteaubriand,* with sauce béarnaise, as Paris ever produced, accompanied by potatoes, string beans, and other vegetables. Then a sweet, and afterwards cheese, fruit, and coffee.

As accessories we had *Monopole* or else an excellent imitation of hock, a good Burgundy-type red wine, and brandy or liqueurs. The Spaniards have a most unfortunate custom of serving red wine straight out of the refrigerator, which accentuates its metallic taste, but the milk-white French rolls at these luncheons more than made up for it. We were not, of course, attempting to provide anything special; our aim was merely to do the comparative, and we knew that our expense accounts would not get past the auditors if we went in for caviar (Spanish caviar is magnificent), lobster, or the other accompaniments of a really first-class meal. At that, the bill per person at our luncheons was always between nine or ten dollars.

I obtained some idea of what a really noteworthy Spanish meal was supposed to be during my visit to the *Führerschule* of the Phalanx at Santander in the summer of 1940. The fixed-rate meals at the Hotel Real were not very exciting, and in order to revive our spirits our hosts took us to a little Santander restaurant where, in good French style, the kitchen was more or less a part of the dining-room. We had been forewarned not to eat too much lunch, and I was able to do a fair job through the hors d'œuvres, various kinds of shellfish, thick fish soup, sole, *paella,* lobster, mutton chops, and *rosbif,* with the appropriate wines and vegetables. But just as I was congratulating myself upon having acquitted myself honourably, if not with distinction, in the competition with my German, Italian, and French colleagues, it developed that these dishes were only leading up to the main course, which consisted of medium-sized chickens roasted whole, one for each person. And my good record up to that point was forgotten as vast quantities of salad, flan, cheese, and fruit followed in steady succession.

There was nothing very wrong with such Gargantuan meals in Santander or in other regions where supplies of food were relatively plentiful. But in Madrid and Barcelona, and particularly the latter, where food supplies for the common people have been restricted in punishment for Catalonia's stand during the civil war, such displays were extremely harmful to public morale. The Franco regime made some attempts to repress the more ostentatious displays of what money could accomplish, but the restaurants did not obey its regulations.

Typical of their disregard of authority was their treatment of a laudable decree, issued to correct the extremely late meal hours prevailing in Spain, which provided that lunch could not be served to a patron arriving after two thirty, nor dinner after nine thirty. The inexpensive restaurants made some pretence of complying, and so did the provincial hotels, which in this way could compel a motorist delayed on the road to take a room—where, following English practice, you could have anything served day or night. But the expensive restaurants paid no attention, for they made a specialty of catering to late arrivals from work or cocktail parties. A group of Americans in Madrid had a luncheon club that used to assemble every Saturday at a bodega for a few drinks beforehand. If we took only two or three rounds, we went to a moderate-priced eating-place, but if there was any serious drinking we always ended up at one of the very expensive establishments. All this was taken into account by the restaurant-proprietors in fixing their prices, and although some disgruntled patron occasionally complained to the police, the forty- or fifty-dollar fine was nothing in comparison with their extra profits.

It was the same with the one-dish day, which like the dessert-less day (abandoned after a few months) was a German importation. The theory was simple. On Mondays you ate only one course, supposedly stew or something filling but inexpensive, and paid the price of a normal meal; half of this went for relief. The restaurant-owners, however, had other ideas. For a time, in the early months after the war, they complied more or less, and their patronage on Mondays dropped off accordingly. It was then discovered that a one-dish meal permitted the inclusion of soup and dessert. Spanish cooking is notable for its excellent stews, and a *paella* consisting of vast quantities of rice, with meat, chicken, or fish intermingled, or a *cocido,* with chick-peas and meat, provided us with as much as we could eat even if we omitted the soup and dessert. This, however, did not suit the Spaniards, who, when the food is there, are magnificent trenchermen. If the restaurant-proprietor was a stickler for law and order, the usual practice was for one person to order *paella* and the other a *cocido,* it being understood that double portions of each would be served. If you were known to the management, however, you ordered what you chose as usual.

Gradually, under the compulsion of Spain's steadily dwindling food supplies, the government has taken some steps to restrain this gourmandizing. Under one decree it was forbidden to serve more than four courses at any one meal. By another, restaurants were ordered not to serve meat to their patrons except on days when meat was being distributed on ration cards in that section of the city. Finally meals à la carte were forbidden entirely. Three different price classifications of restaurants were set up, each allowed to serve a plain table d'hôte and a de-luxe version, costing double. The top classification was $2.70 plain and $5.40 special, plus service of 10 per cent.

Travellers who came through Spain in August 1942 reported that the luxury restaurants were still in operation, and that people who had the money to patronize them were able to avoid the hardships from which their fellow citizens were suffering. And still the hungry peered through the windows of these incredible establishments.

Yet the luxury restaurants, which were, after all, confined mostly to Madrid and Barcelona, did not greatly cut into the nation's food supply. They could serve a few thousand patrons a day, and at the best of times the average Spaniard could not afford any of the delicacies with which the wealthy stuffed themselves. Far worse was their effect upon public morale. Only a regime with a magnificent flair for unfavourable publicity could have believed that such restaurants would aid its standing abroad. At home the results were even more disastrous since the ordinary citizen considered them the final proof that the Franco regime was a government with the sole aim of favouring the privileged classes.

They also contributed greatly to the general lowering of moral standards which followed the end of the civil war. It was every man for himself, with no mercy for the poor, the weak, or the scrupulous. Once, at a time when sugar was particularly scarce, I asked the proprietor of one of the big restaurants how he managed to obtain the unlimited quantities that he seemed to have at his disposal. He said it was quite simple, from the rationing agency. He bought his regular quota at the low official price, and for all above that he paid the high black-market quotation.

My informant did not wish to disclose whether these extra profits were going to the government agency itself, or to some employee who was making extra money on the side. The point did not really matter. What did matter was the general corruption which resulted from the successful effort of the wealthy and strong not to accept the hardships produced by a war that was intended merely to restore their position under the monarchy. The result was that although the nation as a whole retained the fine instincts of *caballeros*—the humblest peasant so considers himself—money was able to accomplish almost anything in Franco Spain.

This was true despite the fact that there was not enough of anything that people wanted, from food, apartments, clothing, public utilities, to the least important details of existence. The efforts that my wife and I had to make in order to get back to Madrid after a visit to Barcelona in March 1941 epitomize these difficulties and the conditions to which they gave rise. The night express to Madrid, which was running only three times a week because of lack of coal, was booked solid for the next three weeks; space on planes was reserved even farther ahead. It seemed that we were stranded permanently, but fortunately Mr. and Mrs. Weddell happened to be at Tarragona, less than sixty miles away, and they agreed to let my wife ride back with them; meanwhile I obtained a ride with someone else. Although we had been in Spain a long time, we supposed mistakenly that it would not be difficult for her to reach Tarragona. She stood in line an hour and fifteen minutes to buy her ticket on the one good train available, a fast Diesel unit which made it in one hour, only to be told that there was no room and that the only train available was a combination freight and passenger train which took five hours. As it left at noon and did not have a dining-car, this meant a thoroughly uncomfortable journey, but there seemed to be no help for it and she rushed back to the hotel to try to have a lunch prepared.

The hotel factotum was shocked when he heard the story. It would be impossible, he told my wife, to obtain even a sandwich before the dining-room opened, but he guaranteed that he could get a place on the Diesel train. He rushed out of the hotel and was back within a few minutes with the reservation. He had obtained it for a small tip from the same clerk who had told my wife there was no room; the clerk regretted the inconvenience he had caused, but pointed out that, after all, he was paid very little by the railroad and had to get something for himself. It was a bad day for the clerk, however, for other travellers had not produced the necessary bonus and my wife found the train virtually empty.

Such dealings were the merest commonplace in Franco Spain, and inevitably they produced a black market on a scale probably unknown in any other country. *Estraperlo* was the general name for this black market and an understanding of its operations is essential to an understanding of present-day Spain. The name went back to before the civil war.

*Estraperlo* was the name of a gambling device which a Mexican promoter had wished to establish, along with roulette and other conventional games of chance, in the San Sebastián Casino. In his efforts to obtain the concession from the Rightist government which was then in power, he bribed a number of politicians, including a relative of the Foreign Minister, Alexander Lerroux. When these facts were disclosed the unusual word quickly became as famous as "the little green house on K street" did when the oil scandals of the Harding administration were revealed. It stuck in the public mind throughout the civil war, and afterwards the frequency of its use was an accurate indication of the practices which it represented.

"Racket" is the nearest translation, for *estraperlo* was a general term for any of the various sharp practices which were necessary to maintain life in Franco Spain. Ladies of good society would boast: "I bought some potatoes *estraperlo*," with the same pride that they said: "I bought this hat at Hélène's" when they returned from shopping excursions to Biarritz. Food was of course the principal concern of *estraperlistas,* as it was of everybody else. But the shortage of everything was so complete that it is scarcely possible to name an article which was not handled in this black market at one time or another.

It extended everywhere, and to every type of activity. On my first visit to Barcelona, for example, in November 1939, I did not go to see any of the big textile manufacturers because they were almost all in jail. Our cotton credit had supplied them with the necessary raw material, but they were still short of the dies, bleaching materials, and repair parts for spindles and looms which were necessary to resume operations. This challenge to Catalan resourcefulness had been met, of course. A factory which for one reason or another could not reopen would sell its stock of dies, for instance, to another that needed them. Naturally the prices charged were far above the 1936 level fixed by the government, and when somebody squealed there were mass arrests—followed by the mass release of the culprits a few weeks later.

Automobile tires were very scarce, and long before Pearl Harbor I was accustomed to the fact that a second-hand tire, which could be sold without restriction, commanded a higher price than a new one, which could be obtained, theoretically at least, only by means of a government priority. But new ones also were to be had *estraperlo* at unbelievable prices.

When gasoline rationing finally came, the *estraperlistas'* field of operations was greatly increased. The gasoline rationing plan was well conceived; there was never such an absurdity as the "X" cards, providing unlimited quantities to the fortunate holders, which our own O.P.A. was guilty of. In Spain nobody could obtain a gallon of gasoline without handing over a coupon to the filling station attendant, who in turn could get no more until he had accounted for every gallon that he had received. Precautions were taken against the issue of extra ration cards in provinces away from home; cards were issued only in the province in which a car was registered. And a flat rate of so much gasoline for each horsepower of your car obviated complications over issuance of supplementary allowances. In fact there were no supplementary allowances, and care was taken to see to it that taxis, trucks, and buses covered the mileage corresponding to the amount of gasoline they received. To further discourage pleasure driving, and at the same time raise government revenues, the price of gasoline was fixed at $1.60 a gallon except for necessary transport services, which bought it at forty cents a gallon.

With all these excellent precautions, however, bootlegging of gasoline flourished. Filling station operators gave short measure on tickets and sold the remainder at higher prices. Taxi-drivers found it more profitable to sell the gasoline that they had bought cheap than to pick up fares. Although use of official cars was sharply restricted, so that a colonel who was driving away from his house would have to leave his wife to take the streetcar, it was usually possible to buy some gasoline from the driver of an Army truck.

The tobacco ration was two packages every ten days for men only; supplies seldom permitted the government to hold to this schedule, and as numerous Spanish women smoked, cigarettes were one of the foundations of the black market. So, of course, were pesetas, which sold at from 25 to 30 to the dollar, compared with the official rate of 11 and the "tourist" rate (copied from the travel mark) of 12.5.

For centuries smuggling has been a common practice in Spain, and the ingenuity which the *estraperlistas* employed in carrying on their trade would have earned fortunes for them in our prohibition days. Food is bulky, and as travellers arriving in Madrid were forced to submit to customs examination at the station, a less resourceful people would have given up the effort. But sacks of potatoes, the contents of which were obvious at a glance, continued to arrive somehow. So did meat. One day the station police were struck by the fact that a peasant woman who frequently came to Madrid for the day always arrived with legs badly swollen, but had neatly turned ankles every evening when she took the train home. The next time she arrived they searched her and found that she had a couple of dozen veal chops bandaged to her legs. There was one apparently very pregnant woman who, because of the Spaniards' respect for propagation of the race, made many a successful trip until it was discovered that her bulk was due to large slabs of beef laid over her stomach.

Determined efforts were made by the government to suppress these practices. The cumbersome machinery of permits and other formalities required for the transportation of food and other products already made this traffic illegal per se, but in October 1940 a special system of courts and prosecutors was set up to handle nothing except infractions of the rationing laws. The definition of offences under this law was very comprehensive. Besides sale of rationed articles without a permit, or at more than the prices fixed by law, it was an offence to hoard stocks beyond the amount permitted by the government. It was even an offence for a private householder to have any reserves of such foodstuffs in his own larder. Heavy fines and sentences to hard labour were authorized, and in order to encourage informing, it was provided that any person denouncing an *estraperlista* or hoarder would receive forty per cent of the fine. The extent of the black market is apparent when one considers that between the establishment of these special courts and June 30, 1941, 87,888 charges were brought. And, despite the notorious slowness of Spanish justice, 1,300 *estraperlistas* were sentenced to labour battalions, and fines totaling nearly $5,500,000 were imposed. In addition, goods to the value of nearly a million dollars were confiscated, and scores of grocery and butcher shops were padlocked for a month or longer.

Even these courts, however, were not drastic enough to meet the situation, and in the autumn of 1941 Franco gave military courts jurisdiction, with power to impose the death penalty upon the worst offenders. This, according to the latest reports from friends in Spain, has at last had some effect. Mountains of chick-peas, thrown away by some frightened hoarder, were found in the Guadalquivir River, and for a time the black market ceased to exist. In some ways Spain's own continued slide downhill has contributed to this development. The ban upon the circulation of standard-size automobiles, for example, has reduced trading in gasoline and tires. The shortages which have begun to hit Portugal, once the great supply depot for the *estraperlistas,* likewise have cut down the amount of this contraband trade. Nevertheless, a black market is inevitable as long as there are not enough of the good things of this world and there are wealthy people who want them. The only cure for bootlegging in the United States, as we finally discovered, was repeal of the Prohibition Law; the only cure for *estraperlo* is a revival of normal supplies of food and other coveted articles. And this, unfortunately for a nation which deserved a better fate, will be long a-coming.

# Chapter IX

## "BREAD, MOTHERLAND, AND JUSTICE"

The condition of the common man under Franco is similar in many ways to the state of primitive nature before there were any governments, and life was "solitary, poor, nasty, brutish, and short." Except that he is not alone in his misery, that description applies with bitter accuracy to the lot of the average Spaniard today. Greece is the only nation in the Western world that is worse off. But in Greece there is little or no food for anybody; in Spain, despite all the mistakes of the Franco regime, hardships would have been endurable if all had been compelled to share them equally, and the regime had lived up to its grandiloquent motto of "Bread, Motherland, and Justice."

This misery certainly was not the result of deliberate policy. Many of the Franco regime's aims were excellent, but by the perversity of fate these often aggravated the effects of the stupid policies. Thus, although the attempt to hold both wages and the cost of living at the 1936 level was commendable, the failure to keep down prices produced even more intense suffering among the poor than would have resulted if the government had not intervened at all. By 1941 the official index of food prices, calculated on the official levels, was twice as high as it had been in 1936. If one took into consideration the *estraperlo* prices, the cost of obtaining the food necessary for health was at least three or four times the pre-war level.

Wages and salaries, on the other hand, had been returned inflexibly to the 1936 level. As early as 1940 the government started giving way and began to authorize increased pay for certain groups, but its concessions were completely inadequate to meet the increased cost of living. Once it started raising wages, it would have to permit further price rises, and it was caught on the horns of the dilemma produced by its costly and fundamental error: the attempt to carry out a collectivist program unsuited to the temperament of the Spanish people.

The result was that the pay increases which were grudgingly conceded by Franco only threw into more relief the failure of his regime. Typical of such highly publicized "favours" to the working classes was the decree raising the minimum daily wage of workers on the railroads to 10 pesetas—90 cents a day. Ordinary day labourers in Madrid were raised to 9 pesetas—81 cents a day. Highly skilled mechanics, who in the United States are making $20 and $25 a day, are paid $2.50 in Madrid. And they were raised to this amount only after their employers saw that their men could not do such delicate work as making jigs or patterns for machine tools when they were half or three fourths starved.

Low wages had always prevailed in Spain, but until the civil war prices were low accordingly. It must be said to Franco's credit that he has been fairly successful in holding stable rents and the cost of utilities and services. Streetcar fares in Madrid, for example, were two cents, and the subway, which charged according to distance travelled, averaged about the same amount. A hair cut was nine cents. While an excellent servant was paid $8 a month, most got less.

Somehow or other even the petite bourgeoisie managed to keep a servant and pay for apartments with a sufficient number of cubicles to contain their large families. To be sure, incredible feats of managing and wangling were part of the daily routine of a Spanish household. If Paquito, for instance, ever was sent outside Madrid on a commission for his employer, you could be sure that he would bring back something to eat despite the combined efforts of the Army and the Civil Guard to stop him. Family ties are strong in Spain, and relatives living in the more prosperous farming regions of the north managed to send a considerable amount of food to families in Madrid.

Another survival factor was the Spanish custom of holding two or more jobs. This was a particularly common practice among government employees, many of whom did not go back to the office after lunch and siesta. Merry del Val, for example, was available to correspondents only in the morning. In the afternoon he became an official of the "Justice" division of the party; on the side he was also the fascist chief of protocol.

Apart from actually accepting bribes, it was always possible to use one's position with the government or even a private concern to help sell insurance or carry on some other individual enterprise. The income of a large household, moreover, was increased by the fact that there were usually two or three wage-earners, at least. Almost the entire family tried to get some kind of employment, no matter how ill paid.

As a result, all except the extremely poor managed from time to time to buy a litre of olive oil *estraperlo,* or perhaps a tiny piece of sausage to cook with their chick-peas. But the prices of these articles, whether they were unrationed or were bought on the black market, were high even by American standards, and for the most part they did nothing to alleviate the hunger of the Spanish people. It profited a government employee earning $45 a month nothing at all to walk by a shop offering ample supplies of ham at $1.50 a pound. A frying-size chicken (minus head, feet, liver, gizzard, etc., which were sold separately) cost $1.80 in 1940 and 1941, but has now risen to $2.80.

*Estraperlo* prices were of course even higher. Stewing meat, the only kind that could be bought, was 75 cents a pound in 1941 and very few families could obtain it at any price; now meat has almost disappeared from the black market. When it was to be had at all, olive oil was a dollar a quart, sugar fifty cents a pound. Flour cost the same as sugar, and coffee (which was very rare) a dollar a pound.

Such prices obviously placed these commodities beyond the reach of all except the wealthy, and the mass of the population had to live upon what they could obtain on their ration cards. Even in normal times, of course, very few Spanish families indulged in such luxuries as meat or coffee; their diet consisted for the most part of bread, rice, chick-peas and other dried vegetables, and large quantities of fruit and green vegetables. Even though the cooking was done in olive oil, this is a diet markedly deficient in fats and starch; according to estimates by Spanish authorities, the food consumed by the average Spanish workingman before the civil war produced only two thirds of the calories contained in the diet of workmen in other European countries. This food deficiency, which perhaps was one reason for the cadaverousness of Don Quixote and many a Spaniard who has come after him, had helped create a serious tuberculosis problem in Spain before the civil war. But on the whole it was a healthy diet, rich in vitamins, and suited to a hot climate. Certainly it was infinitely superior to the bread, molasses, suet, and tea with which the English poor, for example, manage to stifle the pangs of hunger.

Nevertheless it was already on the danger line before the civil war, and afterwards these deficiencies became all the more marked. For the first two years after the war all but the poorest could buy unlimited quantities of fruit and green vegetables, but this was a long way from providing them with the nourishment that they needed. And they were always hungry. These foods had no staying qualities; as my wife and I knew from experience, after a meal of fish, rice, chick-peas, and fruit you felt quite full, but you were hungry again in an hour or so.

As long as there was an adequate supply of bread this problem was not so serious. Spanish bread is very heavy and does keep hunger away. For that reason, when a friendly diplomat gave me some fine white flour with which to make our own bread, our servants did not like it and continued to eat the bread obtainable on the ration card.

In the beginning this was relatively plentiful. Between the end of the civil war and the outbreak of the European war, bread was not even rationed. When rationing was imposed, the amount per person was fixed at 6½ ounces a day, which was much less than the poor usually consumed but still fairly adequate. But as the food shortage grew worse in the autumn of 1939, some localities began to go without any at all; in Madrid the ration was reduced to 3⅓ ounces without any formal announcement. Aroused by the protests which followed, the government then instituted a novel scheme under which the amount of the ration was determined by size of income. Three classes were set up, ranging from eight ounces for the poorest to three ounces for the "wealthy"—including anybody with an income in the neighborhood of $60 a month—who, it was said, would be able to make up for their smaller quantities of bread by buying other and more expensive foods.

This rationing system must commend itself to anyone who knows post-war Spain. Unfortunately, however, the inefficiency in distribution continued. There was never any certainty that there would be bread for either poor or rich, and always there were long lines waiting before dawn in front of the bakeries to be sure of sharing the limited distribution. There were many days when our district got no bread at all.

Even worse was the steady deterioration in the quality of the bread. Soon after the end of the civil war, when the Franco regime wished to emphasize its success in attaining its aim of "Bread, Motherland, and Justice," it was pure white. As time went on, it became greyer as a result of adulteration with barley and oat flour. Afterwards the comparative plentifulness of corn induced the regime to use meal but the bakers did not know how to cook it and the bright yellow loaves were still worse. As the famine grew more desperate in the winter of

1940–1, other expedients were tried. Sawdust was one of the adulterants, and a splinter lodged in my gum one night when I was having an expensive dinner in the Palace Grill. Ground-up chick-peas were also used, and the maximum proportion of wheat flour was fixed by a government decree at thirty per cent.

As the prosecution of a number of bakers revealed, the amount of wheat flour actually used was considerably less than thirty per cent because many saw their chance to make extra money by using a still larger proportion of adulterants and selling the balance of the flour *estraperlo*. The result was bread that was brick-hard and should make an interesting study for a dietician; we tried to eat it by dunking it in coffee or hot milk, but instead of getting softer it disintegrated. Spaniards, who have good teeth and strong stomachs, ate it. But no digestion was capable of deriving much nourishment from sawdust.

The quality of other foods also had greatly deteriorated. Never was there a gram of fat on any kind of meat, whether bought legally or otherwise; it was all trimmed off and used by the soap and nitroglycerine factories. A considerable quantity of the milk on sale in Madrid came from melancholy, undernourished cows who were kept in the gloom of milk establishments scattered throughout the residential section of the capital. To speak of butterfat content, pasteurization, or sanitary precautions of any kind revealed you as a new arrival in Madrid. As a candid operator of one of these urban dairies once told us, the cheapest grade of milk was half water, the middle grade was one third, and only the top grade was more or less as it came from the cow. The poor quality of all grades was recognized, and the Auxilio Social and other relief agencies tried to use dried milk, prepared in the highly sanitary Nestlé plant near Santander—which is operated by Swiss experts—exclusively.

Difficult as it was to obtain potatoes, which were sold by weight, the purchaser usually found a pound or so of stones in every sack. Much of the coal one bought was slate. The sugar produced in Spain was much less sweet than that in other countries, but this supposedly was due to faulty methods of refining rather than any deliberate effort at adulteration.

Even if it had been of good quality, the food available to the poor—namely, that on ration cards—was totally insufficient. Foreigners who lived in Madrid throughout the war told me that except at the very last the average *Madrileño* had more to eat while the capital was besieged than after its "liberation" by Franco. Yet, owing to the extraordinary rationing system, it is difficult to explain just how little food they received under the New Order. Unlike those of other countries, the Spanish rationing books do not provide for the regular distribution of fixed amounts of food over a given period. A household ration book contains coupons for certain amounts of bread, olive oil, sugar, chick-peas, ersatz coffee, and so on. Bread, of course, could be bought (theoretically, at least) every day. But sale of other rationed articles took place only after an announcement in the newspapers that there would be a distribution of such-and-such commodities in such-and-such districts of Madrid. These announcements were made very irregularly, depending upon the varying supplies of food, the crop estimates, and expectation of imports from other countries. As the shops had no reserves to use if something went wrong with the transportation or distribution system, sometimes the food was not available even after the official announcement.

The best over-all figure that I could obtain from the government was the special rationing allotment set up for the coal miners of Asturias, after the weakness produced by their hunger had seriously cut down production. For Franco Spain it was relatively generous. It allotted 15 ounces of bread a day for adults, 10 ounces for children between the ages of seven and fourteen, and 6 2/3 ounces for younger children. For adults, it authorized the following weekly quantities of food: sugar, 4 ounces; olive oil, half a pint; lard, 4 ounces; dried codfish,

8 2/3 ounces; potatoes, 3 pounds 3 ounces; chick-peas, lentils, and other dried vegetables, 1 pound 9 ounces; soap, 4 ounces.

This was by no means a starvation ration, although it was very deficient in sugar and fats, but it was far from being typical of Spain. The reason for the particularly generous ration of potatoes was that Asturias adjoins Galicia, the great potato-producing region of Spain, and the inadequacy of transportation facilities made it difficult to ship them anywhere else. The supreme importance of coal in maintaining the national economy made it essential to keep up production. Moreover, it was necessary to placate the hard-boiled Asturian miners, who, with their mastery of the art of fighting with dynamite charges, constitute the most dangerous nucleus of opposition to the regime.

Other sections of Spain, however, which were less useful or less dangerous, were not so fortunate. We kept records of the food that we obtained on our ration cards for the twelve months ending on May 15, 1941, and the following is the average amount of food per month per person distributed during that period: sugar, 3⅓ ounces; olive oil, half a pint; meat, 3⅓ ounces; dried codfish, 3⅓ ounces; chick-peas, lentils, and other dried vegetables, 6 2/3 ounces; rice, 6 2/3 ounces. In other words, the amount that the Madrid public received *per month* was roughly equivalent to the food that the Oviedo miners were given *per week*.

Potatoes do not appear on this list because, as I have mentioned earlier, the removal of rationing restrictions and other complications abruptly destroyed the relatively abundant supplies that we enjoyed for a time. We did not bother with the soap available on the rationing cards because it was of such low quality that it was not worth buying. For washing clothes and all other purposes we used toilet soap, which, as a nickel-size cake cost fifteen cents, was *de lujo* and therefore could be bought without restrictions. We also could have obtained a special ration for the baby of one kilo of sugar a month, and one small can of condensed milk, but did not desire to use this privilege.

The difficulties which we encountered in obtaining enough food for the baby and for ourselves made us realize the grimness of the struggle that confronted the average Spanish household. By comparison with the mass of the Spanish people, we were the darlings of fortune; we had had some conception of the famine conditions which we would have to confront, and when we shipped our furniture from England we had included large quantities of sugar, flour, canned meat, and coffee, all of which were admitted without the requirement of an import permit. Each time that I came back from visiting my wife in Saint-Jean-de-Luz I had brought small supplies of food, and on my tour of Spain in the autumn of 1939 I had bought potatoes, lentils, peas, and other non-perishable vegetables. When my wife and baby finally came to Spain in February 1940, we brought in enough powdered milk to last for several months, and friends who visited France before the collapse brought still more.

In addition we were helped by the departure of other Americans who turned over to us the remainder of their own scanty supplies. Our biggest windfall came in the late summer of 1940, when the food shortage was so acute that wives and children of American executives of the telephone company were ordered back home. Despite the efforts of Colonel Behn and his large organization to obtain food for them, their growing children were showing the unmistakable effects of malnutrition. Individually their supplies were small, but as they were kind enough to turn most of them over to us, we obtained a substantial total of milk, cereals, and baby food. As other foreign households one by one gave up the struggle, they let us have their last carefully guarded stocks. From time to time various diplomats also helped, and we occasionally managed to have small packages of sugar, coffee, lard, and flour sent in from Portugal. We were determined to hold on as long as possible, and although the restaurant prices were so high that we could not afford to take many meals out, we bought whatever food was offered without regard to price. As a result, I used my entire salary on mere subsistence, and I spent half my time trying to get food.

Yet, despite all our efforts, the threat never lifted that some day the cupboard would be irremediably bare. Thanks to our advantages as foreigners, we were never actually hungry, but fish and rice were our mainstays and I have not been able to eat either since I returned to this country. For nine consecutive weeks early in 1941 there was not an ounce of meat distributed in Madrid; neither for love nor money were we able to obtain a potato for the baby until a young American friend had the brilliant idea of bringing some from Salamanca, where they were plentiful despite the forays of the Nazis. An outbreak of boils from which other Americans and I suffered was clearly the result of food deficiencies, and it was a long time after our return to the United States before my wife and I regained the weight we had lost. The baby, who lived mostly on dried milk, cereals, and canned vegetables from outside Spain, suffered no ill effects. But our continual preoccupation with food left its mark on her: she would burst into sobs when she had finished one course and would not stop even though the next was immediately served; it was months after our return before she realized that now there would always be enough for her.

Spaniards had no such solution available when their children cried for food. Despite all the water it contained, the supply of milk was sufficient to meet only half of the demand of Madrid children. Mothers therefore continued to nurse their children until they were two years old, and in particularly difficult times they gave their breasts to their older children. The mainstay of the poor was bread and the family *cocido* of chick-peas, flavoured with tiny amounts of fish or perhaps some meat bones which the butcher could not sell otherwise. High sales taxes, moreover, increased the prices of even the rationed articles, and many of the poor did not have the money to buy meat when it became available once a month.

The majority, however, already had enough money to buy all the food that could be obtained on ration books. Long since they had lost interest in mere wage increases. What they wanted was food. We paid our laundress, for instance, 65 cents for a day's labour, from which she had to feed herself. But we discovered that the poor woman much preferred the alternative system under which she was paid only 45 cents but was given her lunch. And she made this choice despite the fact that she did not have the money with which to buy coal to cook for herself and her young daughter. She was embarrassingly grateful when she was permitted to cook a meagre supper for herself and her daughter on our stove.

The fact that working people of Spain needed food rather than higher wages was recognized by a remarkable decree which placed upon the employers the responsibility of keeping their workmen from starving. Large employers of labour, particularly in factories or mines, were required to set up company stores to provide most rationed articles for their employees at the official prices or less. They were ordered to provide premises and administrative help at their own expense, and they were compelled to give transportation of these foodstuffs priority over goods needed in the operation of their business. The decree was a tacit admission of the breakdown of the government's own rationing system, an invitation to employers to use their own ingenuity and get the food where they could without too much regard for the source, rather than permit the collapse of the entire economic structure. Circumstances being what they were, it was a wise move, and a Spanish workman would not be able to understand the objections of American labour to the company store.

At best, however, this was only a palliative measure. A Dante would be needed to describe the hunger of the Madrid poor, living in their wretched hovels (or in actual caves off Abascal

Street), with little or no heat against the rigors of the Castilian winter, threadbare clothing, and not even soap with which to wash themselves.

Despite attempts of the police to round them up, crippled beggars, with stumps of arms or legs protruding, were two and three to the block in the business section of Madrid. Mothers, with emaciated children wrapped in their shawls, sat on the stairways of subway stations with hands outstretched for alms.

The hunger was so intense that garbage, meaning food that was thrown out although still edible, almost ceased to exist. Our servants, who apparently had accordion stomachs, each day consumed every morsel of food that was cooked in our apartment, whether we unexpectedly went out to dinner or brought home a guest or two who ate whatever was in the house. But every morning there were scarecrows rummaging for orange peels and anything else they could find in the garbage heap around the corner from our apartment.

All this time, as I knew from Spaniards with relatives in Navarre and other northern provinces, food was relatively abundant in these rich and industrious farming regions. I began to suspect that perhaps I was judging Spain from conditions in Madrid alone, and when news came in February 1941 that the American Red Cross was sending a food shipment to Spain, my wife and I decided to visit the south and see for ourselves how things were.

We discovered that Madrid was a land of milk and honey by comparison with the incredible misery of Andalusia. In the grey dreariness of a Castilian winter this suffering had not been so striking. But in Cadiz, with a warm sun overhead and the bright blue of the Atlantic washing at the white city's ramparts, the famine seemed all the more cruel. For it was a famine. The stevedores who were attempting to unload the American flour and milk from the Red Cross ship, the *Cold Harbor,* were so weak that they staggered under the burden; they had their entire lunch period free for sleeping, for the simple reason that they had no lunch to eat. As the Red Cross representatives went down to the boat each morning, there were lines of women in their inevitable black shawls who extended their hands and whispered: "Bread, bread."

We were staying at the Hotel Atlantico, a lovely white modern building, overlooking the sea, which had been built to attract summer visitors from all of southern Spain. But the famine penetrated even there; for breakfast we had a cup of ersatz coffee, or *malta,* without milk or sugar, and two unwholesome macaroons made of almond paste. Dinner consisted of a watery soup, a small helping of stewed mutton, and a few English peas. But for the fact that during our stay in Cadiz we had lunch every day aboard the *Cold Harbor,* where there were unlimited quantities of fine white bread, meat, and potatoes, we would have gone to bed hungry.

We visited almost all of the grocery stores of Cadiz, and except for a few bananas their shelves were as bare as their tile floors. For the first time in our stay in Spain we discovered that there was not even any fish to be had. Lack of Diesel oil for the boats kept most of the fishermen from going out, while almost all of the reduced catch was shipped under contract to Seville or Madrid. The swollen Guadalquivir, moreover, had inundated thousands of acres planted in vegetables. These extraordinary misfortunes, piled on top of the long-standing hunger of southern Spain, had done their work.

By this time, to be sure, enough American flour and milk had been distributed to the Auxilio Social to alleviate these conditions. But the authorities insisted that because of the shortage of gas, produced by the lack of coal, it was impossible to start using the flour to make bread. They seemed unable to understand the insistence of the *Yanquis* that they use the supplies on hand at once.

In the old people's home operated by the Little Sisters of the Poor my wife and I discovered a different feeling toward the famine victims, although, as the Mother Superior sadly explained, she had been compelled to limit the number of inmates to sixty because she could not feed any more. The people in Cadiz were so poor now, she said, that the Sisters could collect very little alms. In the old days a friend might send them a fat pig from his farm in the country, but now the government's regulations about transporting food were so severe that this also was impossible. Here lately, too, it had been almost impossible to get either fish or vegetables, and the Sisters and their charges had had to live mostly on bread and chick-peas. This was difficult for the older ones, because the bread was so hard for them to chew with their toothless gums. Some of them, she said, could not sleep at night because they were so hungry. But now, with the American flour and the wonderful American milk, everything would be so much better, she told us, her eyes shining with elation. We asked her if she had yet made any bread, and the answer was a quick "*Mais non,* we have a better use for the flour."

The Mother Superior, who had the shrewdness of her native France, explained that after all there was still bread to be had and that although it was not very good, there was no use passing up any possible supply of food. Last night, she said, she had made a wonderful *bouillie* of hot American milk mixed with American flour, and the inmates had enjoyed it more than anything they had had for years. One old man had called on his patron saint, San José, to bless the North Americans; another, afraid that such a luxury could not last, would not eat his *bouillie* until he was sure that there was more flour and milk and that the Sisters would take care not to waste it.

That afternoon a steamer put in at Cadiz with a large consignment of oranges destined for England. Having been frozen by a sudden cold snap, they had spoiled, and the port authorities had induced the captain to donate them to the people of Cadiz. They were gone in a flash, and the starving people, seeing their chance to put something in their stomachs, did not wait to cut them open and gulped down the rotted oranges like animals.

In Seville conditions were nearly as bad. The animation and gaiety which had once made it one of the most cheerful cities in the world was gone. There were a few vegetables and oranges on sale in the municipal market, but they were beyond the reach of the mournful women who stood there, each with an infant in her arms and a brood of young children clutching at her. They were stuffing into their mouths the outer leaves of cabbages and anything else resembling food that they could pick off the floor. Some of the more prosperous were spending a few centimes on small twigs which, when chewed, give a sweet taste. Others were consuming long purplish pods from the locust tree—the same that we have in the south of the United States—which fill up the stomach but cause severe intestinal disturbances if eaten regularly.

But there were few people in Seville who were eating regularly. We were staying with the American consul, John Hamlin, in the pleasant consulate which was built originally for the Seville exposition held by General Primo de Rivera, and we did not have to rely upon the *Cold Harbor* or the meagre fare in the grandiose dining-room of the Andalucia Palace Hotel. This was fortunate, for the famine was well-nigh universal, and when we went to the Hospital of Caridad and were confronted by Valdés Leal's painting of the dead in their coffins, its horrors were a near reminder of the gaunt faces that we had seen in the municipal market. We asked the Sister who was showing us around what the food situation was like among the completely destitute who called on the hospital for help. The worst of it was, she said, that they could not keep anybody more than three days. And when they were turned out to make room for more, only the good Lord could say what became of them.

The stolidity with which these unfortunates endured their sufferings stands out above all other impressions. I would have supposed that these quick-witted, sensuous, and mercurial people would long since have resorted to violence. I could not understand why a mother, seeing her children starve before her, did not rob the first prosperous-appearing individual who came within reach. But they seemed to accept their fate, and there had been no bread riots, no disorders. For a time it had been risky to travel on the road between Seville and Cadiz after dark, but the military courts, exercising freely their power to punish robbery by violence with death, now had the situation in hand. Some day, I reflected, this pent-up bitterness will burst out in a frenzy of cruelty and destruction which will be all the worse because it has been held in so long. But for the moment no one seemed to have the spirit to do anything more than accept the inevitable.

The return journey to Madrid revealed even more desperate suffering. On the way down we had come via Talavera and Mérida, which was longer but a better road. We returned by the main highway from Seville to Madrid, passing through Córdoba. Perhaps the famine was as bad on the longer route, but the car gave us no trouble and we went through the desolate countryside with no more contact with the people than as if we had been in another world. The road back was different. The aged tires on the car gave way irrevocably, and as a result of nine blow-outs, which each time required us to search through village after village until we could find a second-hand tire and tube, we acquired an unrivalled and undesired knowledge of conditions along this route.

Carmona, a charming little town of about 20,000 people which is located on a hillside a few miles north of Seville, was our first stop. Tire trouble had not yet begun, but we wanted to see what the alert and enterprising head of the local Auxilio Social had been able to accomplish with the flour and milk. In Seville exactly nothing had been done, but clearly this was a man with force and vigour. There was no automobile to be had, but *¡Hombre!* a farm cart brought the food just as well. Meanwhile he had made arrangements with one of the local bakers to bake the bread; he was baking anyway for his own customers, and only a small amount of extra fuel was needed. The Auxilio Social loaves were just being taken out of the oven when we visited the baker, a kindly man who seemed genuinely glad that he had had an opportunity to see what he could do with the American whole-wheat flour.

The Auxilio Social official was very proud of the stew that he was giving his clients. There were two large iron pots filled with rice and chick-peas, which had been boiled together. It did not look very appetizing, but we tasted it and found it excellent. He insisted upon showing us his storeroom as well, where the American flour and milk were carefully put away, along with a couple of sacks of chick-peas and a few pounds of dried codfish. Such zeal was heartening, and the extraordinary beauty of the town, with narrow streets, whitewashed houses, and grass-covered roofs that recalled somehow the demure English charm of Rye, almost effaced the memory of the horrors that we had seen. The rolling country on either side was covered with the thin green of young wheat, and hundreds of peasants, wearing their broad-brimmed Andalusian hats and their Sunday best, were standing in the streets. Evidently it was market day.

There was, however, no such pleasant explanation. The flood brought down by the Guadalquivir had wrought havoc in Carmona as well as in Cadiz. The peasants who lived in Carmona could not work, and as the great landowners paid them only when they did work, the entire community was destitute. There was no unemployment insurance for them, of course, no poor relief except what could be provided from the scanty resources of the Auxilio Social. The chief explained to us that he had long since been compelled to give up any idea of helping anybody except children, pregnant women, and nursing mothers. The old people had lived their lives and nothing could be done for them.

As we talked a wretched little girl of four or five, with her skin the greenish parchment colour which carried its own inescapable meaning, came up to us and silently stretched out her emaciated hand. We looked at her in surprise, for it seemed impossible that she could be so obviously starving on the excellent food that we had seen cooking in the Auxilio Social kitchens. Our guide read our astonishment in our faces. He explained that despite the restrictions he had been compelled to impose, there was not enough food to care for all the children. This little girl, he said, had been starved so long that even an optimum diet would not bring her back to normal, physically or mentally. The food that was at his command had to be saved for those for whom it would do some good.

He told us about a case in which his sister was taking a personal interest. When the last baby was born it was discovered that the mother did not have a single article of clothing for it, not even a sheet to wrap it in. And the mother herself had no clothes and was lying naked in the bed which she and the baby shared with the four older children. Naturally, he said, she had had so little food that she could not nurse her child, and the American milk had arrived just in time.

Typhus had broken out recently in a village near by, but thus far Carmona had escaped any serious epidemic. Tuberculosis, the scourge of this sunny land, had taken an extra toll, but most of the deaths were from weakness or plain starvation. In normal times between three hundred and four hundred people died in Carmona a year. This was the end of February, and already there had been that many deaths in two months.

As we drove on from Carmona the desolation assumed a franker guise. The countryside was deserted, except for an occasional solitary peasant digging in the sun-baked fields for roots, or cutting a tall, weedy plant with thick semi-edible stems that grew along the roadside. As we stopped at village after village trying to buy tires, children with emaciated limbs and faces like skulls gathered around the car. They did not say a word, but stuck out their hands for any crumbs we could give them; they pounced on the scraps of bread and sardines which had been our lunch.

At the government tourist hotel at Bailén, where we spent the night, food was plentiful. Next day, however, presented the same desolation as before until we reached La Carolina, where we were able to buy not only tires, but some sardines, which we ate with the bread that we had saved from dinner the night before. When we finished eating in the garage, there were no children standing around the car, and we took away the leavings with the hope that it would be difficult to find any other child who needed them.

About ten miles north of La Carolina, however, we met one who did, a child whom I shall always remember as a symbol of the disasters that afflict Spain. He was stumbling down the middle of the road, so intent upon his problems that he did not even see our car and we had to pull over to the side to get out of his way. I stopped the car and went back to give him something to eat. He was sobbing, and when I asked him what was the matter, he said: "Because I am hungry." He was eight years old, but he was not so large as an American child of four. His ragged clothes, of the nondescript dark grey worn by Spain's poor, were much too big for his thin little body. He had had nothing at all to eat since the day before, and he had left his father's house a mile or so up the road and was trying to walk to La Carolina, where he hoped that his sister might have something for him. When I gave him a can of sardines and the last of the bread that we had saved from our dinner in Bailén, his pitiful little face lit up; then he began to wolf down the food which had so unaccountably presented itself.

In Barcelona the misery caused by the food shortage was aggravated by the unemployment resulting from the lack of cotton for the mills, none of which could run more than two or three days a week. The restaurants were if anything better than in Madrid. I have not been in Almería or Alicante since 1939, but members of the Red Cross mission said that conditions there were even worse than at Cadiz and Seville.

Since I left Spain the food situation has become even worse. This was reflected in the order issued in the autumn of 1941 imposing the death penalty upon incorrigible *estraperlistas.* Now even fish, lettuce, and other vegetables are rationed, and the misery, my friends tell me, surpasses anything that we saw.

Even to this day, however, there have been remarkably few outbreaks of disease. There was one epidemic of typhoid in Madrid, and another in Vigo. In the early spring of 1941 there was a serious epidemic of typhus in Madrid, followed by another at Málaga. The doctors of the Rockefeller Foundation who had been sent to study the epidemics were puzzled that they were not so widespread as they expected, but the effect upon the health of the Spanish people was no less tragic, even though plain starvation, rather than contagious disease, was the result of the famine. The head of the Spanish public service estimated that the death rate in 1941 was double what it had been before the civil war. Obviously the health of the Spanish people has been seriously undermined.

With it all, the Franco regime, according to good fascist principles, has made strenuous efforts to encourage larger families. The Spanish birth rate and the infantile death rate were already higher than anywhere else in Europe, with the possible exception of Rumania; but marriage loans, prizes for the largest families, and all the tried Hitler-Mussolini methods of producing cannon fodder have been employed to give Spain still more mouths to feed. This, it seemed, was the cream of a cruel and stupid jest.

# Chapter X

## SOME NOTES ON DAILY LIFE

Yet life in Spain was not all tragedy. Foreigners, with their privilege of going over to Portugal whenever the difficulties of life in Spain became too unbearable, lived in so many oases scattered over the arid desert of suffering Spain. And desperate as was the condition of the country, the *Madrileños* still sat for hours in the cafés, explaining to all who would listen (including the secret police) just what was wrong with the regime and how perfect things would be if only they were allowed to take charge. As for the humble, they asked little more than to bring down their chairs from their tiny apartments and sit in the sun during the Castilian winter, or find a comfortable place in the shade during the long, rainless summer.

But the attempt to do one's work as a Madrid correspondent involved a constant fight with the censorship and unending efforts as well to cope with the numberless problems of daily living. Food was only one of these difficulties. To explain the manipulations necessary merely to move into our apartment, a task to which the average New Yorker devotes less attention than picking out a suit of clothes, would require a chapter of its own. It was necessary to reach a director of the gas company in order to have the gas turned on, to make numberless visits to the electric company, and to the separate concern in charge of installing meters, before we managed to get lights. We had been staying at Gaylord's, the excellent hotel where the Russian mission was quartered during the civil war, and we could not take a step to obtain ration cards until we had actually moved in. And we could not move in because our furniture was held up at the customs until a guarantee was obtained that if *I* left Spain in less than two years the duty would be paid, regardless of what happened to the furniture.

My tour of Spain during the Primo de Rivera regime did not last long enough for me to say which of the more futile inconveniences of daily life were inherited by Franco and which were part of the fascist dispensation. Why, for example, you were not permitted to post an air-mail letter anywhere except at a certain counter at the Central Post Office, I could never understand. The Spanish postal service had never been celebrated for efficiency or service to the public, and any package or letter arriving with insufficient postage had to be collected at the Central Post Office, which involved still longer waiting. Even copies of *Fortune* were adjudged too heavy for the postman to carry and had to be called for. I suppose this was a pre-Franco custom. Post-Franco, however, was the ingenious practice of some Spaniards who managed to indulge their liking for American magazines (their favourites) by bribing the postman to hand over copies every week.

The war had produced a general breakdown in public utilities as well as public morale. The water in our apartment used to be cut off all day two or three times a week. The lights worked very well except that no bulbs were to be had, but the gas pressure was so low that most cooking had to be done on the coal range—assuming we could get coal. Our apartment was on the top floor, the nearest thing to a penthouse a newspaper reporter will ever get, but our enjoyment of its terraces overlooking the Prado Park was diminished considerably by these inconveniences. And for six weeks in the height of the summer the elevator [1] was broken down, the owner putting the blame

[1] The Madrid wits claimed that Franco was trying to write a new language, and as a first step had renamed elevators *No funciona,* streetcars *Completo,* and grocery stores *No hay* ("Out of order," "full up," and "there isn't any").

on the incorrigible "Red" workmen who finally improvised the missing parts.

These difficulties grew to be just as much a part of the Spanish scene as the eternal *mañana*. Back in the United States, where morning newspapers are delivered in the morning instead of some time after lunch, and it is still possible to find a taxi, life seems rather dull. Life in Franco Spain was difficult, but never boring, and I never grew tired of studying the superb skill with which the fascists tied themselves up in knots.

But the censorship was another matter. It is without a parallel anywhere in the world, and has made it impossible for any correspondent to give his paper the coverage to which it is entitled. Only rarely was I permitted to send anything except the bare text of official announcements, and then the story was usually delayed so long that it was no longer news.

But there were no restrictions like those which made the life of foreign correspondents so difficult in other totalitarian states; we could go anywhere in Spain without having to get any kind of authorization, and Spaniards, unlike Germans, were not afraid to talk to foreigners. At least we had a fair idea of what was going on, even though it was beyond our power to convey it to the American public. It was, of course, easy enough to find someone going to Portugal who would take out a dispatch, but it was equally easy for the authorities to trace it back to us. I did not want to get expelled and miss a good story when the Germans did come in.

Yet the censorship was not too irritating; in its unpredictability it was typical of Franco Spain. Ordinarily, for example, it was strictly forbidden to do more than refer to the shortage of food in general terms. But in the early spring of 1941 the famine was so acute that we were permitted to write about the situation almost without hindrance, the object, of course, being to awaken sympathy in the United States. This busy period was brought to an abrupt close by an article in which I described the bread we were getting in our household. Cardenas, Franco's Ambassador in Washington, could not wait to write and cabled back his protest; the propaganda authorities threatened me with expulsion despite the fact that I was able to show them my copy of the story, duly passed by the censor. Afterwards the censorship was even more rigid than ever.

To complain against censors is an old custom of foreign correspondents, but there is no doubt that the censorship in Spain was ultra-severe. Spanish correspondents in London analysed developments there with a freedom that made us smile when they embarked upon a press campaign against the strictness of the British censorship. Any discussion of events in Spain had to be wrapped up in such cloudy phrases that only experts on Spanish politics could guess what a correspondent was trying to say. For the general public such dispatches were meaningless.

Moreover a really ironclad censorship was imposed whenever there was any spot news. Phalanx zealots would hold their demonstrations against England, for instance, but only once were we allowed to send out a story about them. We got nowhere with our protests to the censors that it was no use to stage a "spontaneous" demonstration if the outside world was not allowed to know about it. In vain we pointed out that as the German and Italian newspapermen were exempted from the censorship, the Axis papers made the demonstrations public anyway. Even information published in the Madrid newspapers, which would become known when they reached correspondents in Lisbon the next day, sometimes could not be transmitted. I suppose the system reached some kind of high when the censor cut out my casual reference in a story to the fact that Serrano Suñer was Franco's brother-in-law.

Nevertheless, something could be accomplished by keeping on good terms with the censors and never giving up trying. Unlike the censors at Gibraltar, for instance, who require correspondents to hand in their copy to an office boy, and never tell them whether all, part, or none of the story is transmitted, the Spanish censors allowed correspondents to look over their shoulder and argue over every mark of the blue pencil. Frequently they were satisfied if you could propose the substitution of the exact synonym for an offending word.

In the early days they handed back your copy after stamping it and you were permitted to take it to the cable or wireless office yourself. After a time, however, it was discovered that some correspondents were restoring the deleted portions of their messages on their way to the transmission office and the system was changed. Correspondents were still allowed to argue over their stories, but the censor kept possession of them and sent them himself to the cable or wireless office.

This new system gave rise to a neat stratagem by the censorship which I was a long time in discovering. My first clue came as a result of my attempt to make a broadcast to the United States in the spring of 1940. The press censorship gave excellent co-operation; I got a reasonably frank talk on conditions in Spain approved by Merry del Val, and I presented myself at the broadcasting office all ready to go. But for some inexplicable reason, although the Madrid station kept calling: "Hello, New York; hello, New York," long past the hour of the broadcast, it never raised the United States. Atmospheric conditions, I was told, were responsible. On consulting other radio companies, however, I found that they were in communication with the United States at that very time and that there were no transmission difficulties. It was obvious that someone had deliberately prevented the broadcast.

This sabotage, as I found out later, was not the work of the Press Office, but of the Radio Office, which was jealous of any invasion of its territory by a newspaper correspondent. But it gave me an idea, and when I discovered months later that several long stories I had written had not been published in the *Times,* I decided to check up. On comparing the wireless company's bill with the dates when I sent the stories, I found that the *Times* had not been billed for any messages. To make sure, I demanded to see the file copies kept in the censor's office, and these too were missing. It was obvious that the stories had been stamped approved in my presence, but that after I left the building both the originals and the file copies had been destroyed. What the purpose of this strange manœuvre was I could never imagine, unless the government wanted to keep us correspondents happy in the mistaken belief that we were being allowed to do our job.

For a time during the winter of 1940–1 I managed to take successful counter-measures. Telephone communication with other countries of Europe had at last been restored, and I obtained permission to telephone my copy to our office in Berne, which forwarded it to New York. In this way I was sure that the story got out. Actually, I could have said anything I chose, for there was no system whereby the censors checked to see whether I was dictating the story as they had passed it. I followed copy, however, if for no better reason than the fact that no story developed during this period which was worth running the risk of being expelled for. Telephone privileges later were abruptly withdrawn from all American news organizations, and again I could never be sure whether my stories were getting out. This development, followed by the German attack on Russia, which clearly would delay Spain's entry into the war, was in fact the principal reason why I came home in August 1941.

I had been sent to Spain with instructions to report the news with complete impartiality, and during the two years I spent there I endeavoured to do so to the best of my ability. The news itself, however, was unfavourable to Franco, for always it concerned some pro-Axis trend or the steadily worsening economic conditions. At least by comparison with the Axis correspondents, or the Vichy-controlled Havas agency, I could not claim to have a pro-Franco attitude. Nevertheless the government and party officials with whom I was in contact always gave me a fair deal and sometimes did me considerable favours.

In the summer of 1940, for instance, I was a guest of the Phalanx, along with one German, one Italian, and one French newspaperman, at the *Führerschule* that it conducted at Santander for the most promising members of the fascist university students' organization. In the same way, I was the only foreign correspondent invited to attend such affairs as the gala performance of *Mocedades del Cid,* with which Franco celebrated in 1941 the anniversary of the union of the Phalanx and the Carlist movements, or the meeting of the Phalanx Council on July 17, 1941, at which Franco delivered his speech denouncing the democracies—a turning-point in our relations with his regime.

No foreign correspondent has obtained an interview with Franco since the end of the civil war, but I came fairly close. I was officially notified that Franco would receive me, had submitted my questions in advance and had them approved, when the anti-Suñer purge of the early summer of 1941 threw out of office the young *Falangista* who had arranged it. Moreover, on such personal matters as helping me get a permit to import food the press officials always tried to be helpful. Their efforts were checkmated by the inertia of Spanish bureaucracy, but they did their best.

All these favours, however, were strictly on a personal basis, of many a drink at Chicote's Bar, or perhaps a common interest in Proust. The Spaniards were not sufficiently propaganda-minded to see that the best way to get a good press was to let foreign correspondents do the work they were paid to do. Until the early summer of 1941 there were no press conferences at the Ministry of Foreign Affairs. Talkative officials were plentiful, but there was no way to guess what the government's real attitude was except by reading the papers and then trying to balance what they said against the personal slant of the editors, the directives issued by the Press Office, and the amount of money that the Germans were paying at the moment.

Characteristically, the censors did not bother to go to the Foreign Ministry press conferences (and some did not even trouble to read the papers). They had no way of verifying our accounts of what was happening. But this system of conferences was at least better than my one previous contact with the Foreign Ministry press officer. This was during a crisis in Franco's long-standing difficulties with the Vatican over the appointment of new bishops. The censor had turned down my story revealing that the Spanish Ambassador to the Vatican had been called back to report, but agreed to send it if the Foreign Ministry official gave out the news. He received me courteously and talked rather frankly about the Ambassador's return and the general question of a new Concordat. I re-submitted my story to the censorship with great jubilation, even though I was using none of the extra details that I had learned at the Foreign Ministry.

The subject of the Vatican was so delicate that the censor decided he must have verification direct from the press officer. The latter could not be found until next day, but then he expressed his utter astonishment that a Yankee journalist could have so abandoned the faith of a gentleman. He said not only that he had not told me that the Ambassador had been recalled, but that during our entire conversation the subject of Spain's relations with the Vatican did not even come up.

Work amid such conditions was very difficult, and it was in vain that I tried to convince the press authorities that a frank discussion of Spain's problems in the American newspapers would arouse interest in the regime and do Franco much more good than his over-zealous propaganda emissaries. The Nationalists were always declaiming against the bad press they got in England and particularly the United States; during the civil war Franco had remarked bitterly that the trouble was that he did not have the gold with which to bribe foreign correspondents as, he said, the Republicans did.

I tried to tell everybody I could reach that whatever might be the custom of other countries, American and English correspondents were not looking for any Spanish gold. The only thing we wanted, I assured them, was to get some stories in the paper and nourish our egos with a few by-lines. But these arguments were useless. The result was that the permanent American and English correspondents in Spain were muzzled, while visiting journalists rushed through Madrid and dashed off articles which were far more prejudicial to Franco's cause than anything we would have written.

Nevertheless the correspondents could not let up in the work of gathering news, even though we knew little or none of it that was of any interest could be sent. The Associated Press and the United Press, each of which had two American correspondents and a large Spanish staff, kept busy sending such non-political copy as bullfight results for publication in Latin America. Reuter's, the British news agency, which was trying to enter the Latin-American field, did the same. Correspondents of the London *Times* and the London *Daily Telegraph* sent stories when they could and otherwise rested on their oars with British calm.

After a year I became the only correspondent of an American newspaper in Spain. The *Chicago Tribune,* which had sent three men to Madrid in succession with instructions to break the censorship, did not have British calm and finally withdrew. Helen Hiett, who for several months did an excellent job of reporting for the National Broadcasting Company, became the subject of another dispute between the same Press and Radio Offices which had fought over my own broadcast. As a result the one station that could relay her broadcasts to New York was closed and she too returned to the United States.

If you could forget that your job was to get out the news, Madrid was plenty of fun. Knowing the statuesque German Ambassadress, we could laugh over the diplomatic incident which resulted when an over-zealous beach policeman at San Sebastián arrested her for indecent exposure and carried her off to the police station despite her protests that she was the wife of Hitler's representative in Spain and that the Führer himself would punish such insolence. Ever afterwards the people of San Sebastián claimed that the "C.D." on diplomats' cars stood for "Naked Body" (*Cuerpo Desnudo*); only by setting apart one end of the beach for diplomats, where they could wear as little as they pleased, could Franco appease the Teutonic wrath. And it was funnier still when the diplomats discovered that as the town sewer emptied into the sea just around the point from their special beach, bathing at San Sebastián was not so very good after all.

It was necessary, of course, to recognize that Franco's Spain was slightly cockeyed and not take things too seriously, if only because the usual means of taking one's mind off one's troubles were almost non-existent. Even the bullfights were no longer what they used to be, thanks to the disorganization resulting from the civil war, and, just possibly, excessive interference by the Bullfight Division of the Entertainments Syndicate, which classified the *matadores* according to its idea of their ability and set up a complicated scale of fees.

Spaniards did not seem to care for their classic drama, and as there was no subsidized State theatre to give them what they ought to have, the plays of Calderón, Lope de Vega, and other great dramatists were almost never produced. The two exceptions were *Don Juan Tenorio,* revived as usual to cap off visits to the cemeteries on All Saints' Day, and the Phalanx's gala performance of *Mocedades del Cid.* Some of the plays which had won Benavente a Nobel prize were revived, but I happened not to like them and in any case the acting and production were wretched.

A young *flamenco* dancer, Miguel de Molina, gave us one of the most pleasant evenings we had in Madrid, and one of my principal grudges against the Phalanx is that it first broke up his performance and then had him sent to prison. Whether this was because he was a "Red" or a pansy was a subject of dispute; there were strong grounds for suspecting that there was some truth in the latter accusation in view of his silk shirts, embroidered by his own white hands, and the fact that the grimy old theatre was scented with his own special perfume. But one would have pardoned almost any crime to hear him sing *Tus Ojos Negros*. And although it could hardly be called entertainment, it was startling if nothing else to go to the Spanish version of Clare Boothe's *The Women* and find that the comedy had been adapted, according to the principles of the new regime, into a sombre diatribe against divorce.

I also gained a new understanding of the United States from *Love Lasts Two Thousand Metres,* an attack on Hollywood by a Spanish author (I have, unfortunately, forgotten his name) who had visited filmland and failed to land a contract. How long his visit had lasted was not very clear, but he had come away with the deep conviction that kidnappings and lynchings were the merest commonplace and that gangsters were always present at the smartest Hollywood parties. I was inclined, however, to question the accuracy of the climactic scene, demonstrating the implacable American persecution of Negroes. This turned upon the fact that the Negro butler had put ice in the highballs instead of bringing them in piping hot as Hollywood etiquette required.

Nothing would have pleased the Spanish public more than unlimited quantities of films from this same Hollywood, but supplies were blocked by exchange difficulties, by the black list of American film stars who had supported the Republican cause,[1] and by the preferential treatment given German and Italian movies. But the Spaniards preferred even aging Amer-

[1] It was characteristic of Franco Spain that the censors allowed *The Life of Pasteur* to be shown, but did not permit the name of Paul Muni, who was on the black list, to appear on the posters.

ican productions, such as *Grand Hotel* or *A Bengal Lancer*, to the latest thing put out by Hitler's UFA. Strangely enough, the Madrid public did not care for two Italo-Spanish films about the civil war, *Frente de Madrid*, and *Alcázar* (the siege of the Alcázar of Toledo), although I found them excellently done and remarkably fair to both sides. The Spaniards preferred to see the Marx brothers over and over again, but we found that they palled after a time.

The night clubs, though plentiful, were bad, and cocktail parties were the principal pastime among foreigners in Madrid. On the surface life was very gay. The usual topic of conversation was the long war between the Spanish government and the united diplomats over their gasoline supplies. These were limited, although not nearly so strictly as those of the general public, but diplomats were allowed to buy gasoline for about 40 cents a gallon, instead of $1.60. There was one condition, however: they had to pay in dollars. There was some excuse for this requirement, since the Spaniards had to pay for the gasoline out of their scanty stock of free exchange. But to pay in dollars was exactly what no diplomat wanted to do. Those from belligerent nations had a good excuse, since each could claim that he did not want to wreck his country's war effort by dipping into its supplies of foreign exchange. On this point the British and German Embassies were as one. Most of the other diplomats, however, had no excuse to oppose the requirement except the real one, that they were buying their pesetas on the black bourse in Lisbon at about half the official rate.

The fortunes of this great struggle seesawed back and forth for months. Once things reached a crisis: an irate chief of mission not only refused an invitation to Franco's annual garden party at La Granja, but informed the Foreign Ministry categorically that La Granja was too far to drive to if he had to pay for his gasoline in dollars. It was a great loss to the foreign colony when Franco won the gasoline battle.

The next best source of amusement was Lieutenant General Queipo de Llano,[1] who had been sent to Rome so that Franco would not have to shoot him for insubordination to Serrano Suñer. There he was having a marvellous time taunting the Italians about their past defeat at Guadalajara and their subsequent disasters in Greece and Ethiopia. Not a man to be satisfied with such easy victims, Queipo was also denouncing Serrano Suñer at every dinner party at which he could be sure that his remarks would be reported back to Spain. How Madame Franco was getting along with Madame Serrano Suñer not only was fascinating but had a bearing on great matters of state; when the two affectionate sisters stopped speaking we knew that Franco's attempt to clip the wings of his brother-in-law had reached a climax.

The social life of Madrid was concentrated around the embassies and the comparatively few Spaniards who had the money and the desire to associate with foreigners. Many of the diplomats who had heard of the brilliant entertainments in the days of the monarchy were disappointed to discover that although Spaniards were quick enough to accept invitations, they were very slow to return them. When they did, it was usually at a restaurant rather than at home, and I could never make out whether the reluctance to ask foreigners into their homes was because they thought them too sacred or too poorly furnished—perhaps it was both. Of course, those who had been Europeanized acted more like people elsewhere. The more important officials of the government and the party, however, almost always refused invitations from the British, American, and other anti-Axis diplomats.

In the course of time Serrano Suñer developed an even better technique: on at least four different occasions he accepted invitations to state dinners at the American Embassy, then

[1] In July 1942 it was announced that General Queipo de Llano had been ordered to Málaga under town arrest, presumably at the instigation of Serrano Suñer.

had his secretary telephone a few minutes before he was due to arrive and announce that he had been detained by government business. Diplomats who had known Madrid in the days of the monarchy sighed and said that the manners of cabinet ministers had certainly deteriorated.

Otherwise, however, the civil war had produced surprisingly little change in Spain's social customs and there was no outbreak of the jazz age comparable with that which the United States and the rest of Europe knew after the end of the World War. Young people, it is true, did the best they could to make up for the fun they had missed during the long war years. Many well-to-do girls had worked as nurses in military hospitals, while the disruption of their normal sheltered life inevitably had had some effect upon daughters of even the oldest families. But the tendency toward freer social life was countered by an even stronger Catholic reaction. Boys still were not allowed to escort girls to dances or, at least in principle, ever to take them out alone; ultra-liberal mothers allowed their daughters to go to a dance with other girls, but those of the old school accompanied them and tried never to allow them out of their sight.

There was, in fact, a definite reaction against all the newfangled and "un-Spanish" customs which allegedly had come in with the Republic, such as divorce and civil marriage. No doubt women suffrage would have been abolished too but for the fact that there were no more elections to worry about. Despite the fact that many *Falangistas* were no better Catholics than the Nazis, the watchword among government and party officials was devotion to the Church. This was illustrated by a colonel I knew who had held strong republican and anticlerical views before the war, and still did. However, he had been on furlough in the Nationalist zone when the war broke out, saw he must join Franco, and had the wit to do so promptly. Now he was making out quite well and he and his entire family had developed into some of the most fervent churchgoers in living memory. Despite their poverty, Spanish women managed somehow to find stockings and at least a wisp of lace to cover their heads, making it possible for them to go to Mass. In Holy Week lines of women waiting to get into church stretched for blocks. But few men except government employees and members of the nobility ever went to church.

Although the jokes on the Madrid stage were still quite rough, the precepts of the Church regarding costumes were faithfully observed; when Josephine Baker, who is no believer in covering herself up, appeared in Madrid in the spring of 1941, she was compelled by the police to wear more clothes than the average preacher's wife in the United States.

Except among diplomats, sun-bathing quickly disappeared from Spanish beaches with the advent of Franco. Men were required to wear tops and shorts reaching to the knees, and the regulations for women were even more strict. A number of women bathers at San Sebastián, Spain's smartest resort, voluntarily wore black dresses with stockings in the mode of 1910. Even these costumes, however, were deemed to provide sufficient covering only when bathers were in the water. The moment they stepped out they had to cover themselves in dressing-gowns reaching from head to foot. Even thus shielded, bathers were not allowed to lie down on the beach.[1] The reaction to the old days was completed when doctors were forbidden to teach methods of contraception. But despite the efforts to popularize the Franco way of life, disillusionment with the results of the war was general. The Republicans were bitter and only awaiting their chance for revenge. But hate kept them keen and eager for the fray, and in some ways I sympathized more with the victors, who were beginning to feel that their sacrifices had been in vain and that Spain was worse off than she had been when the war began. The patriotic exalta-

[1] On the other hand, nobody seemed disturbed by the freedom with which children and even grown-ups relieved themselves on the beach with the utmost lack of self-consciousness.

tion which had held the divergent supporters of Franco together during the war was gone, and quarrels broke out over every move and proposed move by the government.

But for once the Spaniards' incorrigible enthusiasm for political arguments had been overcome by the more pressing necessity of food. Sooner or later all discussions came back to that subject. Cocktail parties were successful or otherwise according to the size of the buffet; hostesses had to feature whole hams or other solid fare in order to establish themselves.

Always when I recall this strange world I turn to the New Year's Eve ball given by the Turkish Minister to welcome in the promising year 1941. Some of the last Piper-Heidsieck I will have for a long time was served that pleasant evening, but only the foreigners bothered with either drinking or dancing.

The Spaniards wanted food, and it was really remarkable to see how the grim old duchesses put it away. Someone told me that night that this was in accordance with the spirit of Alfonso's reign, when the poorer nobility were permitted to take away food from palace banquets without interference, provided they wrapped it in a napkin. Whatever may be the truth of this, the Minister's guests ate so determinedly that I do not think they considered wrapping anything up to carry home. They were not to be lured away by the dancing, and as soon as the footmen brought in a new supply they gathered around the table and swept it as clean as though locusts had been at work. After we had all eaten our twelve grapes at midnight, the cook shifted to scrambled eggs and coffee, which were equally acceptable. When these gave out he sent in his last reserves of lobster and ham, which were more popular than ever. The sound of the duchesses' joyful munching at the buffet table will long remain among my few amusing memories of Franco's Spain.

## *Chapter* XI

### THE LAST EXIT FROM NAZI EUROPE

The Franco regime, in addition, of course, to muzzling foreign correspondents, took other means to keep the outside world from learning of the famine which it brought upon Spain. Its zeal went so far that in the autumn of 1941 the wife of a prominent American resident was imprisoned for attempting to leave the country with a sample of the sawdust bread which was supposed to nourish the people of Madrid. Therefore it might have been supposed that its first aim would have been to expedite the passage through Spain of the thousands of refugees from Hitler, so that they would have little knowledge of this misery to report.

On the contrary, every pretext was used to harass them and to imprison them if they had violated the smallest of the numberless regulations governing the admission and departure of foreigners through this last remaining exit on the west from Nazi-controlled Europe. Well-established usages of international law, which were respected to some extent even by the Nazis, were disregarded. If the Franco regime had deliberately set out to make every refugee a hostile propaganda agent it could have adopted no course better suited to the purpose.

The late Ignace Paderewski was the most distinguished victim of this policy. After months of waiting in Switzerland, he finally obtained a transit visa in the summer of 1940, accompanied by a special guarantee that he would be allowed to pass through Spain without being molested. Accompanied by his sister and his secretary, the aged pianist and statesman got as far as Saragossa without being disturbed. There, however, he and his party were placed under hotel arrest, the excuse being that they had failed to register with the Barcelona police when they spent the night there. The officer of the Civil Guard who had to carry out this disgraceful action told them that as a *caballero* and a music-lover he was ashamed to be involved in it.

Perhaps because of these sentiments, Paderewski's secretary was permitted to telephone to the Polish Minister in Madrid, who at once requested the help of the United States. Thanks to the intervention of President Roosevelt, who sent a personal appeal to Franco, Paderewski was not handed over to the Germans and was finally allowed to proceed to Portugal. But the ordeal undoubtedly contributed to his death a few months after his arrival in the United States.

More drastic measures were required to obtain the release of Hubert Pierlot, the Belgian Prime Minister and now head of the Belgian government-in-exile, and Paul Henri Spaak, his Foreign Minister, who also put themselves at the mercy of the Spaniards at this time since there was no other way for them to reach London. They and their entourage also had a personal guarantee of safe passage, but it was even less efficacious. Barely had they entered Spain when they were stopped. The Spanish police, supposedly in order to salve their consciences, at first did not formally arrest them, but returned them to the Port-Bou frontier and informed them that they would have to go back to France. The Belgians, preferring the risk of being handed over to the Nazis by the Spaniards to the certainty that Pétain would surrender them, refused to go. They remained without shelter in the no-man's land between the two frontier posts for more than a week, according to officials of the Belgian Embassy in Madrid; the Spanish military authorities issued a strict order that they should not be allowed a morsel of food or even a drink of water, and of course if it had been obeyed hunger and thirst eventually would have compelled them to surrender to the Vichy authorities.

Perhaps with the connivance of the Spanish officers, they somehow did get enough food and water to hold out, and they were finally readmitted to Spain and put in jail. Afterwards they were transferred to Barcelona, where they were placed under guard in a second-class hotel. Again there was a happy ending to the story, for after six weeks of captivity they escaped by automobile to Portugal, and from there reached London without further difficulty.

At about the same time former King Carol of Rumania, accompanied by his mistress, Madame Lupescu, also started through Spain after his overthrow by Rumanian fascists. He also found out what the pledges of the Spanish government were worth. He got as far as Barcelona without difficulty, and he was watching as his special car was coupled to the regular Madrid express when he was suddenly informed that Franco sent him his most cordial salutations and entreated him to remain in Spain as his guest. Carol was still meditating the terms in which he would refuse this undesired hospitality when railroad employees uncoupled his car and he realized that he was a prisoner.

He was not, however, an ordinary prisoner, for he was allowed to spend the remainder of the summer at Sitges, a coast resort near Barcelona, and when winter came he obtained permission to go to Seville, where he lived in comfort at the Andalucia Palace Hotel and was even permitted to take an occasional drive in one of his high-powered automobiles. It was on one of these drives that he and Madame Lupescu, according to the account published in the Franco press, "outdistanced" the police escort car and crossed into Portugal, at last safe from Hitler's vengeance.

Several governments played a part in this "escape," and no

useful purpose would be served at the present time in revealing the circumstances behind it. Carol had richly deserved anything that Hitler or relatives of slaughtered Rumanian fascists would have done to him, and the humble refugees who every day were thrown into Franco prisons had far more claim on the sympathy of decent people.

From the standpoint of international law, however, the arrest of Carol was equally deserving of condemnation, especially since he too had been given a specific safe conduct. In all three instances these pledges were given by Colonel Beigbeder, the Foreign Minister, and in each case the detention order was issued by Serrano Suñer, who as Minister of Government was in command of the police. Franco, as I have pointed out, lacked the will to impose any coherent policy upon his warring supporters, and Serrano Suñer took advantage of this chaos in the hope that he could embarrass Beigbeder, who with all his faults was a man of honour, into resigning.[1]

Carol's "escape," however, took place after Serrano Suñer had succeeded Beigbeder as Foreign Minister. As Serrano Suñer at the same time had retained control of the police through his henchmen in the Ministry of Government, on this occasion there was no question of divided responsibility. Various proposals were made by interested governments in order to save Carol, but I never learned why Serrano Suñer heeded them. Supposedly he hoped that by not committing the final infamy of handing over such a prominent refugee he might have a claim to mercy if ever he were in a similar predicament.

The inexplicable, however, was the merest commonplace in Franco's Spain. He and Serrano Suñer were supposed to be completely under Hitler's thumb, and in many respects so they were. Yet Franco maintained diplomatic relations with

1 The general suspicion that Beigbeder had had a part in arranging the escape of Pierlot and Spaak was, in fact, one of the reasons why Franco at length yielded to Serrano Suñer's insistence and dismissed him in the following October.

the governments-in-exile of Norway, Poland,[1] the Netherlands, Belgium, and Greece long after they had been overrun by his Nazi patrons. It is true that the Belgian Ambassador was expelled and the Embassy closed in retaliation for the escape of Pierlot and Spaak. And after the surrender of Greece the Greek Minister was declared persona non grata and had to leave. But a tactless statement in the Greek Legation's propaganda weekly was primarily responsible for the latter's recall. The Norwegian and Netherlands Legations, however, are still functioning in Madrid, and even a representative of the former Czechoslovakian government enjoyed quasi-diplomatic standing with Serrano Suñer's Foreign Ministry.

I can make no attempt to account for such phenomena, any more than I can explain why the Franco government, instead of interning the crew of a British bomber which had made a forced landing in northern Spain, allowed the aviators to proceed to Gibraltar. For that matter, a remarkable number of British soldiers, who had been hiding out in France ever since Pétain capitulated, managed to evade the Spanish police and get back to England. Many were aided by the common people of Spain, whom Mr. Chamberlain had allowed Franco to crush. Most of the British were still in uniform, had no money, and did not speak a word of Spanish. But friends of liberty helped them to hide on railroad trains, warned them when the police were about to search hotels, and put them in touch with agents who helped them to get across the border into Portugal. Sometimes help also came from high quarters, and even Franco Spain has produced no more bizarre incident than the use of a cabinet minister's official car to smuggle three British officers across the country.

The most revolting of all the shameful articles that I read in Serrano Suñer's newspapers was one gloating over the fears of the rich Jewish refugees who had managed to get as far as Portugal but feared they would be caught at Estoril when the

[1] Closed a few months ago.

Germans came. Yet every one of these refugees had gone through Spain, and it had been in the power of Serrano Suñer's police to stop them. But I never heard of anything happening to Jews who were carrying enough gold bullion or dollar bills to satisfy Franco's agents at the frontier.

Other prominent refugees who fled through Spain after the collapse of France were the Duke and Duchess of Windsor, who intended to return to England but were ordered instead to exile in the Bahamas. Count Haugwitz-Reventlow, who had met the American woman he has since married while they were waiting for days on the International Bridge at Irún, and other members of cosmopolitan society jammed the Ritz Hotel in Madrid in those tragic June days and renewed their friendships with Spaniards whom they had met in casinos and night clubs all over Europe.

But the ordinary refugee, like the ordinary Spaniard, got harsh treatment under Franco. Prodigies of cajolery and patience were necessary in order to induce the consulates in Marseille, Berlin, Berne, or other refugee centres to submit the applications to Madrid. Then followed months of delay, and as often as not, as I knew from several refugees who had some connection with the *Times* and called on me to intercede for them, some careless employee would make a mistake in the order granting the visa and the whole process would have to be repeated. The visas were usually granted for only a short period, from five days to two weeks, and some refugees made the mistake of entering Spain without already having a Portuguese visa. The Portuguese also took their time, and police headquarters in the Puerta del Sol was thronged continually with excited refugees who were begging for prolongation of their permits to remain in Spain.

Whether these anguished petitions were granted depended entirely upon the whim of a little man with a little moustache who was in charge. He would grant one refugee an extension, then reject the request of another whose case was identical, with the same maddening little smile of superiority. He enjoyed his nefarious power, and the refugees knew that if they overstayed their time they would first be placed in the dungeons of police headquarters, then shipped off to a concentration camp for a minimum of three months. The same penalty was applicable for anyone who violated other regulations, such as the requirement that upon arrival in any city a traveller must present himself to the police (the period of grace varied from city to city). For many refugees, who had been delayed by the necessity of obtaining exit permits from the Vichy government or the Nazis, imprisonment threatened utter catastrophe. A stay in a concentration camp meant at least the loss of steamship reservations that had been obtained only with the greatest difficulty and perhaps could not be changed. In the case of those whose long-awaited permits to enter the United States were about to expire, it sometimes meant the destruction of all their hopes of reaching a free country. Owing to the inefficiency of the police, many who overstayed their permits were not imprisoned, but they were never able to breathe easily until they had crossed the frontier.

As though looking for an opportunity to make trouble, the Spanish police were not satisfied by compliance with all their own regulations. A traveller who arrived with his Spanish papers in order, but without a German or French exit visa, was more sure of a stay in concentration camp than if he had violated some Spanish ukase. This apparently was a device of the Gestapo. Nazi agents were installed in police headquarters of important Spanish cities and checked the papers of all travellers. But in view of the complete confusion which prevailed in the Franco police headquarters as well as throughout the regime, extra precautions were necessary. With all their care, they sometimes found a leading anti-fascist German or Italian in the concentration camp for foreigners at Miranda de Ebro, or at liberty, and took him away under their special agreement with Franco authorizing blanket extradition of political refugees.

Miranda de Ebro is a small Castilian town between Burgos and Vitoria, on the highway from Madrid to Irún. I had driven through it several times before I learned the purpose of the small collection of whitewashed huts alongside the railroad. My idea of a concentration camp was a huge collection of grim buildings, with electrically charged barbed wire all around and machine-guns continuously trained upon the prisoners. There was nothing of this. The camp was surrounded by a low stone wall, which any reasonably agile man could easily climb, and only two or three unshaven sentries in their blanket capes were lounging about the entrance.

There were usually four hundred or five hundred prisoners in the camp, most of them foreigners who had violated the visa regulations in one way or another, but including some Spaniards who had been influential enough to have themselves sent to Miranda instead of to the much worse conditions in a Spanish jail. Except for the climate, which was notable for its blow-torch heat and biting cold, it was very nearly a model concentration camp. The huts were not heated, but prisoners were given blankets at least; the food was deplorable, but it was not much worse than that of their guards. These treated the prisoners fairly well, although I heard of one bad case—a British soldier who had been wounded in the leg and was severely beaten because he could not do the work that had been imposed on him. But otherwise few prisoners complained about either their treatment or the amount of work they were compelled to do. They suffered most from boredom, although they were allowed to receive letters and magazines if there was anybody sufficiently interested to send them.

There was no attempt to copy Dachau methods of breaking men's wills; when the prisoners assembled at sunset for the lowering of the flag, they marched as sloppily as the guards. Escape was easy, but few took advantage of the opportunity; with the exception of those who knew they were on the Nazi list, all expected to be liberated sooner or later and meanwhile they were better off than they would have been outside with no money. Certain prisoners were even allowed to go out unguarded to do shopping for the camp.

For those who had money, life was relatively agreeable. Cigarettes, candy, and sandwiches, although in extremely limited quantities, were on sale at the canteen. British, Polish, Dutch, and other prisoners whose governments were represented in Madrid received spending money and warm clothing from their embassies. Some of the miscellaneous prisoners, who had no one on whom to call, benefited from the generosity of Mrs. Weddell, who hired a secretary with the sole duty of supervising the distribution of food, clothing, and money among Miranda prisoners and other foreigners who had been stranded in Spain.

No man ever came out of Miranda with any surplus flesh, but the camp physician, an Austrian prisoner who had been sent there on suspicion of not liking the Franco regime, told me that in the winter of 1940–1 there were only two deaths among the prisoners: one from pneumonia, and the other from a burst appendix. Common colds, which prisoners had difficulty throwing off because of their weakened condition, were the worst health problem, he said. There were, of course, very few drugs, but this deficiency was general throughout Spain. Once accept the idea that an innocent man is to be sent to a concentration camp, and Miranda de Ebro should get a high mark.

But Americans do not accept this idea; our aim in fighting Hitler is the establishment of a world order where such injustices shall not exist. And even if one were in accord with the twisted principles of the Franco regime, there was no justification for the way one prisoner was held indefinitely while others were released after a week or so. At the time I left Spain there were still about a hundred Belgian sailors there, crews of several small patrol boats which, in the confusion resulting from the collapse of France, had put in at Spanish ports. The Belgian Ambassador was not popular with the Spaniards, and after the Embassy was closed there was nobody at all to intercede for them.

And there they remained, while numerous Polish soldiers, who had escaped into Spain just before the Nazi troops reached the frontier, gradually were released. Both countries had been at war with Germany, both had been over-run, both had governments-in-exile functioning in London. But, fortunately for the Poles, the Polish Legation was still operating in Madrid and its members kept in touch with the right officials. So quick were the Spaniards to release Polish prisoners that sometimes they did so before the Legation officials had arranged the necessary papers for them to go on to Portugal, and they stayed on at the camp on something approaching a voluntary basis.

There was, in fact, no semblance of a uniform policy toward the unfortunates passing through Spain. A refugee who had overstayed his allotted time, or for any other reason had incurred the displeasure of the police, would suddenly disappear. If he had anyone influential to start looking for him, he probably would be traced to the Puerta del Sol headquarters within a day or so and released. If he had no one to help him, he stayed there for a few days, without being permitted to communicate with anyone, and then was sent to Miranda de Ebro—women ended up at the incredibly sordid jail at Figueras, near the French-Catalan frontier. However, in the case of a prisoner with money with which to bribe a guard, or who otherwise managed somehow to get word of his imprisonment to his embassy, almost always some arrangement was made permitting him to remain at liberty until he could leave the country.

This was a bad system, even if one considered the question solely from the viewpoint of Franco. All travellers who violated minor regulations should have been imprisoned, or none. But favouritism and corruption permeated the entire Franco regime, and it was only natural that it found one of its purest expressions in the treatment of foreigners by the Spanish police.

Although there were exceptions, in general the secret police were if possible as incompetent as they were corrupt. They were, for example, over a month in tracking down a desperate American "spy" who was exploring Spain's military works along the Mediterranean. They took this long despite the fact that the "spy" was not trying to hide and filled out papers giving his name and occupation and the make and licence number of his car at every hotel where he stopped. It was characteristic of the Spanish police that when they did catch him they held him incommunicado and it was a week before he was able to communicate with Madrid and establish the fact that he was prospecting for oil at the special request of the Spanish government.

Although the anti-Semitism imported from Germany had not stopped the principal members of the Rothschild family from making their way through Spain, it plagued the existence of ordinary Jews. As one way of making life more difficult for them, the Franco government refused to give a work permit to any German subject who could not present a letter of recommendation from the Nazi Embassy, which of course was not available to Jews. I knew well a German Jew who was thrown into despair by this order, which cost him his job with an American film company in Madrid. Yet he became an official photographer for the Phalanx, and even was given the much-desired commission to photograph Serrano Suñer and his entire family as they relaxed in the grounds of the Pardo. No further commentary upon the vigilance of the secret police surrounding Serrano Suñer and Franco should be necessary.

On the other hand, just because they were so incompetent, there was never any way to know when they would suddenly arrest you and hold you incommunicado on some fantastic charge. One night the police went to see an English woman who was employed at the British Embassy and therefore was supposedly immune from arrest. The police, after desultory questioning, asked her to walk around the corner with them, and almost before the frantic woman knew what was happening she had been thrown into the dungeons under the Puerta del Sol. There she was held for three days in a damp, cold cell, with nowhere to sleep except on the floor, and with prostitutes her only companions. At no time was she given an intimation of what offence she was supposed to have committed, and she might be in prison yet if the British Embassy had not managed to trace her and obtain her release.

It is difficult to convey to Americans the atmosphere of doom that hung over every foreigner, with the exception of Germans and Italians, who found himself in Spain. Actually, only twice to my knowledge were Americans arrested in Madrid: one was the woman carrying bread; the other was the wife of an official of the National City Bank, whose whispered attempts to quiet her restless children at the movies one afternoon were thought to be hisses directed at the Führer, because he happened to appear in a news reel at that moment. One of the children got away and reported it, and the woman was quickly released. But there was never any knowing when you, like anybody else, might simply disappear and never be heard of again. Misgivings were the greater since all over Madrid there were forlorn lines of relatives waiting to see the prisoners. When the wife of an embassy porter complained too loudly about the treatment her son was receiving, she too was put in jail.

In addition to the worry over what the Spaniards might do there was always the gnawing fear of being imprisoned by the Germans. I knew one distinguished diplomat who made no secret of his belief that if they came in, the Nazis would hold him in a concentration camp for the remainder of the war. Detailed plans to evacuate the entire British colony at a moment's notice were worked out, and for months at a time every Britisher in Madrid kept his suitcase packed with the indispensable necessities in case sudden flight should be necessary. Even with all these precautions it appeared highly likely that in the general confusion nobody would be able to get away.

Looking back on it from the security of the United States, this constant fear seems rather ridiculous. The Germans, after all, have still not invaded Spain; the relatively comfortable internment of American diplomats and newspapermen who were caught in Berlin and Rome, and their exchange for their opposite numbers in the United States, have demonstrated that some of the amenities of war have survived. At that time, however, these exchange arrangements had not been worked out, and a number of British foreign-service officers caught by the Blitzkrieg, including at least one minister, were being held prisoner by the Nazis. The utmost caution therefore was observed by diplomats and private citizens alike. Newspaper correspondents, who were regarded with especial suspicion, were accordingly prudent.

For example, although I went to Spain resolved not to give the fascist salute, since it was not required by law, I soon found myself compelled to do so or leave the country. I tried to avoid all public gatherings where it was required, but I gave it whenever it was inescapable. Substantially the same policy was followed by other newspapermen and by the staffs of the various embassies, although chiefs of mission did not give it unless they wanted to. And knowing how sensitive the Franco regime was to any photographs which would bring home to the outside world the extent of the misery in Spain, my wife and I only once took snapshots anywhere except from the terrace of our apartment.

The experiences of Miss Therese Bonney, who made some

excellent photographs of suffering Spain in the early spring of 1941, seemed to show the wisdom of these precautions. As she told me the story, her exhibition of photographs of life behind the lines in Finland during the war with Russia had won the admiration of both the Spanish Embassy and Dr. Thomsen, the German chargé d'affaires in Washington; he had urged her to communicate direct with his friend Otto Abetz, German Ambassador in Paris, if she found the slightest difficulty in obtaining a permit to go to occupied France. Miss Bonney, who told everyone she was an ardent admirer of Franco, had been granted special facilities to enter Spain; once she reached Madrid, she was given all possible help by Merry del Val, the head of the Foreign Press, who accompanied her on her camera tours of the worst affected sections of Madrid.

But the distrust of the Spanish police for cameras and photographers was such that despite her special visa she was held five days at Badajoz, a Spanish frontier post, before being permitted to proceed to Madrid. As soon as she had started taking pictures, someone robbed her station wagon; although the police quickly recovered her valuable cameras and unexposed film, the thief, curiously enough, had made away with all her exposed films. Miss Bonney brushed aside suggestions that the police might have had a hand in the robbery.

Despite this co-operative attitude, however, Miss Bonney, and Mrs. Weddell, who had accompanied her while she took pictures, were promptly denounced by a Madrid newspaper in the vilest language that I have ever seen in print. The pretext for the attack was that Mrs. Weddell had taken along some bread from the Embassy ovens to give the starving children after the pictures were made. Although Merry del Val's presence had been a guarantee that no reflection upon the Franco regime was intended, the editorial was devoted to the general thesis that the two American women thus were deliberately mocking the suffering of Spain. An accompanying cartoon showed one woman handing a morsel of bread to a starving child while another took the photograph; out of respect for Mrs. Weddell, I will not quote the obscene abuse which was used in the editorial.

Spanish newspapermen told me that Miss Bonney and Mrs. Weddell had merely been caught in the sniping which was always going on between the Auxilio Social, which they had visited, and its bitter rival, the Feminine Section of the Phalanx, and that no harm was meant. But if the Spanish fascists felt no gratitude for Mrs. Weddell's innumerable gifts to starving Spain, her position as the wife of the American Ambassador should have protected her from such indignities. Mr. Weddell would have been fully justified in asking the State Department to recall him. With the press censored so rigorously, anything published in Spain had to be considered an expression of government opinion.

Thereafter Mrs. Weddell discontinued her charity work among the Spaniards, but she never turned down any foreign refugee who appealed to her for help in getting out of Spain. She and the Ambassador quietly kept in touch with the continually diminishing American colony in Madrid; their interest was an assurance that if the worst happened they would do everything within their power to help.

For this reason I was not too concerned by the visits of the three detectives who honoured me with separate calls during one particularly anxious week in April 1941. The first asked me everything from my mother's maiden name to what political party I belonged to in the United States. The second, besides covering all of these points, also wanted to know the street address of the *Times* office in New York; he seemed genuinely surprised when I told him about the visit of his predecessor. The third came after I had complained to Foreign Press authorities to stop all these goings-on; he too asked the same questions, and assured me that although he had not been able to trace either of the other two, I only had to call on him if I was disturbed in the future.

The most difficult moments, however, came at the frontiers, and as I was usually travelling alone, there was no way to let anybody know if something happened. Always I had a moment of uneasiness at the frontier military headquarters when the clerk checked my name against the list of individuals who were not allowed to cross. Only once, however, was I arrested, and this was under circumstances which in retrospect are fine comic material.

This was at the end of January 1940, when I was on my way to Saint-Jean-de-Luz to bring my wife and baby back to Madrid. By this time I knew by heart the complicated routine of baggage examination, money declaration, pass from military headquarters, and the rest of it, and I was saving American and English stamps for the police officials at the frontier. I was travelling with a foreigner who was even better acquainted with them than I, and our passage through the frontier routine was accompanied by exclamations of "*Hombre, que tal,*" with warm handshakes. Everything had been done, and we were in the car, with a cocktail at the Bar Basque in Saint-Jean-de-Luz only fifteen minutes away, when one of the officials came up and asked my friend, whom I will call Joe, to have the kindness to drive back to military headquarters for a moment. We supposed it was merely a request for Joe to bring back something from France for the commander, and Joe drove away alone, leaving his wife, his two sons, and me to wait for him at the customs shed.

An hour went by, and then someone phoned that Joe had been detained but would be back in five minutes. Another hour, and this time the chief customs inspector, who had been particularly cordial in greeting us, came out looking rather embarrassed. He asked Joe's wife to step into the dressing-room, where a woman searched her. A *carabinero* meanwhile searched the two boys. We knew then that Joe must be going through the same thing at military headquarters. In another half-hour the search was repeated, and this time it included me. I was still free to go on across, however, and I could not decide whether it would be better to go while the going was good and notify Joe's friends, or stay on with his family. As I was deliberating, an inbound traveller came up speaking Spanish with a Middle Western accent, and I asked him to report the incident to the American Embassy when he arrived in Madrid.

Finally, just as the frontier was about to close, we were all ordered back to military headquarters, where we were told that we were under arrest but would be permitted to stay at a hotel in San Sebastián on condition that we did not leave the town. A soldier who pretended not to speak any English went along with us, but it was not until we were at a table in the deserted dining-room of the Hotel María Cristina that Joe explained what had happened. Madrid police headquarters had suddenly decided that he was smuggling out a secret document, and the suitcases and the car itself had almost been taken apart in the search. When that failed, Joe was then questioned on a series of fantastic charges, obviously based on reports of agents whose faulty knowledge of English had garbled their report of his telephone conversations during the past six months. And so we would be held until the matter was cleared up; we were told that we could telephone our friends in Madrid.

The next two days were among the longest I have ever spent. The luxuriousness of our hotel suite was in ludicrous contrast to our depressed spirits. I left the hotel once, to telegraph my wife that I had been delayed, but otherwise we stayed close to the telephone for word from friends trying to get us out. Finally on the third day came the news that although Joe and his family must stay, orders had come from Madrid for the release of the North American journalist. Joe and I must report to military headquarters at once.

The *comandante,* a tall, handsome Spaniard in an immaculate uniform, with boots and spurs polished to an unbelievable brilliance, received us with the utmost suavity. He deeply regretted the necessity of inconveniencing us, and hoped that Joe and his family would soon be able to continue their journey. Turning to me, he said I could go on to France after I had cleared up one little matter. He then produced the telegram to my wife, in which I had said that if there were any orders for me from the paper, she must relay them to me in San Sebastián. He wanted to know what orders I was expecting.

I broke in to ask if this meant that he had stopped the telegram, leaving my wife, who had been ill, wondering all this time what had happened to me. He said that he had, and I began a tirade in Spanish, later shifting to French, in which I was then more fluent, that doubtless did little or no credit to my discretion. The *comandante* smilingly heard me out, then remarked that although he did not wish to hurry us, he supposed from my remarks that I much preferred Saint-Jean-de-Luz to San Sebastián and he had given the appropriate orders to let me pass. By a nice irony, this time nobody made a move to search me or my baggage, and if any of us had been carrying any secret papers, I could have carried them out with no one the wiser. Joe and his family were released a few days afterwards.

This incident, and the trials of many a foreigner passing through Spain, came to my mind when a sudden and apparently insuperable difficulty arose that jeopardized my final departure from Spain nearly a year and a half later. Some time before, in accordance with my practice of always having an exit visa ready in case of an assignment to go to Portugal, I had obtained one from the little man at police headquarters. I had made sure that he had put on the authorization for my return to Spain—his favourite trick was to leave it off, thus making it necessary to spend weeks in Portugal waiting for a special authorization from the Foreign Ministry—but I had not noticed the date. Only three hours before my train left, a friend who was thumbing through my passport happened to see that the visa had been dated June 15 instead of July 15. An exit visa was valid only if used within thirty days after being issued, so this was useless.

This mistake, intentional or otherwise, might cost me my trip home. I could just catch the boat as it was, and if I missed it I could not get another reservation for weeks; in that case I could not return soon enough for a possible German invasion in the autumn. On the other hand, it would be useless to try to get anything at police headquarters.

Suddenly my two years in Franco Spain produced a dividend; it came over me that the difference of only one letter separated the very bad month of *Junio* from the very good month of *Julio*. Having been arrested once at the French frontier, I was willing to take a chance at the Portuguese border; a friend produced the same shade of green ink favoured at police headquarters, and a stroke of the pen was enough to make an *N* into an *L*. The Spanish officials did not question the visa, but it was not until I was out of Spain beyond all doubt, and was standing in the Portuguese frontier station that I realized what a relief it was to breathe free air again.

# *Chapter* XII

## THE GERMANS FIGHT US IN SPAIN

Although Rumania, Hungary, Finland, and other small European countries have since bowed their heads to the yoke, Franco's was the first European government that willingly became an Axis vassal. It was clear to the generalissimo and everyone else that the Axis had won the war for him, and Germany, Italy, Japan, and Portugal—the channel through which German troops and war supplies reached Franco in the early days of the civil war—were hailed as the partners that they were.

The partners were not all, to be sure, entitled to the same consideration by the regime. If the jittery officials of the Portuguese Embassy in Madrid reflected the views of their government, Salazar must long since have repented of his own participation. The Portuguese dictator, swallowing Franco's claim to be the defender of Europe against Communism, did not realize that annexation of his own country was the ambition of the regime. While the Republic was anathema to Salazar and his "corporative" or semi-fascist State, at least it did not attempt to do anything against Portugal.

Without Salazar's help in its early days the uprising might have been defeated, since Franco at that time lacked adequate Atlantic ports to receive his supplies from Hitler. For this reason the flag of Portugal was draped with those of the Axis in the lounge of the Hotel Condestable at Burgos, the provisional capital, as a notice to the world that Franco would remember his friends; along with Axis representatives, the Portuguese Ambassador and his military and naval attachés are invited every year to the dinner on April 1 at which Franco relives his triumphs; representatives of Salazar's uniformed youth movement visited Spain as honour guests of the Phalanx, and the Franco press often spoke of the community of purpose existing between the two young and virile regimes.

Unfortunately, however, these editorials had a distressing tendency to emphasize the charm of the days when Philip II ruled both Spain and Portugal and their vast Empires. Every now and again a fire-eating *Falangista* announced that Portugal must be taken over, and this was unpleasant reading for a little country with no natural defences or other protection except the British and American fleets. When Hitler reached the Spanish frontier he became master of the entire Iberian Peninsula, and all Salazar's efforts since 1939 to keep Franco neutral stand exactly the same chance of success as those of Britain and the United States.

The Japanese also were listed by Franco as allies, for the two far-separated dictatorships were united by their feeling toward the democracies. Because of the thousands of miles which separated them, however, Franco was not particularly successful in effecting the desired strengthening of relations. He sent a Spanish trade mission to Tokyo soon after the end of the civil war, but the Japanese, busy with the preparations that bore fruit at Pearl Harbor and Singapore, had few commodities to spare for an ally so far away. The Franco press nevertheless did the best it could to show that Spain and Japan had been linked since the earliest times by the efforts of St. Francis Xavier and other Jesuit missionaries in the Orient, and that they were now joined even more closely in their common enmity for the democracies and the "Asiatic hordes" of atheistic Russia.

The continuance of Spanish influence in the Philippines,

where a large number of sugar plantations are owned by Spaniards, was a more effective tie. A branch of the Phalanx existed in Manila, and great honours were rendered to the rector of Manila's University of St. Thomas when he came on a pilgrimage to the fountainhead of *Hispanidad*. The fascists boasted that the conquistadores had left their mark in the Philippines as well as in Latin America, and the Franco regime fought "Yankee domination" of the Filipinos with the same weapons that it opposed us in other former Spanish possessions.

What has happened in the Philippines since the fall of Corregidor is still a closed book, but it may be presumed that Franco's men, for the moment at least, find Japanese rule more to their liking than was ours. With no geographical limitations upon their visions, the more ambitious Spanish fascists even envisage the ultimate restoration to the *Imperio* of the Philippines and other former Pacific possessions now held by the Japanese. This is not, however, a matter to be pressed until the United States is knocked out of the war.

Italy's influence over Franco had required artificial respiration since the Republicans defeated Mussolini's legions at Guadalajara. Matters were not improved by the selection of General Gambara, commander of the Italian expeditionary force, as Ambassador to Spain when the war ended. Whatever may have been the qualifications of Gambara for military command, he was too frank in his criticisms of the regime to be a successful diplomat. At times in the winter of 1939–40 Franco was on the point of demanding his recall, and a visit by the president of the Royal Italian Academy was necessary to restore identity of purpose between the two "sister" nations. It was a relief to the Spaniards when Gambara was called home for service in the war with Greece.

The ignominy of Italy's performance in Greece and Africa was a deadly blow to Italian influence in Madrid, and the final blow was Mussolini's claim to a lion's share of the spoil that Franco expected to get for himself by entering the war. Making things worse was the fact that both regimes were so obviously dependent upon the Nazis for anything they did get.

Nazi prestige in Spain, on the other hand, after weathering the difficult time between announcement of the Russo-German alliance and the collapse of France, has grown stronger. The Führer's pact with Stalin, supposedly his mortal enemy, did weaken Germany's standing for a time, and a few unquiet spirits in the Madrid Phalanx even talked of demonstrating against the German Embassy. The severance of trade between Spain and Germany after the war began created serious inconveniences for Franco, who had set out to orient Spain's entire export trade toward Germany, and eventually Franco was compelled to make limited commercial agreements with both France and England.

But Hitler's military success more than counterbalanced these setbacks. The Nazi pilots and tank crews were even better than they had shown themselves in Spain, and Franco, who had denounced the "absurd" conflict resulting when Britain and France declared war on behalf of Poland, crowed over the Nazi successes as if they had been his own.[1] The Russo-German alliance, however, still stood in the way of full understanding, and the Franco press could relieve its feelings only by praising the stout resistance put up by Finland to Soviet attack.

The last obstacle to complete fascist accord was removed, however, when Hitler invaded Russia in June 1941. The happy little barks of the Franco pfennig-a-liners showed what a strain it had been to lay off the "Marxist assassins" who were allied with Hitler in the restoration of the unity of Christian Europe. Promptly the "Blue Division" of "volunteers" was formed to take part in the new crusade. I was at the North Station in Madrid on the day that the last contingents left for the Russian front. As they waved good-bye from their freight cars they seemed to have a presentiment of the massacre that awaited

[1] In a speech before the Fascist Council on July 17, 1941, Franco declared that the Allies had already lost the war.

them in the Russian winter, and they were a pitiful group in their red berets and dark blue shirts. The crowd of fascists that was staying behind was, on the other hand, supremely enthusiastic. Their own officials went almost unnoticed, but the German military attaché was cheered to the echo as he paraded stiffly up and down the platform. The fascists shouted: "Viva Germany!" and "Death to Russia!" with vicarious ferocity.

The fascists, and stay-at-home fascists at that, were, however, the only Spaniards that displayed any enthusiasm. Despite the prevailing misery, the promise of high pay was insufficient to attract more than a handful of "volunteers," and many of these were starving workmen who were not permitted to hold jobs because of their record as Republicans. The Civil Guard was used as a press-gang throughout Spain, but popular resistance was so great that it was able to produce only a few thousand recruits. Chiefs of the Phalanx were ordered to enlist *en masse*, but, in accordance with the usual custom of Franco Spain, those who were in favour managed to obtain their discharge for more pressing duties on the home front. The bulk of the division was composed of officers and men assigned from the Army. General Muñoz Grande, one of the few fascist Army officers, was relieved of his post as commander of the Gibraltar area and placed in charge of the division.

That such methods were necessary was a striking demonstration of the failure of the Nazis to back up their dominance over the Franco regime by establishing any ground of solidarity with the Spanish people. The failure assuredly was not due to lack of skill or effort by the two principal representatives of Hitler in Spain, Baron von Stohrer, the German Ambassador, and Hans Lazar, the press attaché.

Von Stohrer knew Spain well, for during the World War he had served as a secretary to the Madrid Embassy until his activities in organizing German propaganda and espionage made him unacceptable to Alfonso's government. This time, however, his work was subject to no restraint. Von Stohrer, who is at least six feet four and built in proportion, had a six-foot baroness, and they towered over the Francos in more ways than one. Both speak perfect Spanish, French, and English, among other languages; they are charming, and a beach picnic they gave in San Sebastián was one of the most pleasant affairs that my wife and I attended while in Spain. It was appropriate and diverting that von Stohrer's house adjoined that of his great rival, Sir Samuel Hoare, but there was never any doubt in the *Caudillos's* mind of the Ambassador upon whom he relied.

Fully as important a cog in the Nazi machine was Lazar, a swarthy cynic whose combination of brutality and polished manners made him an excellent choice for his work in handling the Franco journalists. Lazar, who was generally believed to be a Jew, was born in Bulgaria and served the Austrian government after the World War as a press attaché in Budapest and Berlin. He had anticipated Hitler's successes, and after the Anschluss he was taken over by the Nazis when most of the Austrian diplomatic service was dismissed. He was about to retire to his wife's estate in Bessarabia when his qualifications for the work in Madrid were realized. He is a propaganda technician, and an extraordinarily good one; as far as I could gather from several talks with him, he would have been just as industrious if he had been directing propaganda for—or against—the liquor traffic. He liked his work, though his contempt for Spaniards, and particularly for the fascists who did his bidding, was unsurpassable.

Lazar had an important aid in the Franco regime, which was always ready to crack down upon any newspaper that, for one reason or another, printed an article or a headline not in complete accord with the German propaganda line. This seldom happened, because the Franco government, in addition to telling its newspapers what not to print, issued daily instructions ordering them where and how to display the news. Sometimes, Spain being what it is, an article would appear suggesting, for example, that perhaps the war might last a long time because of the coming entrance of the United States into it. I regret that I no longer have the original of a letter from Lazar to one offender; I gave it to our Ambassador, thinking it was time that our government understood how Lazar worked, and did not retain a copy because I was determined to avoid trouble with the Spanish police. Although I do not recall the exact language, it went something like this:

*Dear Mr. So-and-so*:

When I read the —— today I was surprised to see your article, which, if I may be allowed to say so, was contrary to easily determined facts about the Reich.

Accordingly I have taken the liberty of sending you the enclosed article, which I feel confident will set the matter right. Perhaps you would be good enough to see to it that it appears in —— tomorrow. I suggest that it be placed on page 1, column 5. In order to avoid such regrettable incidents in future, I suggest that you do me the honour of calling on me at your early convenience.

In the background was the certainty that if a newspaper writer proved recalcitrant, Lazar or von Stohrer would go to the press authorities and obtain his dismissal. Usually, however, Lazar did not feel it necessary to show the iron hand. He was equally expert with the velvet glove, and he specialized in small stag dinners in his apartment at which there was always excellent food and drink. Spanish newspapermen, who are not even supposed to live on their salaries, were easily won over by such affairs and the substantial bribes which were to be obtained by faithful observance of orders.

The result was that the Spanish newspapers hewed to the Nazi line as determinedly as if they had been published in Berlin. *Alcázar,* a Madrid afternoon sheet which was supposed to be the mouthpiece of the Catholic Church, followed his guidance almost as completely as *Arriba,* the spokesman of the Phalanx. The one-time monarchist *ABC,* which though a tabloid was the only newspaper in Franco Spain making any pretence to competent writing and mechanical production, was just as much under his thumb. The articles by *ABC's* London correspondent, Luis Calvo, were particularly effective anti-democratic propaganda, and the capacity of the opposition Lazar had to face may be judged from the fact that the British allowed Calvo to stay on apparently because the *ABC* once was a monarchist paper and might one day help win over the conservatives, who would in turn win over Franco.

Lazar's dictatorship of the Spanish press was, moreover, so unquestioned that when the Minister from a certain European country had a complaint to make, he went direct to Lazar rather than to the official press department. Only the week before, he told Lazar, all the newspapers had been lauding his country, and now they were making one bitter attack after another; he pointed out that although internal developments did seem to indicate a shift away from German influence, the issue was not yet decided and the German propaganda machine had not yet gone into action. He saw no reason why the Spanish press should be so precipitate, and Lazar agreed. "These swine," he said, "are always trying to anticipate my orders, but I will show them that they must stop this nonsense." He was as good as his word, and thereafter the Franco press concentrated its attention upon England, the United States, and other known foes of Hitler.

Lazar's activities extended as well to periodicals, moving pictures, and the government radio, and his general propaganda line was that of the Phalanx, with variations to suit German interests at the moment. He has been highly successful in producing a definite orientation and timing in the midst of the prevailing chaos.

Propaganda naturally covers much more than the routine mediums of influencing public opinion, and it was Lazar who arranged a German Book Week every year, brought Nazi scientists and technicians to Spain, and sent Fascist newspapermen and party officials on expense-paid visits to Great Germany.[1] Probably most important of all was his success in organizing the Germans and pro-German Spaniards into unrivalled propagandists and rumour-mongers. This made it possible to give quiet explanations that would have perhaps produced complications if published. Thus Lazar passed the word during the period of Hitler's alliance with Russia that although he was speaking only for himself, the Russians had wrecked his wife's estate and he was sure that the Führer would take an awful vengeance. After the Russo-German war began he promised that the wheat of the Ukraine and the oil of the Caucasus would be available in a few weeks to relieve Spain from reliance upon England and the United States. And it was Lazar who interpreted every move of Anglo-American appeasement as proof of our weakness, who fathered the continual rumours that the Germans were coming, that they had actually reached San Sebastián. These rumours had a considerable effect upon even Allied diplomats, and their panic over what the Germans might do to Gibraltar is perhaps the most creditable explanation of the policy that we have followed.

At several times since the spring of 1940 there has been abundant reason to justify these fears, and there can be no doubt that if they need her, the Germans will try to completely take over Spain. Meanwhile the efforts of Lazar and the Nazi organization are an important element in a war of nerves which has two main objectives: to convince Franco that he can save himself only by carrying out Hitler's orders; and to frighten the democracies into granting fascist Spain raw materials and other goods which directly or indirectly can be

[1] The British attempted to copy his methods and gave some journalists a free trip to England. The principal result was just another book attacking England's "materialism" and lack of the finer fascist instincts. It was interesting to learn, however, that in England every workman had a car and that clubs of the Pall Mall standard were to be found on every street corner throughout London.

employed for the benefit of the Axis. Each aim helps the other, for the more we fear a German invasion, the more we are tempted to give Franco what he and the Nazis need. And this in turn bolsters Lazar's argument that we would not be trying so hard to buy Franco off but for our realization that the entrance of Spain into the war would be a fatal blow to our cause.

If Spain were not so hard to handle, Hitler would have marched in long ago, without waiting for Franco to give the go-ahead signal. We can have no doubt that when the Führer decides the time has come, a fifth column of great power will be ready to take whatever action circumstances require. In Portugal plans have been made with equal thoroughness. In both countries, however, the Nazi organization is so successfully masked that few signs are apparent. Once when a group of Americans were speculating on this subject a bit too audibly in a Lisbon bar, a stocky individual with shaved neck came over from a near-by table and said with an unmistakably guttural accent: "The fifth column, it is *hier. Ja*!" The "tourists" in Madrid and the rest of Spain, however, were less boastful, and casual visitors saw little tangible evidence to justify the pall of foreboding which hung over Spaniards and citizens of non-Axis countries.

There was, to be sure, ample evidence of "peaceful" German penetration. The Franco regime's solidarity with Germany was evident in speeches by Franco, in the place of honour given the German Ambassador at all ceremonies, in the state visits of such dignitaries as Heinrich Himmler. It was apparent in trivial happenings as well. Over and over, in the course of automobile trips through Spain, my car was stopped by the police for examination of documents, passengers, or whatever. In Spain any person with fair hair was always considered a German unless he was known to be otherwise, and almost invariably when the policeman came up to the car he would announce: *"Usted es aleman,"* with a deference that did not justify a denial, and wave me on. (German citizenship did not, however, produce equally happy results among the Spanish shop-people; only once did I encounter an unaccommodating shop-keeper, and when I asked why he acted with so little *cultura,* he replied that he assumed I was German.)

That there were large numbers of Germans in Spain was clear beyond question. Before the war there were thousands living in Seville, Barcelona, and other commercial centres, and although the Fatherland presumably needed every one of them for the war, they stayed to the last man. "Hisma," the Nazi organization that handled the trade between Franco Spain and Germany during the civil war, kept its staff intact after the outbreak of the European war, even though commercial relations were virtually cut off. The German Railways Information Office in Madrid, and offices of German steamship lines both in the capital and in the principal ports, also remained open despite the lack of customers. German business men (using the abundant pesetas that the Nazis, who printed most of Franco's bank notes, had obtained by the simple process of running off two sets of one issue and keeping one for their own use) continued to buy mines and factories wherever they were offered for sale, then proceeded to import engineers from Germany to operate them.

The German Embassy, which overflowed into buildings once occupied by the Czech, Austrian, and other legations of liquidated countries, had between 150 and 200 employees. There were more German newspaper correspondents in Madrid than from all other countries combined, though one or two whom I knew told me that they sent home very few articles. Those that I saw published were mostly technical descriptions of factories and mines which were of little interest to the ordinary reader but of absorbing importance to anyone planning to take over Spanish industry.

German officers, presumably on leave from the occupying forces in France, were to be seen roaming around the Basque country as far as Bilbao, and occasionally in the Palace Bar and other gathering places of Madrid. The German school, to which all good Spanish fascists sent their children, taught its pupils the *Horst Wessel Lied* very loudly, and the Deutsches Kultur Institut operated just across the street from the American Embassy.

But this apparent openness only served to mask the grave danger that was invisible. As early as December 1939 the British estimated that there were 80,000 Germans in Spain, and since that time the agreement for the exchange of German engineers for Spanish labourers has considerably increased the number. There were more dangerous arrivals. The Lufthansa operated—still does, according to the latest information I have received—a fast daily passenger and freight service from Stuttgart to Lisbon, with stops at Barcelona and Madrid. I do not know what passengers got off in Barcelona, but frequently I saw big and tough young Germans, whose hands seemed to be itching to take a control stick, riding in from the Madrid airport. From that moment they seemed to disappear into thin air. Never did I see them on the streets, and the only clue I obtained was on a visit to Seville, where a boarding-house keeper told me that she would be able to give us lodging during crowded Holy Week because the young fliers who had been staying there had unexpectedly moved into the barracks at the military air field. They had been hard-working young men, for the living-room and one or two bedrooms just vacated were littered with German and Italian aviation magazines.

That night we went to a bleak little night club, Las Cadenas, which is the only place in Seville where *flamenco* dancing is available for mixed company, and were considerably put off by six of the most sinister Gestapo men ever to be encountered outside Hollywood. It was a relief when they started talking among themselves in German about us; at least there was no longer any mystery about them.

For it was the unknown strength of the German fifth column

that inspired the most worry. No one could say where the Germans were, what they were doing, when they would strike. Nazis were installed in Spanish frontier outposts, and at the Madrid headquarters of the police. That I knew because I or my friends saw them there. But where else they were was a mystery. An anti-Nazi German who was hiding in Spain told me that a car filled with Gestapo men drew up at the door of his rooming-house and he escaped out the window just in time. But afterwards he frequently went out in the streets and was not molested. And no one could say why the pursuit was abandoned.

Supposedly the aviators and Gestapo undercover men kept out of sight in apartments of German residents, but rumours had it that two entire divisions of German troops had arrived in Spain. If this was so, where were they? And did the Gestapo have its own separate jail, to which luckless refugees from Hitler were taken before being returned to the Reich? I was assured that it did, but I did not see it. And was it the Gestapo that listened in on the telephones of every American and Britisher in Madrid so expertly that no official of the British Embassy ever discussed confidential matters in his office without disconnecting his telephone entirely? Again I do not know, but it would appear extremely likely in view of the fact that few Spaniards had the technical knowledge necessary to tap telephone lines away from the central exchange.

I do know, however, from my own experiences and those of other Americans in Spain, that the Franco police were incapable of gathering accurate information about foreigners, at least. On the other hand, officials of the German Embassy gave friends of mine among neutral diplomats some very accurate information about my own movements and sources of information—of course in the expectation that it would be passed on to me and I would take warning. It may be presumed that if they went to this much trouble over one newspaper correspondent, their knowledge of the activities of important personages was even more comprehensive.

Pending the occupation of Spain much of this thoroughness seemed rather pointless, but the Nazis' long-range preparations have justified themselves in other countries and it must be assumed that Hitler knows what he is doing. While they are waiting the Nazis are making good use of Spain's position as a "non-belligerent" or, as *Arriba* prefers to call it, her attitude of a "moral belligerent" for Hitler.

Despite the emphasis that has been given the question in the United States press, the amount of food that Hitler has been able to obtain from Spain is the least of these advantages. The meat, eggs, milk, and other dairy products taken out of the provinces nearest France represent a considerable loss to starving Spain, but are of comparatively small importance by comparison with the staggering amount of food required to feed German-conquered Europe. It is likely, in fact, that Portugal has supplied more of these products to Germany than has Spain.[1] Since the western Mediterranean became untenable for Allied shipping, the Germans have taken almost all the oranges and other fruits that Spain exports, but England has found it possible to get along without them, and Germany could also if it were necessary.

The two Spanish food products in which Germany is most interested are olive oil and rice, and there is no question of the fact that large quantities of both have been exported in the years since land communication with Germany became possible through France. Olive oil is particularly important to the Nazis because of the scarcity of fats, and the Russians discovered that some of the German planes which they shot down were lubricated with olive oil. A certain amount of

[1] The Germans obtained Portuguese money cheaply by selling French francs on the black market in Lisbon.

wool, hides, and medicinal plants was shipped out by the Nazis during the civil war, and this trade also has continued.

Far more important, however, are other Spanish products used directly in Reich war production. Together with Italy, Spain has almost a monopoly of the world's supply of mercury; she is one of the principal producers of cork, and she is an important source of iron pyrites (used in making sulphuric acid, one of the indispensable bases of war industries), wolfram (the ore from which tungsten is derived), lead, and manganese.

Years ago Spain was a large producer of copper, but as the mines have been nearly worked out it is unlikely that they are producing much more than her own requirements. Until now, at least, the Nazis have not troubled to import much of the high-grade iron ore produced by the Bilbao mines, which were their principal interest during the civil war, and have even permitted Spain to ship considerable quantities to the British. This is because of the fact that the Belgian, French, and Swedish mines are more conveniently located for the Nazis' purposes; apart from the distance from Bilbao to the Ruhr, handling costs are high because the Spanish railway lines are broad-gauge—approximately the same width as those of Russia—and it is therefore necessary to reload the ore cars at Hendaye. Should it become necessary, however, the Germans could obtain considerable quantities of both iron and copper from Spain; they do not haggle over the cost of vital products, and at times they hauled iron pyrites by truck all the way from the mines near Huelva, in southern Spain, to the French frontier.

Spain also provides almost the sole route for transportation of food, cork, and wolfram from Portugal, and particularly for articles imported from the outside world. Despite the efforts of the British and American blockade authorities, it is impossible to prevent the Germans from getting their hands on some of the goods acquired by Spanish and Portuguese firms. Great shrewdness has been shown by Franco's government in obtaining the necessary permits. The British, for instance, were supremely confident that for over a year they had permitted Spain to import just enough gasoline and other petroleum products to meet her minimum needs. But when American officials investigated in November 1941, they found that the Franco government had exaggerated Spanish consumption and had obtained enough extra gasoline to fill every storage tank in the country. It is unlikely that much of this has gone on to Germany, since it is more useful to the Nazis to hold it as a Wehrmacht reserve at strategic points within Spain.

The Nazis have been very much interested, however, in lubricating oil, which, although scarce in Germany, was so abundant in Spain that it was not even rationed. In the spring of 1942 a vigilant official of our Board of Economic Warfare discovered that one Portuguese importer was on the point of acquiring from the United States enough Fuller's earth, employed by the Nazis to purify airplane engine oil for re-use, to meet Hitler's requirements for an entire year. Through Spain and Portugal the Nazis have endeavoured to obtain many articles which, though used only in small quantities, are necessary to keep their armies and planes in the field. How successful they have been we shall probably not know until after the war; but to judge from the quantity of goods which reached Germany via neutral countries in the World War, the amount must be considerable despite everything we can do.

Owing to the fact, moreover, that there are fewer neutral countries this time, Spain and Portugal also are particularly useful in maintaining the Nazi espionage and propaganda network in the United States and other American countries. As an alternative route of communications the Germans have had the African colonies of the Vichy government, but Spanish and Portuguese ships supply a more convenient means of sending out agents and the money to support them.

Except for German agents of Spanish nationality, it is unlikely that many get through on the passenger ships, since the British check the passports before sailings and do not permit suspicious characters to go aboard. Freighters, however, are less easily supervised and it was revealed early in 1942 that not only German agents but American money confiscated by the Nazis when they burst into France were reaching Latin America by this means.

Also an extremely favourable circumstance, from the German point of view, is the co-operative attitude of both the Phalanx and the Franco diplomatic service. Although the ultimate aims of the Franco regime in Latin America differ slightly from Hitler's, the Nazi and the *Falangista* propagandists are working together. Spain is an excellent means of communication for Nazi spies in North and South America, who otherwise would have to resort to more difficult means of transmitting their reports. Investigations of German spy rings in this country have demonstrated the frequency with which such reports are sent to agents within Spain despite our censorship.

How much more help the Franco regime is giving the Nazi spy organization is another question to be settled positively only after the end of the war. From Brazil and other Latin-American countries there have come frequent reports that Spanish ships communicate to U-boats the positions of all Allied shipping that they encounter. This has, of course, been denied by the Franco government. Equally naturally, it has denied that its diplomatic representatives abroad utilize their privilege of sending dispatches in code to report information of value to the Nazis. The Cuban government, however, remained convinced that they were doing so, and in the summer of 1942 it ordered Spanish diplomats to stop using code for their cabled reports.

Only a moment's reflection is necessary to show that all

our censors are valueless if such information is in fact leaking through Madrid to Berlin. The greatest efforts were employed to keep secret Molotoff's visit to the United States, but the news of his arrival was at once cabled by a Latin-American emissary in Washington to his home government, leaked into the newspapers there, and thus became known to the Axis long before the American public was informed. This report was transmitted by a diplomat friendly to our cause; although Franco's ambassadors may all be just as sympathetic with the American way of life, there is at least a possibility that officials of Franco's Ministry of Foreign Affairs are not. From the fact that Spain, rather than Switzerland or some other neutral country, has been chosen to represent German interests in many of the Allied nations, it would seem that the Franco foreign service is expected to make itself useful as long as we permit.

But although such activities, from their very nature, are difficult to prove, there can be no question of the fact that Germany is already using Spain as an advanced base of military operations. It was by hugging Spanish territorial waters, in defiance of the rules of neutrality, that most of the German merchantmen which evaded capture by the British reached the ports of occupied France from Vigo, the principal port of northwestern Spain. The deserted coast of Galicia, with its many small harbours, provides superb opportunities for fuelling U-boats, and the evidence available would indicate that plans to utilize it were worked out by the Nazis before the outbreak of war. In the last two weeks before the invasion of Poland over thirty-five German merchantmen, including two heavily loaded tankers, put into Vigo in order, it was announced, to escape capture by the British. At least one of the tankers, however, had time to get home before the war began, and the failure of its captain to do so was a clear indication of the purpose for which its cargo of Diesel oil was to be used. When I reached Vigo in October 1939, both tankers were already riding much higher in the water than they were when they arrived, and port gossip had it that a submarine had been seen standing out to sea in the early dawn.

On my next visit, at the end of May 1941, the evidence was conclusive. Both tankers were riding so high that they were presumably empty, but they were being used as submarine depot ships. Extraordinary quantities of food, particularly fresh fruit and vegetables, were going aboard, and although the men who came off wore the uniforms of the German merchant marine, it was always a different group.

Throughout this book I have attempted, for obvious reasons, to avoid identifying any informant who is still in Spain or otherwise exposed to Axis reprisals. But although I cannot name my sources, I was convinced that relief crews of the U-boats stayed aboard the tankers while others kept the submarines at sea. Fueling supposedly was done from lighters outside the port, but occasionally a U-boat took advantage of a particularly dark night to come all the way into the harbour.

Whether the Nazis also were making use of El Ferrol, which has some of the finest shipbuilding and repair facilities in Europe, I was not able to determine because the dockyards are screened from outside observation. It seems clear, however, that the Axis has bases in the Balearic Islands, where the Italians first took over during the civil war. Land-based airplanes for a time compelled the British to send reinforcements to Egypt all the way round the Cape of Good Hope, and they avoid the western Mediterranean whenever possible. In 1942 even heavily armed convoys were getting through to Malta only with severe losses. Most of the planes which inflicted them seemed to be based on Sardinia, but the Balearics also certainly were used.

Franco's supreme value thus far to Germany, however, is not to be told in terms of bases or such easily definable services. Because of our exaggerated emphasis on keeping him "out of the war" we were extremely slow to launch the North African operation, paving the way for an attack on Italy and the Balkans, the two most vulnerable points in Hitler's domain. And now that Hitler has lost the free use of Vichy's African empire, Spain and Spain's agents are his last reliable means of maintaining his commercial, propaganda, and espionage networks in the outside world.[1]

Other and less obvious factors have been equally important in staying the Führer's hand. At any time, of course, since his troops reached Hendaye it has been within his power to occupy Spain and Portugal by writing out an order. What Franco thought about it would scarcely halt the onrush of the Nazis. But large numbers of occupation troops and Gestapo men would be required to hold down unruly Spain, it would be necessary to take over the thankless task of governing the country, and the problem of maintaining the long lines of communications back to the Fatherland would be extremely difficult without the help of Franco in combating underground resistance. That Spain would starve irremediably matters nothing at all to them, but the Nazis are concerned over the possibility that their imports might be cut off by unsettled conditions.

Pending the moment when Spanish territory becomes absolutely essential to the Axis war machine, the Führer has been content to leave Franco a certain amount of room to manœuvre, trusting that in the end the bait of empire will do its work. Should this strategy be justified by success the problems of the Nazis in Spain would be considerably simplified.

At times, as we shall see, the Franco government has been on

[1] Marquis Luca de Tena, Franco's Ambassador in Chile, who is a royalist and does not want the Nazis to march into Spain, was jubilant over the Rio de Janeiro conference, which adopted a resolution calling on Latin-American countries to break off relations with the Axis. This action inevitably hampered the activities of Axis agents in every Latin-American country except Argentina and Chile. Everywhere else the Axis has had to rely mainly upon Franco's representatives. Luca de Tena told a friend of mine that he was certain Hitler would have taken over Spain shortly after the Rio de Janeiro conference but for the proof it gave of Latin America's solidarity with the United States.

the point of acceding to Hitler's desires. Always thus far, however, the fatal example of Mussolini, who thought that he would have a short and enjoyable ride on the Axis victory chariot, has stopped the generalissimo in time. The latest blows Mussolini has suffered, coupled with the Allied landings in French North Africa, have certainly impressed Franco.

Hitler's intentions regarding Spain are much clearer, and it may be that at any moment he will decide that the advantages of taking over the Iberian Peninsula outweigh the disadvantages. The possibility is now remote, but a crushing Allied defeat in some near theatre, giving Hitler the opportunity to attain a lasting success by marching into Spain, might bring the final decision. Thus it appears likely that Spain's turn would have come next if Rommel's drive against Egypt in the summer of 1942 had been successful, making it possible to bottle up the Mediterranean by closing the Strait of Gibraltar.

A staggering reverse for the Axis might have the same result if Spain seemed the only means of saving the situation. Our occupation of North Africa seems to bring that situation near, particularly if the Nazis should find the alternative of a drive through Turkey inadvisable. Conditions in December 1942 seemed remarkably similar to those of February 1941, when Wavell reached El Agheila and there was some slight ground for the belief that General Maxime Weygand would vindicate our government's hopes and bring French North Africa into the war on our side. Wavell, however, was thrown back, and as German land-based planes soon virtually closed the western Mediterranean to British shipping, it turned out to be unnecessary to take over Spain. This was fortunate for our cause, for then Gibraltar was much weaker than it is now, and Hitler was left free to invade Russia. The example of Napoleon did not deter the Führer from marching on Moscow, but if he is guided by Napoleon's equally disastrous invasion of Spain, he will stay on the other side of the Pyrenees. It remains to be seen what page of history is a guide to the future.

# Chapter XIII

## FRANCO FIGHTS US IN LATIN AMERICA

Although many gallons of printer's ink have been spilled to awaken us to the danger we are in from Axis manœuvres in Latin America, little attention has been given to the no less menacing efforts of Franco. There are, beyond question, far too many Germans, Italians, and Japanese in the Latin-American countries, and it would be idle to minimize the necessity of strong measures to prevent them and their henchmen from organizing fifth-column movements. But unless we also understand what Franco is trying to do and take adequate measures to stop him, his minions may overcome our newly won influence before we know what is happening.

How great a danger the Latin-American policy of Franco represents for us was not clearly apparent in Spain despite the clear statement of aims contained in the Twenty-Six Points of the Phalanx. Only when, after my return to the United States, I went to Chile for a three-month stay did I begin to realize how effectively Franco Spain is attacking where we are vulnerable, on the innate differences between the Protestant, Anglo-Saxon, English-speaking civilization of the United States and the Catholic, Spanish-speaking civilization of South and Central America.

Despite the admiration that many Latin Americans feel for Germany, the Nazi system of government is too much for most of them to swallow. But the Franco regime is a diluted form of fascism, uncomfortably similar in its operations to some of the dictatorships which have flourished among our southern neighbours in recent years. Should fascism ever gain a real foot-hold in Latin America, it will show the clear inspiration of the propaganda which Franco has hurled against us continuously ever since the end of the civil war.

The German press in Chile and elsewhere also has emphasized our bad behaviour in the past toward the weaker nations of the Western Hemisphere, the ulterior motives behind our Good Neighbour policy, and other points stressed by the Spanish fascists, but this does not mean, as many Americans believe, that Franco's agents are mere Nazi stooges. Our problem in Latin America probably would be simpler if they were.

For the moment, of course, their propaganda is very much the same, since the aim of both the Nazis and the *Falangistas* is to turn Latin America against us. But Franco's speeches have revealed over and over again his full sympathy with the *Falangista* ambition to reassert Spanish influence, to give Spain that "pre-eminent place in all common tasks" to which she was entitled as "the spiritual cradle of the Spanish world." In the spring of 1940 he wrote with a flourish: "Before the ashes of our dead Empire, and with the promise of another," in the visitors' book of the Archives of the Indies at Seville, which houses the early charters and papal bulls under which the conquistadores extended Spanish rule to the New World. Despite its military and economic weakness, the Franco regime is pursuing its own ends in Latin America, although the aid of the Nazis is acceptable for the present just as it is needed to acquire the desired portions of the French Empire in Africa. The statement by General Varela, already cited, on the extent of Spain's future power as head of the Latin-American countries, indicates how generally these ambitions have permeated the entire Franco government.

In his early career the generalissimo himself was primarily

an *Africanista,* the term applied by the Spaniards to those who insisted that Spain must make up for the prestige lost in the war with the United States by recovering Gibraltar and staking out a new empire in the wastes of Morocco. The ambitions in Spain's backyard need not detain us. Despite all Franco's tub-thumping, he has thus far acquired only the International Zone in Morocco, with an area of 225 square miles, which contains only the 60,000 inhabitants of the city of Tangier. His ambitions, to be sure, reach much farther. But as they are dependent solely upon the success of Nazi arms, they need not disturb us here.

Franco's policy in Latin America, however, is another matter. It must be conceded, of course, that it is nothing new for a Spanish government to fight the United States in Latin America; whenever a strongly nationalist regime takes power in Madrid an effort is made automatically to revive Spanish control of the former colonies. General Primo de Rivera had much the same idea as Franco; the expositions which he held simultaneously in Barcelona and Seville, and Ramón Franco's goodwill flight to South America, were part of his effort to give Spain a position of leadership comparable to that of England in the English-speaking world. Even the Spanish Republic, which was so different from the Primo de Rivera regime, tried to revive Spain's position and attacked efforts of the United States to extend its influence in the countries south of the Rio Grande.

The Republic, however, had little to offer except the general concept of the unity of blood and civilization. As it was committed to breaking the hold of the privileged groups in Spain, it did not appeal to the governing classes of Latin America, who for the most part held privileges very similar to those of their opposite numbers in the mother country. When Franco came to power after overturning the Republic, the stage was set for a new effort under much more favourable auspices. In the Phalanx he had a relatively effective instrument, for its Foreign Division (*Falange Exterior*) was modelled directly upon the *Auslandsdienst* of the Nazi party, and by the end of the civil war it had more than 250 branches outside Spain, including units in Berlin, Rome, Istanbul, New York, and Manila, but with the majority, of course, established in Latin America. And Franco deliberately cast himself in the role of protector of everybody in the world who spoke Spanish, some 70,000,000 in Latin America alone.

These efforts were a constant source of amusement to the Latin-American diplomats in Madrid. To them it seemed incredible that a government so manifestly incompetent to rule Spain should take it upon itself to tell its former colonies what to do. In the United States there has been a somewhat similar current attitude to the mother country; some Americans who think of the Revolutionary War as only yesterday still do not like the British. But they do have to respect them, for England is certainly our equal in vim and vigour. The Latin-American countries still gloried in their struggle to throw off the yoke of Spain, and the contrast between the continued weakness of Spain and their own large territories and hopes for the future made their representatives in Madrid resent Franco's pretensions even though they could not take them seriously.

Soon after the end of the civil war, however, his government's quarrel with Chile produced a startling demonstration of Franco's determination to attain his "pre-eminent place in all common tasks." On July 16, 1940, using as a pretext some anti-Franco speeches delivered at a mass meeting in Santiago, Franco abruptly broke off relations with Chile, claiming that the presence of a member of the Popular Front had given the speeches government endorsement. A contributing factor, although unmentioned in the Franco press, was Chile's stubborn refusal to hand over for execution several Republicans who had taken refuge in the Chilean Embassy on the day that Franco occupied Madrid. The Republic had permitted Chile to extend the Embassy right of asylum to 1,500 Rightists, and Chile, applying the same principle, refused to give up these Leftists.

What Franco hoped to attain, however, was much more ambitious than merely a rebuke to the Chileans for such temerity. With the exception of Chile and Mexico, all the Latin-American governments had supported his "crusade" against Communism, and, as the Madrid newspapers made clear, he saw an opportunity to isolate the two Leftist governments and prepare the way for the full assertion of Spain's leadership. The result, however, was entirely different from what had been expected. All of Latin America, regardless of what side it had taken in the Spanish civil war, was up in arms against this arbitrary act. The reaction was so unfavourable that the Franco government soon realized its mistake and was compelled to permit all the refugees in the Chilean Embassy to leave Spain. On October 12, the "Day of the Race," Chile and Spain resumed diplomatic relations.

Other no less harmful blunders were committed after Serrano Suñer took over the Foreign Ministry. The Phalanx organizations already acted with a conspicuous lack of regard for the susceptibilities of Latin Americans, and the ill feeling was increased by Serrano Suñer's attempt to fuse the diplomatic service with the Phalanx by appointing party leaders as Spanish consuls in the different countries. For months a bitter dispute raged between the Franco government and Cuba over the appointment of one Riestra, the island Phalanx leader, as consul general. Although this appointment was finally revoked, Cuba nevertheless proceeded to outlaw propaganda organizations sponsored by any foreign governments—a bitter blow to the *Falange Exterior,* whose officials in Madrid had boasted to me that the party had made more progress in Cuba than in any other of Spain's former possessions. Although Cuba's attitude was the most pronounced, the Spanish fascists were compelled by hostility in most Latin-American countries to adopt other names, such as the Circle of Spanish Catholic Action. Mexico, which, though it still has not recognized the Franco regime, permits the Phalanx to operate quite openly, is in fact the only important exception.

Despite these blunders the Franco regime has proceeded with its vigorous efforts to win back the Latin Americans. Honours were showered upon Marshal Benavides, the former Peruvian dictator, when he arrived to take over his country's Embassy. The severe climate of Madrid promptly gave the marshal an almost fatal case of pneumonia, and he had himself transferred elsewhere as soon as he was strong enough to leave, but Franco kept trying, taking advantage of the anniversary of Pizarro's conquest of Peru to hold grandiose celebrations at Trujillo, his native village. Similar celebrations were staged in Peru itself, and the aged Marchioness de la Conquista was sent there to represent the Conqueror's family.[1]

When Dr. A. C. Escobar, the new Argentine Ambassador, arrived, the Franco regime outdid itself. Flags of Argentina and Spain were flown along the entire route from his hotel to the palace when he presented his credentials, and he promptly attained a position of influence surpassed only by that of the German Ambassador. A musical comedy purporting to show the gaiety of life in Argentina was produced soon afterward in his honor. When Argentine wheat and corn began to reach Spain under a credit arranged by England and the United States, the expressions of gratitude to Dr. Escobar were sufficient proof that the Franco regime was not lacking in this virtue although it was a trifle mistaken about the nations which were entitled to the thanks.

Activities in Latin America are now directed by the Council of Hispanidad, Franco's equivalent to our Office of Inter-

1 This tour also encountered a mishap, as I discovered when I was in Lima: the marchioness refused to go home after the celebration, declaring that in Spain there was simply nothing to eat. As Peruvian upper families were tired of paying her hotel bill, this created a difficult situation, which was finally solved by inducing her to start back by way of Santiago.

American Affairs, which was set up in November 1940, under the direct control of the Foreign Ministry, then held by Serrano Suñer. Older organizations, which had been engaged in improving relations with Latin America, were subordinated in order to give the council undisputed jurisdiction in the work of establishing Spain's claim to be the "spiritual Axis" of the Hispanic world. This claim was not based on "land alone," or on the claim of "a special race," stated the decree creating the council. "Spanish America" was assured that Spain "asks nothing and claims nothing, it only wishes to restore to Hispanidad its feeling of unity." Nevertheless, it was proclaimed that the council would be a successor of the Council of the Indies, "father of just laws, governor of nations, creator of culture," which had governed the American empire from Seville. And the new organization would have charge of "all of those activities that tend to the unification of the culture, economic interests, and power" of the Spanish-speaking world.

The council, following Nazi methods, proceeded to send out as goodwill emissaries such spokesmen as José María Pemán, a poet and member of the Spanish Academy, whose praise of the Inquisition, the expulsion of the Jews, and other old Spanish customs makes his *Child's History of Spain* (now used in all elementary schools) a pure delight. To the extent that its funds permitted, it also made plans for a library of literature in the Spanish language, films showing life in the mother country and the Latin-American republics, radio programs, and other routine propaganda activities.

For the most part, however, the Franco regime has sought to advance its prestige in Latin America by attacking the United States. Even before the establishment of the council the Spanish newspapers were in the habit of printing first-page articles to commemorate the sinking of the *Maine,* the defeats of Santiago and Manila Bay, and other events intended to show the depravity of the *Yanquis.* As a delicate attention to the American delegation at the Havana Pan-American conference in 1940, *Alcázar* reprinted a hymn of hate against Theodore Roosevelt, written a quarter of a century ago by Rubén Dario, the Nicaraguan poet, to give the impression that it was directed at the present occupant of the White House. A poster, bearing the imprimatur of the Undersecretariat of Press and Propaganda and displayed throughout Madrid, contained a despicable cartoon attacking President Roosevelt and a map asserting Spain's claim to the Philippines, Cuba, and the territory we took from Mexico. Still more violent anti-American posters were issued by the S.E.U., the university fascist organization.

A few days after the creation of the council the new forward policy went into action over a newspaper report that Uruguay was about to cede Punta del Este, the point of land which dominates the Rio de la Plata estuary, to the United States for a naval base. The outcry in the Spanish press was as usual, but the significant new element was the protests of the fascist intelligentsia, who are strongly represented on the council. The S.E.U. cabled to students throughout "Hispano-America" protesting against cession of Punta del Este, which, it said, would thus become the "first Gibraltar" of South America. Dr. Pio Zabala, rector of the University of Madrid, added the weight of Spanish scholarship with cabled appeals to the heads of universities in which he emphasized "the indestructible and profound links" uniting "Ibero-America" with "the peninsula that gave it Christianity and today is its best sister." He urged that no "alien influence be allowed to install itself within the spirit or body of *Hispanidad*."

After such an outburst of rhetoric it was rather an anticlimax for the Legation of Uruguay in Madrid to issue a flat denial that any such cession was contemplated, but from this time no opportunity was lost to oppose every move proposed by the United States toward a common front against the Axis.

Franco propaganda has been hampered by one fact: the

majority of Latin-American countries, realizing their military weakness, are sensitive to anything resembling an attempt to reimpose the once hated Spanish regime. All except the small group of the wealthy were a long way from accepting the fascist thesis that wherever a conquistador had trod, or the Spanish language was spoken, Spain automatically had special rights. They looked with suspicion upon the Nazi-style maps listing all of South America (including Brazil, for if Spain is entitled to annex Portugal she has an equal right to dominate Portugal's former colonies), Central America, and Mexico as her natural sphere of influence.

Nor were they conciliated by Spain's own weakness, which certainly would make difficult the fulfilment of these grandiose aims. Some thought that Spain was merely a stalking-horse for Germany, and all realized that she was not in a position to give them any help against the Axis in times when they needed a powerful friend.

Economically Spain was of still less importance. Even in the days when she held a trading monopoly with most of the New World, and to this end held back the commercial and industrial advancement of her colonies, she had not developed her own resources. They were still not developed, and although Franco Spain needed almost every article exported from Latin America, she had almost nothing with which to pay for them and was a suppliant for any small favours that Brazil, Chile, and particularly Argentina might care to extend. This economic weakness, joined with her military incapacity, made the Latin-American countries resent her noisy propagandists all the more.

These weaknesses would not have been so important if Spain had held the intellectual leadership of her former Empire, as England long held the leadership in the English-speaking world.

But Spain has had little influence upon the main currents of Latin-American intellectual life. With the exception of an occasional outstanding scholar, such as Menéndez y Pelayo, or a novelist of the world renown of Blasco Ibáñez, Latin America had received little from Spain since attaining its independence. The independence movement in Latin America had been inspired principally by the writers of the French Revolution (although Thomas Jefferson, Tom Paine, and other champions of freedom in the New World also exerted a powerful influence), and France has ever since been a dominating cultural influence. Madariaga has quoted somewhere the remark of a Latin American who announced to his Spanish hosts that "we think in French but talk in Spanish," and this typifies the way that most upper-class Latin Americans have looked toward France rather than Spain for everything from philosophy to the furnishings of their luxurious homes.

For French influence has not been confined merely to books. Good Argentines and Panamanians, like good Americans, hope to go to Paris when they die, and French civilization has provided the pattern for gracious living in far-away Bogotá. The influence of France extended to political affairs as well. Although Latin-American countries have copied many forms of our own government, the multiplicity of parties was a sign that the Third Republic was a controlling influence in the few nations of the south where an attempt was made to carry on true popular government. The Leftist parties, in particular, have borrowed much from the anti-clerical measures adopted by the French Radical Socialists.

French influence has diminished in recent years, and particularly since the abrupt collapse of France in 1940 under the Nazi onslaught. Except for a handful of Latin Americans who are on sufficiently good terms with the Germans, the races at Auteuil and the finery in which they used to show themselves no longer exist. But the United States, rather than Spain, has been the gainer. The Chileans, for example, are reading a fine mixture of American writers, ranging from

Pearl Buck and Zane Grey to John Dos Passos and Walt Whitman. American cars and radios already had been adopted by the Latin Americans, but now, with the great French couturiers out of reach, American dresses are as eagerly sought after; and favoured Latin Americans go to New York now with almost as much enthusiasm as they used to leave for Paris.

Spain, with most of its intellectuals imprisoned by Franco or in exile, and its poverty increased by the civil war, cannot challenge this growth of our influence. In those countries, in fact, where the middle and working classes have any political power, there is a powerful anti-Franco movement. Our large investments in Latin America had been a long way from making us popular, but now the cries of "dollar imperialism" and "Yankee blood-suckers" have mostly been silenced by the genuineness of our efforts to help Latin-American countries defend themselves. It might seem, in fact, that with the help of Franco's mistakes our own Good Neighbour policy had put us in an impregnable position. We have assumed the role of patron and protector of Latin America, which was too heavy a load for Spain; the Office of Inter-American Affairs provides hundreds of millions of dollars where the Spaniards spend thousands. The value of our credits, lend-lease shipments, and other favours to Latin America during 1941 was probably more than Franco spent on his entire government. Since Pearl Harbor our good-neighbourliness has increased, and the high prices that we are paying for Brazilian and Central American coffee, Cuban sugar, and Peruvian cotton—which could be sold nowhere else—are in contrast to Spain's dependence upon the bounty of Argentina for her daily bread.

We have made equally strenuous efforts to undo the harm which resulted from our readiness in the past to land the marines whenever a Latin-American country defaulted on its bonds, which was often. Under the Good Neighbour policy we have renounced the collection of debts by force, and we have accepted the virtual expropriation of American oil interests in Mexico, for example, with scarcely a murmur of protest. The second President Roosevelt has spared no effort to eradicate the unpleasant impression left by the big-stick methods of the Rough Rider of San Juan Hill. We have all the cards, it would seem, and since every Latin-American country, with only two exceptions, has taken our part in the struggle against the Axis, Franco's challenge might appear supremely unimportant.

Although this was the opinion that I held before going to Latin America, I found there that despite our progress in winning the friendship of Latin Americans, we are not as strong as some Americans, who have the impression that the Latin Americans are as enthusiastic about us as we are about the conga, may think. The nations to the south are still somewhat puzzled by our changed policy, and some attribute it to Machiavellian designs upon their independence or whatever they value most. And despite goodwill on both sides, there are fundamental differences between us and the Latin Americans which make it difficult to attain the common understanding that has grown up without any forcing between us and the Canadians and still exists between the American republics and Franco Spain.

Distance is not the only reason, although the 6,000-mile journey from New York to Santiago or Buenos Aires is itself a powerful obstacle to good-neighbourliness. Distance has not prevented us from developing a well-grounded liking for Australians, who are even farther away. Far more important is the gulf between the civilization of the United States and that which developed under Spain during a period of three and a half centuries. These differences have been well summarized by Nicholas John Spykman in his *America's Strategy in World Politics*: [1]

[1] New York: Harcourt, Brace & Company; 1942.

While Canada is in many ways a northern extension of the type of society found in the United States, the lands below the Rio Grande represent a different world, the world of Latin America. It is perhaps unfortunate that the English and Latin speaking parts of the continent should both be called America, thereby unconsciously evoking an expectation of similarity which does not exist. Only if it is realized that the countries to the south are different from the United States in essential geographic features, in racial and ethnic composition, in economic life, and in social customs, ideology, and cultural tradition can we evaluate the significance of this area for our national life and estimate correctly the likelihood of an effective co-operation in a common policy of hemisphere defense.

These differences are not apparent at first glance. Expecting perhaps to find himself in the exotic surroundings portrayed by Hollywood, an American on his first arrival is impressed by the tall buildings, the moving-picture palaces, and other symbols of our own civilization. Buenos Aires in many ways is a glorified Chicago, and an Argentine or Chilean cowboy doubtless could handle a roundup in the Texas panhandle without having to do so much as adjust his spurs.

But Latin America is also a world of baroque churches, siestas and fiestas, harem-like seclusion for women, and poverty for almost all except a privileged few, that in many respects is another Spain. The great families drive around in Buicks and read French novels banned by the Index, but their manner of life is much like that of the upper classes in Spain—some of whom also indulge in both uncanonical reading and big automobiles. The lasting power of Spanish civilization has been demonstrated by the completeness with which it has been accepted by Latin Americans not of Spanish descent. With the exception of the Germans, most of whom keep to themselves, few immigrants have been able to resist the influence of Spain. Latin America is even more of a racial hodge-podge than the United States, but after a generation or so the British, Swedish,

Swiss, Yugoslav, Irish, Italian, and Dutch families have adopted the Spanish way of life.

Very much as in Spain, the Army, the Church, and the landowners are the dominant forces in most Latin-American countries and constitute problems which cry for solution. Although none of the twenty Latin-American countries is so unfortunate as to be without the forms of republican government, few have been more successful than Spain in making popular government work. Democratic government as we know it scarcely exists outside of Chile, Colombia, and possibly Uruguay and Mexico. Most of the remainder are controlled by the propertied classes or are out-and-out dictatorships. It cannot be said that all of these are simply old-fashioned dictatorships, of the type that Spain had in the nineteenth century, for several have displayed distinct fascist tendencies.

The Franco regime's strength in Latin America therefore is out of proportion to its own weakness at home. Its influence is being thrown solidly against us, and although the Spanish fascists are concerned primarily with the ambitions of Spain, this influence is no less beneficial to Hitler and the Japanese. Franco propaganda, which is based upon Spanish language and culture rather than Nazi racial dogmas, is aimed at strengthening Latin-American isolationists rather than pleading the Axis cause directly. Just as the Nazi propagandists in Spain used the mediæval unity of Christendom to justify Hitler's New Order, the Franco agents in Latin America insist that the American republics must look to Europe rather than to the alien Yankees; that if ever the time comes for closer inter-American relations, the United States should be excluded.[1]

[1] Argentina, whose government's attitude to the United States so closely resembles Franco's own, is sometimes put forward as the leader of this movement, which rejected the term "Pan-American" because this was said to imply the hegemony of the United States. Franco and Argentine propagandists reached a new high in audacity with the claim that Chile and Argentina are united, rather than divided, by peaks of the Andes soaring over 20,000 feet above sea level.

Depending upon the audience, they sometimes lamented the prospect that the entire post-war world would be under the heel of the United States; on other occasions they revived the bogy of Communism which had been used so successfully in England and France during the Spanish war.

This propaganda, reinforced as it is by the special appeals of the Nazis and the Japanese (the Italians resident in South America make little effort to spread the Fascist gospel and apparently want most to be left alone) is unquestionably effective among the upper classes of Latin America. There is little chance for us to fight it without ourselves copying the Franco regime—too high a price by far. On the other hand, as long as we fail to take a firm stand against Franco, we are hampered in our efforts to win over the people, who really control the government in Chile and could, with sufficient encouragement, assert their control in Argentina.

We have, therefore, an opportunity to win the adherence of two of the leading countries of Latin America, which until now have continued diplomatic relations with the Axis and have provided excellent bases for espionage and propaganda. We have also an opportunity to obtain a far more genuine backing in the countries that have already broken with the Axis or even declared war. It is a people's war that we are fighting, and we must show unmistakably that it is. For the people of Latin America can scarcely be expected to disregard the differences in language and customs existing between us if we do not raise an unblemished standard of liberty.

It is true, of course, that many of their statesmen were and still are sympathetic with Franco; from this it could be argued that a break with Franco would weaken our standing with them, and would even be used by Axis propagandists to claim that we intended to overthrow non-democratic Latin-American governments. But the statesmen who broke with the Axis did so knowing full well that Franco is fighting us and that, although we may still be unable to see it, we must sooner or later strike back. And although the Latin-American countries as a whole have not been so successful as we have in making democracy work, liberty is their ideal as it is ours. This aspiration to liberty is in truth the only means, apart from narrow self-interest, that we have with which to unite our southern neighbours in the fight against fascism. The governments of Latin America are with us for a variety of reasons, including the sound one that if we do not all hang together we shall be hanged separately; there seems no reason to expect that a realistic policy toward Franco, recognizing his hostility, would weaken our position. Certainly we should make it clear that although we will fight fascism wherever it shows itself, we recognize that different nations take different roads toward freedom and we have no desire to interfere with the internal affairs of any country of this hemisphere. This, however, is not a difficult task in view of the excellent Latin-American record of the Roosevelt administration, and we can be sure of far greater support of the war effort by the people of Latin America when we prove beyond dispute that we are in the war not merely for ourselves but for the rights of all men.

# *Chapter* XIV

## BRITAIN AND FRANCE TRY TO APPEASE FRANCO

Since Munich the word "appeasement" has become a term of abuse; it has been used to condemn almost any kind of conciliatory policy with which a critic is not in agreement. Such reproaches occasionally are made too freely, for under some conditions *Realpolitik* demands the grant of concessions to a fence-sitter, as Turkey has been thus far in the war, or even to a probable enemy. Those responsible for such a policy should not be branded as appeasers unless their very methods make it unlikely that they will attain their objective.

Under different circumstances the effort to avoid war with Germany which culminated in Munich might have been justified by political realism. Chamberlain will be condemned by history, not for the mere fact that he gave way on Czechoslovakia and other issues, but because from the very nature of the Nazi regime it was impossible to buy Hitler off. Each retreat by the democracies, instead of placating the Führer, caused him to place his next demand that much higher. When Chamberlain decided to make a stand on Poland, a general war became inevitable because his concessions in the past had overstimulated both the appetite and the self-confidence of the Nazis. Appeasement thus produced the very catastrophe which it was intended to avoid.

After examining every argument advanced to justify the

efforts of the democracies to make up to Franco since the end of the civil war, I think it is fair to call them another example of the same disastrous policy. Franco, because of numerous interrelated factors which never quite produced the situation required, is still not formally in the war. But this is in spite of, rather than because of, the way that England, France, and the United States have tried to conciliate him.

The strictly one-way concessions that we have granted him are completely the opposite of the policy which he would have followed if the situation had been reversed. For this reason it was not until the autumn of 1941, when we at last cracked down on his imports of oil, that he seems to have had a suspicion that perhaps we were not as soft (and stupid) as we looked. His behaviour thereafter improved enormously, but any sign of renewed weakness on our part will be an invitation to him to join with Hitler completely.

Our concessions and attempts at concessions are in fact part and parcel of the original error by which Britain and France, with the United States a sleeping partner, allowed the Axis to destroy the Spanish Republic. Over six years have elapsed since the Spanish civil war began, and at this date it is not worth treating in detail the methods by which the democracies fought themselves. In the light of subsequent events, however, it is useful to recall the two major premises upon which supporters of Chamberlain and Daladier justified their policy toward Spain: (1) if the Spaniards were allowed to fight it out without foreign interference, neither side would win, Spain would be split permanently into two hostile zones, and England and France would be able to play off one against the other; (2) if Franco won out nevertheless, the democracies would be able to take advantage of Spain's weakened condition to compel him to get rid of the fascist "wild men" and cut his ties with the Axis.

The first premise, although it implied a continuation of the outlook which produced the Hoare-Laval deal, did indicate a certain amount of political realism. The Bourbon sovereigns of France and Spain had aided our cause in the War of Independence, not because they were admirers of Thomas Jefferson, but because they saw an excellent opportunity to break up the British Empire. If the British and the French had had sufficient backbone to stop Axis help for Franco, their amoral objective might have been attained. But they did not, and at the end of January 1939 the success of Franco's Catalan offensive destroyed all possibility of a peace without victory.

Thereafter only quick and decisive intervention by England and France, which from the nature of the two governments was impossible, could have saved the remnants of the Spanish Republic. Upon the British Foreign Office and the Quai d'Orsay, therefore, rested the responsibility of developing a joint policy which would put Spain back under Anglo-French control, or at least reduce Franco's opportunities to harm the democracies when the general European war began.

By this time many true-blue British Tories had become aware of the danger that fascist Spain constituted for the Empire, and they joined with liberals in demanding a strong policy. These imperialists were especially concerned over the advantage the Axis would derive from control of Minorca, in the Balearics, which with Gibraltar is the key to the western Mediterranean. The island, with the great base of Port Mahon, was still held by the Republic, and they urged that England and France occupy it as a guarantee of Franco's good behaviour. Later, when the Republican fleet mutinied and went to French Africa, they insisted that it also should be held as a hostage.

Chamberlain and Daladier, however, held fast to their second guess: Franco had won, but they thought that suitable concessions in the form of credits for the reconstruction of Spain would win him away from fascism both at home and abroad. The appeasers thought that Mussolini could be "detached" from Hitler by kind treatment, and the same arguments were used for concessions to Franco. It was even supposed that France would be able to bring both dictators into a Latin and Catholic bloc which would offer just as determined resistance to fascism as popular governments.

Events have demonstrated that the appeasers were mistaken in this belief, but the theory is worth noting because it has taken on new life again and again and still exerts a powerful influence upon our policy toward Franco. Until Hitler reached the Spanish frontier, at least, this point was arguable. Even now its wisdom is not a matter that can be settled with mathematical precision, for every opinion has to be based on one's own views of the aims entertained by Franco and the men around him. If Franco were merely another Spanish general who had grown tired of democratic government, and if he had no aims beyond the restoration of "order," the democracies should not permit a certain amount of sabre-rattling to halt the work of appeasement.

During my two years in Spain, however, I formed an entirely different opinion of Franco. From observing both his actions and his words, I am convinced that he is far from being just another Spanish dictator. His brand of fascism is not, it is true, an exact copy of that favoured by either Hitler or José Antonio Primo de Rivera, and his regime has been kept at cross-purposes by disputes among his supporters. But he is no less a fascist, with unshakable imperialist aims and an intransigence toward the democracies which, unlike Hitler, he has never attempted to disguise.

His community of purpose with Hitler and Mussolini has been strengthened by the fact that only the overthrow of France, England, and the United States will permit Franco's regime to attain its ambitions in Africa and Latin America. These ambitions are a part of Franco himself and were not wished upon him by Serrano Suñer or anybody else. If the situation were reversed, if Germany and Italy were democracies, and fascism were in control of England and the United

States, he would, it is true, be pulled by divided loyalties. But in his view the road to Berlin leads to both fascism and empire, and I do not believe that he could have been appeased in 1939; with the Nazis at Hendaye there is no possibility of making him a loyal convert now.

Certainly the methods followed since 1939 destroyed whatever chance of success existed. Prestige is important in Spain, and the persistence with which London, Paris, and Washington have sought his good graces ever since the fall of Barcelona played no small part in their failure. The full story of the last days of the Spanish Republic has not yet been told, but it seems clear that Britain and France had a hand in the failure of many of its leaders to go back to Valencia after escaping into France from Catalonia. And the British, instead of taking Minorca for themselves, proceeded to hand it over to Franco.

The gift was the more valuable because the generalissimo, who knew well the strength of Port Mahon from the days when he was commander of the Balearics, still lacked the naval and air strength required to capture it. A British cruiser, H.M.S. *Devonshire,* therefore was provided to carry a Franco representative to Minorca to demand its surrender. The men in the garrison, impressed by this demonstration that England, their last hope, was now supporting Franco, saw it was useless to hold out any longer. There still remained a few bold spirits, however, who knew they were marked men and preferred to sell their lives dearly rather than die before a firing squad. The resulting difficulty was neatly solved by the kindness of the *Devonshire's* captain, who promptly offered to take them to safety in France. After 450 of the leading Republicans had been taken off Port Mahon the entire island surrendered on February 8, leaving Franco the relatively simple task of overcoming the last Republican resistance in metropolitan Spain. And on February 27, 1939, while Franco with his customary deliberateness was still preparing for his final offensive against

Madrid, England and France recognized his regime as the rightful government of Spain.

The following month was memorable for Chamberlain, for it brought the occupation of Prague and shattered his boast that from Munich he had brought back peace in our time. But though Hitler had let him down, appeasement went on unhindered in Spain. The Casado *coup d'état,* which overthrew the Negrín regime in the last days of Madrid and installed a government determined to surrender to Franco at once, was the next move. Alvarez del Vayo indicates very clearly in *Freedom's Battle* that the British government, repeating the service that it had rendered at Minorca, helped engineer this stroke, which made possible Franco's bloodless entry into the capital on March 28. On April 1 the generalissimo was able to announce that the Republican armies had been crushed and the war was over. A week later, as an expression of his gratitude to the Axis, he joined the agreement against the democracies which to this day masquerades as the anti-Comintern Pact.

And now England and France rushed to pave the way for the great loan which was to save the situation. As her Ambassador France had named Marshal Pétain, her greatest living soldier, who was thought to be particularly acceptable because of his acquaintance with Franco and his part in working out the combined French and Spanish Moroccan expedition which laid Abdel-Krim by the heels. Britain's choice was Sir Maurice Peterson, then Ambassador in Baghdad and one of the coming men in the British Foreign Service. The United States, which was tardy and did not recognize Franco until April 1, also sought a representative sympathetic to the new regime. Claude G. Bowers, our far-seeing Ambassador to the Republic, probably was unacceptable to Franco, and certainly Franco was unacceptable to Bowers. Finally Alexander W. Weddell, our Ambassador to Argentina, was named to complete the trio that was to match its skill against von Stohrer and Lazar.

Soon after my arrival in Spain an invitation to dinner at Mr. Weddell's summer residence in San Sebastián gave me an opportunity to see the three representatives of the democracies together. They were a remarkable contrast. As the venerable Marshal Pétain sat in the place of honour, paying little attention to anything except the food, none of us suspected that within a few months he would become head of the French government and disgrace his noble career by abandoning the fight. When he first saw the absurd little machine-gun nests that Franco was putting up on the road to Hendaye he burst out laughing, and I had the impression that the defender of Verdun would know how to deal with the braggadocio which inspired them. But it was merely a tired and rather choleric old man who sat through the formal dinner, then, after a short conference with his British colleague, drove back alone to his villa in Biarritz. Long before he left Spain, I came to realize that the marshal was not only a defeatist but an extravagant admirer of the Franco "authority" and "order," which he is now trying to instil from Vichy.

Nobody could accuse Sir Maurice Peterson of being overimpressed with the Franco regime. A brilliant and sardonic man, he conformed very neatly to the idea of British diplomats that one forms from reading Somerset Maugham. Members of his Embassy had told me that his dispatches displayed such a deep understanding of the Franco regime, and were written with such distinction, that they deserved a place in literature. With a few people Sir Maurice unbent and was completely charming. But his career in Baghdad, where as representative of the might of Britain he was monarch of all that he surveyed, had given him perhaps a shade too much of British ambassadorial arrogance. He detested Spaniards almost to the point of refusing to have anything to do with them; when, long afterwards, he was induced to entertain Franco's cabinet, angry fascists claimed that Lady Peterson, as informally as if she were in her English country house, had fed one of her favourite dogs from her plate in the middle of the state dinner.

Mr. Weddell, a scholarly Virginian who had risen to the rank of consul general in our foreign service before his retirement in 1928, had been called back into service by President Roosevelt in 1933. His transfer from Argentina to Spain, presumably a sign of approval of his work in Buenos Aires, had pleased him very much. He and Mrs. Weddell liked both Spain and the Spaniards, and they spared no effort to develop friendly relations with the Franco regime. Unfortunately, the fascist officials were not to be converted from their love of the Axis, while the high aristocracy which frequented parties at our Embassy had used up its influence in regaining its ancient privileges and had little more control over the conduct of Spanish affairs than citizens of Omaha.

The hopes of the democracies were, however, concentrated upon Marshal Pétain. His coming had been prepared by the Bérard-Jordana agreement, under which (Georges Bonnet was in charge of the Quai d'Orsay) France agreed to give Franco both the Republican fleet and $40,000,000 in gold which the Spanish Republic had deposited in the Bank of France several years before the civil war. Soon the fleet was duly handed over, and so were the jewelry, stock certificates, and other movable valuables shipped to France during the civil war.

But French Leftists, taking advantage of various legal technicalities, for a time prevented Pétain from delivering the gold, and this produced the first notable setback for the democracies. For although the appeasement press of London and Paris had discovered a remarkable friendship between Franco and Pétain, dating back to the days when the generalissimo was a pupil of the marshal at the French War College, the missing $40,000,000 made Franco remarkably cool. As punishment, the former pupil kept a marshal of France waiting for more than a week before allowing him to present his credentials.

Any doubt concerning Franco's continued dislike for the democracies should have been removed by this incident, but the British and French nevertheless did not lose their eagerness to give him the $40,000,000 and even larger sums. A reconstruction credit, they were convinced, would still bring him into the fold. Spain had to have hundreds of millions of dollars to import the articles she needed, and certainly she could not get it from Hitler. With the backing of London and Paris a syndicate of Dutch, Belgian, and French banks, headed by the Mendelsohn private bank of Amsterdam,[1] sent Paul Van Zeeland, a former Belgian Foreign Minister, to make the offer. The only condition was that Spain would remain neutral in the European war.

To the surprise of London and Paris, this attempt to make friends was flatly rejected. As though to emphasize his resentment of this interference with his government, Franco and his spokesmen gave pledges of eternal friendship in speeches commemorating the departure of the German and Italian expeditionary forces. Serrano Suñer went to Rome to thank Mussolini, and Göring set out to receive the thanks due Hitler but was called back by the steadily growing tension over Germany's demands on Poland.

Perhaps because their attention was required by the approach of the general war, England and France did nothing further. It was the United States that stepped into the breach late in July with a $13,350,000 credit, granted by the Export-Import Bank, to supply Spain with cotton, then her most urgent need. The credit ultimately provided Franco with nearly 250,000 bales, enough under post-war conditions to meet the needs of the Catalan mills for an entire year. Presumably our objective was goodwill, but if so we failed. Not for the last

[1] Its sudden failure a short time before the outbreak of the European war seems to have been connected with some sort of Nazi financial offensive.

time, the Franco press gave only a few inconspicuous lines to this American generosity, and although the arrival of the cotton ships was duly publicized as a "work of the *Caudillo*," the Spanish public was left to guess where and how he had wrought so hugely. None of the problems outstanding between Spain and the United States, such as the refusal of the Franco regime to hand back the Spanish telephone system to the International Telephone & Telegraph Corporation, was even discussed. The credit was granted without conditions, and although it did make possible the ultimate liberation of some twenty Americans who had been captured while fighting for the Republic, Franco was bound by international law to release them in any case.

Nevertheless, Warren Lee Pierson, head of the Export-Import Bank, came to Spain a month later to discuss still more unilateral concessions, and though his conferences were cut short by the outbreak of war, this inexplicable desire to press favours upon a hostile regime has continued for a long time to dominate our government.

It is highly likely that the $40,000,000 handed over by France, which gave Franco almost his only gold reserve, and the cotton provided by the United States, destroyed the one chance of the democracies to make their appeasement policy work. But for these favours the Franco regime would have been in direst straits in the months that intervened between the outbreak of the war and the re-establishment of trade between Germany and Spain made possible by the collapse of France. Until then communications were almost cut off, and if Franco had been left to his own devices he would have had to accept whatever terms England and France chose to impose as the price for the cotton, gasoline, coal, rubber, and other commodities required to keep Spain going. But the three governments gave him just the help that permitted him to defy them; although in the end Franco was compelled to consent to a trade agreement with France in January, and with England two months later, he gave no pledges and obtained credits from both. It must be granted that the two agreements, like the dismissal of Serrano Suñer over two years later, did constitute a small gain for the Allies, but they failed conspicuously to yield the lasting benefits which the democracies should have won by demanding the dismissal of the Phalanx as a prerequisite to any deal.

Still greater advantages could have been obtained if Chamberlain and Daladier, dropping their hopes of appeasement, had taken advantage of their unique opportunity to overthrow both Mussolini and Franco while Germany was engaged in Poland. Influential members of the French government did give this proposal serious consideration in the last days of August. With the Maginot Line an impregnable defence against the Nazis (as it was before France slowly went to pieces behind it), the invasion of Italy and Spain would have presented few difficulties. Apart from the considerable advantage of removing the threat of invasions from the Alps and the Pyrenees, the heightened morale of the French would have more than made up for the cost in men and matériel. Even if the Germans had afterwards reached Hendaye, at least part of Spain might have been held as an invaluable bridgehead on the continent. There are, in fact, grounds for the belief that the training in the field which the French armies would have received, and, above all, the demonstration that free men can beat fascists, would have so invigorated the fighting spirit of the Allies that they would have won the Battle of France itself and the history of the world would be different.

Chamberlain and Daladier, however, were not to be taken off the road to destruction, and the moment was allowed to slip. The French Army and the small British Expeditionary Force did nothing while the Germans were throwing everything they had in the drive to crush Poland—just as the British nearly missed almost as heaven-sent an opportunity to open a second front while the Nazis were still battering themselves against the unsurpassable courage of the Russians. From September 1 until the fateful May 10 the Sitzkrieg was on, and the British and French governments used their time to continue the work of appeasing Mussolini and Franco.[1] The two dictators shouted their sympathies with the Nazis, but they did not declare war, and this omission was supposed to show how right Chamberlain and Daladier had been all along.

The 10th of May brought remarkable changes in the Allied diplomatic representation in Madrid. Pétain was called home first to advise and then to take over the French government.[2] An even more extraordinary result of the Blitzkrieg was the appointment of one of the most determined appeasers, Sir Samuel Hoare, as British Ambassador to Spain. Apparently the Foreign Office, feeling that somehow all was not going as it should, had come to the conclusion some time before that more flexibility was needed than was being provided by Sir Maurice Peterson. And flexibility was, or should have been, Sir Samuel Hoare's middle name. He was available for the job because the British people, at last seeing the situation to which they had been brought, overturned the Chamberlain government after the Nazis invaded Holland and Belgium. The arch-appeaser hung on for a time as a supernumerary of Churchill's government, but Hoare was out. The British, however, have a habit of keeping their old-time politicians on the public payroll in one way or another until they are proved guilty of some

[1] The efforts to avoid offending them went so far that, on orders from the British blockade authorities, a French warship turned loose an Italian ship which was bringing Franco his victory gift from Hitler, a six-wheeled Mercedes that was a replica of the Führer's own. As a further proof of goodwill, the Allies allowed Franco to import the German sugar beets he needed through France. The blockade was nothing among friends.

[2] The British maintained contact with Vichy through the French Embassy in Madrid, but it has had no further influence upon Franco. François Pietri, the present Vichy Ambassador, is a fine example of the type of Frenchman to be avoided.

crime such as treason, or shooting a fox. And so Hoare took over the Madrid Embassy.

The situation when he arrived was far from promising, and although the Ambassador and Lady Maud Hoare brought their butler along, they left their winter clothes in England. It was just before Dunkirk, gangs of fascists shouting: "Gibraltar is Spanish" were holding demonstrations against the Embassy, and Manuel Aznar, then Franco's press spokesman, unequivocably demanded return of the Rock. It appeared certain that Franco, like Mussolini, would stab France in the back once she was too weak to parry the blow.

As the days went by, matters got even worse. The French fell back from the Somme and the Aisne, their last line of defence, and for the first time it was realized that France was utterly defeated. No one, of course, could dream of a defeat so crushing that it would bring the Germans to the very borders of Spain within a matter of days. But as the Panzer divisions drove on this soon became a definite possibility. Naturally, everyone assumed that the French government would escape to one of its colonies in northern Africa to continue the fight; in that event, Spain was irrevocably in the war, for she offered the best route for a Nazi attack on French Africa.

Sir Samuel Hoare has much to answer for before history, but it must be conceded that he met this extraordinarily difficult situation with great ability. He met it, however, not so much with further appeasement [1] as with the sang-froid that was one of the supreme virtues of British statesmen in the past; there is no doubt that he has made an excellent Ambassador to Spain. Aznar sneered that the British idea of foreign policy was to make a commercial treaty, but Hoare demonstrated that

[1] Sir Samuel and Lady Maud had not, however, permanently forsaken the cause of appeasement. After Crete the *embajadora,* in a signed article in the Embassy propaganda bulletin, said the disaster showed what a pity it was that the United States had been so slow in providing Britain with the necessary fighting equipment. "Thank God for Mr. Chamberlain!" Lady Maud continued, because he had "gained a year" in which England could prepare.

although this was one of his methods, he had other strings to his bow. With the utmost deftness he dangled the prospect of the restoration of Gibraltar—after the war, of course—before Franco. Assuming the role of Admirable Crichton, he busied himself ironing out small kinks in the Anglo-Spanish trade agreement while the German armoured divisions raced to Hendaye. Above all, he maintained the magnificent inperturbability which befitted a veteran of British politics. Drake had continued to bowl while the Invincible Armada was approaching, and the Ambassador played his excellent game of tennis every afternoon on the American Embassy court as though to emphasize his confidence that no matter how hopeless the situation appeared, there would always be an England.

The Spaniards, who have adopted the word "bluff" into their language as a standard description of British foreign policy, recognized Hoare's air of unshaken optimism for what it was. But nevertheless this serenity inspired doubts. "Sir Hoare," as Spaniards unversed in British etiquette insisted upon calling him, clearly was one of the great statesmen of Europe. He had, after all, demonstrated his acumen by working out the scheme for the partition of Ethiopia with that other realistic statesman, Pierre Laval. Franco seems to have reasoned that if Hoare was so sure that Britain would weather these storms, perhaps it would be better for Spain to wait and see whether another deal could be worked out for Gibraltar and French Africa. After all, the French were beaten anyway. . . .

Naturally Sir Samuel Hoare's personal influence was only one of the factors which kept Spain from going into the war when the Nazis reached the frontier. If Laval had not broken up the plan to continue the fight from Algiers, the Germans unquestionably would have rushed into Spain. Once Laval had done his work, and Pétain asked for an armistice, Franco seems to have expected that he would be able to play the part of an honest broker. The marshal had forwarded the request through Franco, who was so convinced that the negotiations would take place in Madrid that several floors in the Palace Hotel were suddenly reserved for the various delegations. Certainly it was to be supposed that the Franco regime, as the friend of both sides, could gain some small piece of French real estate when so much was changing hands.

To the dismay of both Pétain and Franco, however, it gradually developed that Hitler had no intention of giving definite peace terms until the end of the war. As Germany was not yet in a position to take over either France or the French colonies, it was necessary to keep the French in nominal control. This scheme had the additional advantage of eliminating broker's fees to Mussolini as well as Franco, and it is to be presumed that Hitler, realizing the burden he had incurred by permitting the Italians to enter the war, did not wish to saddle himself with another liability. As a result Franco limited himself to announcing that Spain had now become a "non-belligerent," as Italy was before the Duce finally hurled himself upon prostrate France. German troops did not cross the International Bridge in force when they reached Hendaye, and Sir Samuel Hoare felt strong enough to demand, and obtain, the dismissal of General López Pinto, the commanding general at Irún, who had welcomed the Nazis with extravagant cordiality.

The prospect that Spain would enter the war had not, of course, disappeared. The Spanish press continued to revel in predictions that the British, now left without an ally to face the might of "an awakened and united Europe," would be overwhelmed in their turn. General López Pinto soon was quietly restored to his command, and from time to time demonstrations demanding the return of Gibraltar, and of the British-owned Rio Tinto and Huelva mines in the south of Spain, took place "spontaneously." Had the Free French been successful in their attack on Dakar it is likely that the Germans would have come through immediately to forestall an Allied offensive. But the de Gaulle forces were too timid, and the summer of 1940 dragged past and still the Germans did not come.

By a fortunate coincidence, the exact combination of circumstances necessary still was lacking on several important occasions in succeeding months. As though Franco's and Hitler's aims were on a seesaw, when things were going well for the Axis, Franco was disposed to come in to get his share of the booty. But for that very reason Hitler was not particularly anxious to have him. On the other hand, on the occasions on which Hitler needed him most—that is, when things were going badly—Franco for that very reason was reluctant to get himself involved in what must obviously be a long war. When the decisive moment came, Hitler might of course take over Spain regardless of Franco's position. But he preferred to gain his satellite's consent in order to minimize difficulties with the population. Until the time was right, therefore, Franco retained a certain freedom to manœuvre.

The latter factor was noticeable particularly in the autumn of 1940, when pressure by Hitler was renewed because of the failure of the Blitzkrieg against England. Besides the more obvious reasons, Hitler was anxious to include Spain definitely in the New Order at once as a part of a continent-wide scheme to discredit President Roosevelt's "war-mongering" policy and assist the candidacy of Wendell Willkie—whom the Nazis then considered an isolationist. The plan was to bring all Europe under Axis dominance before the American presidential election, and to this end an elaborate campaign was worked out by the Nazis. Serrano Suñer went to Berlin early in October to discuss Spain's participation and the reward she would receive for entering the war; he then arranged for an immediate visit by Heinrich Himmler to aid in reorganizing the Spanish police along tried lines. Beigbeder, the anti-Nazi Foreign Minister, was still in the way. But the escape of Pierlot and Spaak, to which I have already referred, had weakened his position; the finishing blow was his indiscreet outburst to a group of Latin-American diplomats that he would be absent from Madrid during Himmler's visit because "I won't shake hands with that assassin." With this to reinforce his arguments, Serrano Suñer was able to drive his rival from office a few days later, so that Beigbeder did not, after all, have to take any part in entertaining the Gestapo leader.

This pleasure fell to Serrano Suñer, who meanwhile arranged the interview between Franco and Hitler, their first meeting, at which Franco's share of the spoil was to be determined. Mussolini's competing demands for Casablanca and Algeria, including Oran, marred the tone of the gathering, however, and Hitler in effect washed his hands of the matter. A second visit by Serrano Suñer to Axis-land a few days later did not solve these problems, and at the end of October all hopes of carrying out the Pan-European scheme in time were destroyed by the Italian invasion of Greece.

Although it involves getting ahead of the story, it will be useful to note here the four occasions in the following twelve months during which Spain was under the greatest pressure, internally or externally, to enter the war. The first was in the period from January to February 1941, when things were going very badly for the Italians in Greece, and Wavell's drive into Libya was threatening all that was left of Mussolini's African empire. The Axis needed Spain in order to close the Strait of Gibraltar, shutting off reinforcements for Wavell's army, and there even seemed a possibility that General Weygand would vindicate Washington's trustfulness and join the Allies if Wavell chased the Italians all the way to French territory. Mussolini was so frightened that this time he was willing to yield Franco a much larger share of French Africa than before, and Hitler also was willing to give better terms: the fall of Laval in December 1940 seemed to indicate that the Vichy government was not sufficiently manageable, and always German interest in Spain has increased or decreased in direct relation with the closeness of relations with Vichy.

On New Year's Day von Stohrer therefore presented Franco with a formal demand that Spain enter the war. When this was rejected he went to Berlin for new instructions and made another demand at the end of January. This was again rejected, and, as Wavell's drive was gathering momentum, Mussolini next appealed to Franco. The two dictators met at Bordighera. Again the answer was negative, for it was obvious to Franco that if the British were that strong, there was no prospect of the war's ending quickly. Saboteurs caused one railroad wreck after another as a warning, but the decisive factor was Spain's food shortage, which was so desperate that only the cargoes of Argentine grain that were beginning to arrive could save her from starvation. The British might be doomed, but their blockade was still strong enough to bring Spain down in the common ruin. All that Mussolini received from the interview was Franco's assurance of "moral support."

What would have happened if Wavell had continued his drive all the way across Libya is anybody's guess, but very possibly the Nazis would have taken over Spain and opened another front in Algeria. Instead, however, the troops and equipment Wavell needed were detached to aid in the hopeless defence of Greece against the Nazis. Meanwhile, using shore-based planes to make British surface craft keep a healthy distance, the Nazis poured troops into Libya, and Wavell was hurled back into Egypt. These same land planes then began to inflict heavy losses upon British shipping passing through Gibraltar, and the British were compelled to use the 14,000-mile route round the Cape of Good Hope to supply their armies in Egypt. The Strait of Gibraltar, in other words, was almost as good as closed and there was no longer a pressing need for Franco's services.

The late spring produced another crisis. After subjugating the Balkans, Hitler for a time was apparently undecided what action he should take next. Spain seemed his choice, the German troops at Hendaye were reported to be preparing, and in May Mr. Weddell ordered the only American Embassy official with children in Spain to send them home at once. To the general surprise, Hitler invaded Russia instead, and the immediate prospect of Spain's becoming involved in the war vanished.

The quick victory expected was not attained, and although Germany did conquer most of the Ukraine wheat region, transportation difficulties made it impossible for her to consider delivering wheat to Franco as had been promised. Nevertheless, November brought another crisis, this time so severe that we cut off exports of oil and called Mr. Weddell home to report. Again, however, the Germans decided not to come in.

They were again poised to strike in the summer of 1942, when Rommel's army seemed about to capture Alexandria and close the eastern gateway of the Mediterranean. The British last-minute rally, however, relieved the situation in Spain once more.

Throughout these crises Sir Samuel Hoare went his unperturbed way, protesting whenever there was a particularly insulting newspaper article or demonstration, and between times liberalizing the workings of the trade agreement to enable Franco to obtain a few thousand tons of Canadian wheat here, some Portuguese sugar there. It was not in his character to take the steps that might have got rid of a hostile government, and indeed the golden opportunity was gone once the Germans reached Hendaye. But Sir Samuel Hoare carried out a delaying action with admirable skill and self-possession.

Above all, he retained Franco's respect by making sure that Britain, in appearance at least, always received something in return. At that time the British were interested chiefly in Bilbao iron ore, and although this was and is valuable to them, it was more important that in insisting upon it Hoare showed Franco that England was not so far down in the world that she had to buy goodwill at any price. And when Franco violated a gentleman's agreement with Hoare and began to annex Tangier formally to Spanish Morocco, Hoare did not hesitate to shut off Spain's imports of gasoline and other petroleum products from the United States.

Negotiations for the removal of this order proceeded calmly in the midst of Germany's air assault upon the British Isles. The invasion of England seemed inevitable, but despite the diatribes of the Franco press the embargo was not lifted until Franco agreed to content himself with the occupation of Tangier and promised not to fortify the city. At that, Spain received permission to import only enough gasoline to meet her minimum requirements, or so the British negotiators thought.

Sir Samuel Hoare's conduct of British policy was not, however, without faults. His propaganda was aimed exclusively at the Catholic conservatives, and no effort was made to enlist the support of the democratic forces. Hoare did not see that the Allies must win the support of freedom-loving Spaniards if ever Spain is to be anything but a danger to our cause. That the Nazis were fully alive to the effectiveness of such a policy was evident in their counter-propaganda, which claimed that Hoare was plotting to bring back the Republic. A resolute anti-fascist line should have appealed to Catholics as well as Republicans, for certainly the Church in Spain was aware of Hitler's implacable efforts to stamp out the Church in Germany. Some effective work was done among the Catholics by Dr. Walter Starkie, an able Irish fiddler (as he preferred to call himself) and scholar who knew Spain intimately. Starkie, however, was not a Foreign Office representative, and Hoare failed to give him adequate co-operation. Instead, he leaned upon a press attaché lacking in the imagination and enterprise to combat Lazar. The efforts to win over Spanish Catholics with donations of church vessels from British Catholics thus made little impression. It was significant that the Carlist representative in Franco's cabinet was the only important government official at the presentation ceremonies,[1] and the press almost ignored them. But when the Germans countered with a gift of vessels looted from Poland, both government and press outdid themselves.

It was more serious that his absorption in day-to-day events apparently caused Sir Samuel Hoare to forget his early firmness and revert—as we shall see when we come to his influence on a credit offer to Franco by the United States—to outright appeasement. Though he has fought an effective rear-guard action, the grand strategy has been beyond him. Essentially this defect was a result of his remoteness from the great moral principles that move free men and keep them free. Despite his superlative abilities, he had failed to understand that a nation with a genuine belief in collective security and the rights of small nations would not accept the cynical realism of the Hoare-Laval pact. And because his aim was merely to keep Spain quiet for a few days or a few months, it was inevitable that his mission would remain limited in achievement as in objective.

But although Sir Samuel Hoare could scarcely be blamed for this failure to achieve a lasting settlement, the United States had no such excuse. While Hoare proceeded with his piecemeal concessions to keep Franco going, we were free to adopt a bolder policy, and require the generalissimo to give adequate assurances of good behaviour before he received anything from us. This did not necessitate the genius of a Talleyrand; we had only to sit quiet and wait for Franco to come to us hat in hand.

[1] Sir Walter Scott, my host at Abbotsford, came to Madrid with one of the delegations. He was looking so unhappy already that I did not ask him if he had changed his mind about Franco and the way to win the war. Probably he hadn't.

# *Chapter* XV

## THE UNITED STATES TAKES OVER THE JOB

Although Sir Samuel Hoare is still doing excellent work, according to his lights, the United States now dominates Allied policy toward Spain as much as we did the policy toward Vichy, which was finally abandoned with our occupation of North Africa. The change, which was gradual, first became unmistakable in the early autumn of 1940, when Hoare asked us to provide certain products that Franco needed. As we have seen, our cotton credit of July 1939 had been poorly received, and thereafter we had confined ourselves mostly to working out our own private disputes with Franco.

There was, it is true, one deal that might be termed appeasement by anyone of a suspicious nature. Early in 1940 the Maritime Commission approved the sale to a Spanish steamship company of two 12,600-ton ships of the Dollar Line, the *President Wilson* and the *President Lincoln*. We allowed them to go under the flag of an avowed Hitler lieutenant at the bargain price of $650,000 each. Although they were over twenty years old, they are today the pride of the Spanish merchant marine and would be even more valuable to us. The sale, however, was said to have been approved on the ground that the Dollar Line could thereby have more efficient ships built, and perhaps it does not rank in the appeasement list.

Meanwhile our own negotiations with Franco certainly did not seem to encourage further favours to him. Foremost among the issues involved was the International Telephone & Telegraph Corporation's $65,000,000 controlling interest in the Spanish telephone system. British and French investors long since were in full charge of their properties in Spain, but a government "delegate" had taken over each segment of the telephone system as Franco conquered Spain, and continued to exercise his power for a year and a half after the end of the civil war. Colonel Behn and F. T. Caldwell, his general manager, were allowed in the *Telefonica* solely by virtue of their position as members of the board of the Spanish company. The highly trained American engineers whom they had waiting to take over were not permitted office space and had to pass their time in a rented building.

This was the only important formal investment that we had in Spain, but probably fifteen or twenty million dollars in frozen credits were owing to American automobile manufacturers, film concerns, and other business interests since before the civil war. Their representatives were busy trying to get their money out of the country, but they were no more successful than American interests have been in salvaging property in Hitler's domains. Colonel Behn's superb diplomacy, backed in the end by the State Department, finally put his men back in control in the fall of 1940, but the others were not so fortunate.

We could have compelled Franco to regulate these questions as a condition to the cotton credit, but we were apparently confident that unalloyed goodwill would pay us more in the long run. Our confidence was not justified by the result. In addition to the general pro-Nazi and anti-democratic tone of the press and official speeches, we were singled out for attacks that in some instances were more bitter than those directed toward England itself. Every move by the United States toward closer relations with Latin America produced scurrilous criticisms, and I have already noted the anti-American posters which were pasted up throughout Madrid. The Spanish newspapers, like those of Germany and Italy, enthusiastically supported Wendell Willkie's presidential candidacy against President Roosevelt, and to bystanders, at least, Franco did not appear to be yielding to kind treatment. The State Department did not formally order the wives and children of Foreign Service officers home, but in the autumn of 1940 took the precautionary measure of paying the way of those who went voluntarily. Several took advantage of the offer.

Hoare meanwhile had been having his own difficulties with the Spaniards and finally cut off Franco's imports of gasoline in the summer of 1940. This dispute was settled in September, and soon afterwards he appears to have broached the idea of the new credit to our Embassy. At that time, as at various times since, we were following our own policy, and the suggestion did not get anywhere. A few weeks later, however, it was proposed more definitely that the United States supply Franco with the gasoline, wheat, meat, rubber, and other products that he needed, the wheat and meat to come from either the United States or Argentina. A short time afterwards Lord Lothian, the late British Ambassador to the United States, passed through Lisbon on his way back to his Washington post, and Hoare went over to explain at first hand the proposal that was to be submitted to President Roosevelt.

Whether Lord Lothian had an opportunity to do so before his unexpected death I do not know, but meanwhile events in Spain seemed to make any sort of deal out of the question. For Serrano Suñer's elevation to the Foreign Ministry was quickly followed by a visit to Berlin, Franco's interview with Hitler, and a series of events which indicated that the regime was not to be bought off by any concessions that we or the British could grant. The tension in Madrid was heightened by the dispute between Serrano Suñer and our State Department over the admission of one of his protégés, Giménez Arnau, director of the Foreign Service of the Phalanx, to the United States. It was at first proposed that he should establish himself in Washington as press attaché of the Spanish Embassy, and when this was rejected, he applied for a visa as a correspondent of *Efe,* the official Spanish news agency. The revised application had been in only a few days when a brother of Giménez Arnau, who held the post of Director of Press and Propaganda under Serrano Suñer, announced a gag order forbidding all American correspondents in Spain to send dispatches. His order was withdrawn the next day, and Giménez Arnau has not arrived to direct the fight against us in Latin America, but the incident seemed to indicate that the Franco regime was not particularly anxious to be on good terms with us.

A second incident, which was a direct insult to the American government, seemed to confirm this impression. This was the stoning of the American Embassy by a gang of fascist students from the University of Madrid. Notices had been posted on the university bulletin board announcing an emergency meeting of the student syndicate, and Mr. Weddell had informed Serrano Suñer that a hostile demonstration was planned and had even named the day. No extra guards were provided, however, and even the two usually stationed in front of the Embassy were absent when the gang came up and started shouting its opinion of the United States. When Mr. Weddell came out, one of them grabbed his arm and tried to hold it up in the fascist salute while the others sang the party anthem, *Face to the Sun.* The Ambassador then broke away and started back to the Embassy. This was the signal for the stone-throwing, and although he was not hit, one stone struck the emblem of the United States over the Embassy doorway. Only a few flakes of enamel were chipped off, but this did not alter the fact that the demonstration had been allowed to take place despite the Ambassador's specific warning. When Mr. and Mrs. Weddell entertained the diminished American colony at Thanksgiving dinner later in the day, there was general agreement among the guests that the Ambassador had no choice but to demand an apology and ask for his recall if it was not forthcoming.

Over a week elapsed before Mr. Weddell was able to see Franco, and meanwhile the only step taken by the government to express regret was the suspension from office of the leader of the Madrid University fascist organization. At last, however, the interview took place, and we offered the once famous $100,000,000 credit instead of demanding an apology. This sum was to be used for the acquisition of wheat, gasoline and petroleum products, rubber, cotton, and meat—the five commodities necessary to prevent the Franco regime from collapsing. At the same time Mr. Weddell offered assurances from the British that navicerts for these commodities would be forthcoming immediately. The sole condition was that Franco should pledge himself to remain neutral.

Perhaps suspecting that some elaborate Anglo-Saxon plot was lurking behind this ingenuousness, Franco was not over-enthusiastic. He agreed, however, for Mr. Weddell to discuss details with Serrano Suñer the following week. The interview went off rather well, and Serrano Suñer agreed on behalf of his brother-in-law to accept the credit if the United States would be satisfied with the phrase "it is not foreseen" that Spain would enter the war instead of a flat promise. This distinction was rightly considered of little importance, and a preliminary agreement was reached, with quantities of the various goods and other details to be worked out by American and Spanish trade experts. My story of the credit offer was stopped by the censors, but our Lisbon correspondent obtained a full account and the American public learned of this astonishing transaction nevertheless. The reception was highly unfavourable, and Secretary of State Cordell Hull announced that although Franco had requested a $100,000,000 credit, he had been refused. If Spain got anything from us, Mr. Hull said, it would take the form of small quantities of food to be donated by the American Red Cross.

Exactly what prompted the offer, then caused it to be withdrawn, is one of the government's secrets. According to a later report by Drew Pearson and Robert S. Allen in their "Washington Merry-Go-Round" newspaper column, Sumner Welles, Undersecretary of State, telegraphed to President Roosevelt, who was not in Washington, and obtained a direct presidential veto. This assertion incensed Mr. Hull, who then, in addition to denying that Mr. Welles had ever made such an appeal, stated that the subject of an American credit had not been discussed with the Franco government.

Whatever may have been the disagreement within our own government, it seems to have been the sudden veto by Hoare that finally brought its rejection. At the beginning, of course, the British Ambassador had supported the proposal enthusiastically. His change of heart apparently resulted from the fact that the Franco regime, interpreting the offer as a sign of weakness, suddenly resumed its forward policy in Tangier in defiance of pledges to the British. At the same time several of the most prominent British business men in Spain were arrested and ordered expelled from the country on fantastic charges.

The general idea, however, that Franco could be bought off was not dead, and when it re-emerged it was in the even more undesirable form of a credit by Argentina—to be partly underwritten by England and the United States. Dr. Escobar, the new Argentine Ambassador, arrived in Madrid in mid-December, just when the Franco government was at last beginning to realize what foreign experts had been trying to demonstrate all the time: again, as in the preceding year, there was not enough wheat to last until the next crop.

Exactly how much of the Argentine credit was underwritten by the democracies has not been disclosed, but I do know that the two credits, totaling $110,000,000, which we had recently made to Argentina were involved. The British, with their billions of dollars invested in Argentina, also endorsed part of the credit. A third factor in this closely screened deal was a considerable sum of money owed by an Argentine electrical supply company to Spanish concerns. Finally, the Argentine government also had a hand in it, because at that time there was almost no market for Argentine meat and cereals; for ideological reasons it was willing to take a chance on the possibility that some day Franco Spain might be able to supply iron goods or other products in return.

Argentina later rejected our $110,000,000 credit, and how this development was taken care of is still a secret. The deal went through in January 1941, at a time when Spain had just two weeks' supply of wheat left. Some eighty ships, comprising every seaworthy vessel in the Spanish merchant marine, were taken off their runs and sent in ballast to Argentina. Argentine wheat and maize started pouring in when the nation was down to her last stocks, and Franco was saved to fight another day. Since then Argentina has supplied Spain with over a million and a half tons of agricultural products, including cotton, meat, and casein as well as grains. It would be possible, of course, for the United Nations to cut off Argentine exports to Spain at any time. But this is now an established trade and any such brusque action might have serious effects upon our relations with both countries. The best way to get out of such scrapes is not to get in.

The United States was not, however, to be kept from doing something for Franco on its own account, and the gift which we substituted for the credit produced some of the most maladroit episodes in the history of American philanthropy abroad. It consisted of a million and a half dollars' worth of flour, dried and condensed milk, and medicines to Franco Spain, paid for out of a congressional appropriation to the Red Cross for the relief of war-stricken countries. Appropriately enough, the gift to Spain was lumped with a larger gift to Vichy France—also in the name of goodwill, although two of the Red Cross freighters, after being welcomed at Marseille with much rejoicing, were seized by the Vichy government in retaliation for our confiscation of the *Normandie* and other French ships.

Before making our gift to Spain we had managed at last to obtain Franco's pledge that none of the food or medicine was to be exported to Germany, nor was Franco to export their equivalents from stocks of food or medicine that he already had. As a further precaution, we sent only whole-wheat flour, which is supposed to spoil more quickly than white flour and be less useful to enemy armies. And a special mission, headed by Colonel Cary I. Crockett, U.S.A., retired, went over to see that all this was faithfully carried out.

It seems to have been thought that the mission, as though it were operating in America, would itself distribute these supplies from house to house, thereby impressing upon the Spanish people our goodwill and at the same time guarding against the Germans' getting the benefit. This plan ignored two facts which were apparent to anyone having the slightest knowledge of Franco Spain: there was nothing the commission could do to prevent the Spaniards from exporting equivalent amounts to the Germans even if the American food really stayed in Spain; and Franco, who had refused to allow American relief societies to handle the distribution of food in his territory during the civil war, certainly would not permit us to do so now that he had restored peace and allegedly brought back prosperity. This attitude was quite reasonable according to the well-known principles of international fascism, and if it had been understood in Washington, many of the resulting difficulties would have been avoided.

My wife and I met the *Cold Harbor,* which brought over the first shipment, at Cadiz. Just before our arrival, Colonel Crockett, who had learned to speak Spanish while serving in the Philippines, had fought a major engagement. One cause of the battle was the fact that the Cadiz authorities, for no discernible reason, were constantly interfering with the trucks carrying the flour and milk to warehouses in Seville, and were even trying to make the Red Cross pay a transportation tax. Even more annoying to Colonel Crockett was the fact that the

Cadiz newspapers at first ignored the arrival of the *Cold Harbor,* and when one did print something it took the form of an editorial entitled "We the Hungry."

This started off with a reference to the Sermon on the Mount, then proceeded to denounce in the name of the unfortunates of the world a certain red-faced foreigner who had mocked the misery of Spain by ostentatiously giving a piece of bread to a poor workman who was standing on the Cadiz dock. The editorial stated that the workman would have been justified in throwing the bread on the ground, or the red-faced foreigner in the water, but that with the dignity of a *caballero* he had finally done neither, but given the bread to two or three hungry children who were watching from near by.

The colonel had won the battle by staying in his hotel room and sending word to the *Cold Harbor* to stop unloading and prepare to go to sea. This brought action more quickly than one might have thought was possible in Spain, and upon receipt of assurances that the Cadiz customs agents and editors would improve their behaviour, the unloading was resumed.

But for the route followed by the *Cold Harbor,* which apparently had been determined by someone far from salt water, it would have been necessary to unload at Cadiz only the small quantities needed for its own population. The main cargo was going to Seville, Barcelona, and Marseille. Of these ports, only the channel up the Guadalquivir River to Seville offered the slightest difficulty, and as the *Cold Harbor's* draft had been increased by her heavy cargo, she should have gone first to Barcelona and Marseille, then to Cadiz, and up to Seville last. But orders were to take these ports as they came, and when the *Cold Harbor* reached Cadiz it was discovered that even after unloading everything she had for that port, she still was too heavy to reach Seville. Lightening her involved a needless haul by truck of a large quantity of flour and milk, but this should not have been difficult since she also brought twenty new Ford trucks and two station wagons, with plenty of gasoline. However, they had been loaded as deck cargo, and sea water had to be cleaned out of their transmissions before they could run, while one station wagon and several trucks had been damaged severely when their lashings were torn loose during the voyage.

Our gift perhaps deserved obscurity. Although it was later increased, the original consignment of flour was only enough to provide one day's supply of bread for the population of Spain. The forty-nine-pound sacks of flour bore the inscription in Spanish: "Gift of the American people to the people of Spain," but the ordinary public never saw them. The trucks bore nothing to indicate that they were from the Red Cross, or even from the United States. These markings were painted on later, but they were so small that it was barely possible to see the Red Cross and impossible without close examination to see that it was the American rather than the Spanish Red Cross that was responsible. The Spanish Army, which provided trucks to move the food from Cadiz to Seville, loaded the sacks with the side bearing the gift inscription turned down.

The Red Cross mission were well liked and did their work as well as they could in view of their ignorance of Spanish. But they had a task impossible to carry out. In order to placate American public opinion, the orders were to hand over the supplies to church or government charitable organizations in preference to the Auxilio Social, which was unpopular with us because of its connection with the Spanish fascist party. The Auxilio Social, however, was the only relief organization in Spain that could begin to care for the needy, and we would have avoided many disputes with the Nationalist government if we had simply consigned the supplies direct to the Auxilio Social. As it was, it received considerably more than half of the food that we gave Spain.

A few impressions of this strange experiment stand out: members of the Red Cross mission arming themselves with cigarettes in order to induce Spanish officials to accept the food with more alacrity; the distinguished old gentleman at the head of the Auxilio Social for Seville (father of Gamero del Castillo, once a leading fascist), who seemed to think that he was doing the *Yanquis* a favour by making a slight move to speed up baking of the bread for the starving people; the attempt by the civil governor of Barcelona to commandeer the shipment and add it to the general supplies (paying for it in pesetas); the similar attempt of Franco's oil monopoly to take over the high-quality gasoline we had shipped to Vigo for our trucks, reimbursing the Red Cross in tickets which might or might not be redeemable in Spain's low-grade gasoline; the sale by Spanish officials of American Red Cross supplies in the black market; and the warehouse fire that was set by customs officials in Seville in a vain effort to conceal how much had been stolen.

The newspaper attack upon Mrs. Weddell and Miss Bonney, already mentioned, was part of this episode, since Mrs. Weddell was using Red Cross flour to bake the bread that she distributed; and so was the attack upon Colonel Crockett, the Red Cross functionary. With these exceptions, the publicity, if that was the objective, which we obtained was almost as scanty as that from the cotton credit.

It was part of the agreement that the Franco press should give plenty of space to our gift, and the American correspondents in Madrid used to take turns writing out announcements, which were then sent to the Foreign Ministry for distribution to the press. But this system was a long way from matching the direct methods of Lazar. The Nazis obtained more publicity for their offer—which, incidentally, they never fulfilled—to aid victims of a fire at Santander in the summer of 1941 than we have from all our appeasement efforts since the end of the civil war.

No one with a heart could avoid sympathizing with the plight of starving Spain, and if it had been solely a question of a boorish and ungrateful government, these incidents would not have mattered. But the Red Cross donation was a mistake even if one considered solely the welfare of the Spaniards. The amount of food involved was not large, to be sure, and even if all of it had gone to the Germans it would not have made much difference; a more serious possible aid to Hitler was one whole ton of quinine, needed for malaria victims in the marshlands below Seville, but needed just as desperately by the Nazis.[1]

But even if everything we had sent to Spain had reached the people who needed it, our donation would have been none-the-less harmful to our interests—and theirs—for it strengthened a regime which, like those in Germany and Japan, must be overthrown in order to bring in a decent life for the world. The harm we thus inflicted upon the Spanish people more than cancelled out the good they received.

Particularly disastrous were the circumstances under which the Red Cross shipments were made. They came at a time when there was a unanimous expectation that the Germans would invade Spain at any moment. That Washington had some inkling of the situation may be gathered from its care to send only whole-wheat flour, but this was one of the few concessions to reality. Personal relations between Mr. Weddell and Serrano Suñer were at their worst, and a gang of young fascists even broke the windows of the British Embassy.[2] Plans had been ready for years to evacuate the British colony to Gibraltar, but the United States apparently intended to send ships to French Morocco, assuming we could get there, or to Cadiz, where the *Cold Harbor* had made its first call. The basic principle of diplomacy—which even Chamberlain professed to respect—is not to give concessions under threat of force. And yet

[1] Even the British were worried about the quinine and required the United States to obtain all sorts of special guarantees before they would permit it through the blockade.

[2] There was a limit to the patience of Hoare, and that same evening he took his entire staff, in diplomatic uniform, to call on Serrano Suñer and demand an apology. His firmness carried the day; not only was the apology given, but the windows were replaced the next morning in a country where supposedly there was no window glass.

the United States was still pressing these favours upon a government which from its very beginning had announced its implacable enmity.

But the Nazis did not come despite our appeasers. Suddenly, as in a Western thriller, Hitler late in June turned on Russia, and the immediate danger of Spain's entering the war was removed because all the Axis efforts were required for the "crusade" against Communism. Franco did not leave us in any doubt, however, concerning his future intentions. Promptly he issued the order for the formation of the "Blue Division" to serve with Hitler, ordered Spanish labourers sent to German war factories in exchange for German engineers to operate Spanish railroads and industries, and gave a definitive statement of his position in a speech before the Fascist Grand Council on July 17.

For weeks Mr. Weddell, who apparently feared that Serrano Suñer was not transmitting to Franco our government's views, had been endeavouring to obtain an audience with the generalissimo to emphasize once again that the United States was committed to a British victory but that Spain could still get friendly treatment if she would give assurances of her future policy. The speech was Franco's answer, and in the course of it he paused frequently to see whether Mr. Weddell, who, with other chiefs of mission, was present, was getting the full effect.

The Allies, he said, after a grandiloquent tribute to the might of German arms and the skill of Nazi generals, had lost the war. Of that there was no doubt. There remained only the question of Spain's justified resentment against nations which had attempted to take advantage of her distress to infringe her sovereignty. This, of course, was a reference to the various attempts by the democracies to obtain pledges that Franco would remain out of the war if he received the credits he wanted. The generalissimo went on to denounce in particular the bad treatment he had received in the case of 100,000 tons of wheat which, he said, he had bought in America but had been prevented from obtaining by the machinations of a hostile power.[1] Finally, assuming the right to speak for the nations of Latin America and for all countries not in the war, he admonished the United States not to get into it. He explained in sonorous tones that we would only prolong the war without altering the result, and that in the process the noncombatant nations would be put to great hardship and inconvenience.

The tone of the speech was a clear enough indication that with Hitler's energies now absorbed on the Russian front, no move could be made by Spain for the time being. But the contemptuousness with which Franco referred to the democracies made it clear beyond all doubt that he was only awaiting a more favourable opportunity to strike. From this moment all American business concerns in Spain that could, led by the National City Bank of New York's Spanish subsidiary, the International Banking Corporation, hastened to wind up their affairs. The changed situation was heeded in Washington for a time: physicians sent to Spain by the Rockefeller Foundation to introduce a new typhus vaccine were withdrawn[2] in

[1] No one at the American or British embassies could ever explain what transaction Franco was talking about. Hoare had ranged far afield in his efforts to keep the regime going, and had turned over to Franco a few thousand tons of American wheat, bought by the British but still warehoused in American ports, because the food situation was so critical that there was not time to bring it from Argentina. Apparently, however, this was all delivered. Perhaps intentionally, Franco's grammar was so loosely constructed that it was impossible to say whether he considered the United States or England the "hostile power," or, indeed, whether the wheat had been produced in Latin America or the United States. Naturally he did not make any reference to the considerable credits and donations that he had received from both democracies.

[2] One of the unsung heroes of post-civil-war Spain is Dr. John C. Snyder, who contracted typhus while showing Spanish physicians how to prepare the vaccine from infected rats. According to the Rockefeller Foundation report, the vaccine was found to be of no use in preventing infection by typhus, but Dr. Snyder's recovery after a severe illness perhaps was a tribute to the value of the vaccine in resisting the disease. One of the mental hazards of Madrid life in the spring of 1941 was the necessity of travelling in crowded streetcars

the late summer; no more Red Cross flour, milk, and drugs were sent, and the mission finally wound up its affairs amid a renewed burst of silence in the Franco press. (One station wagon, along with the remaining supplies of American gasoline, was given to the United States Embassy to haul food; the other was turned over to the British Embassy for the same purpose, and the trucks were shipped to England and charged to Lend-Lease.) Our relations with Spain steadily deteriorated, and in November, under prompting from the newspaper *PM* of New York, we cut off exports of gasoline and oil. The recall of Mr. Weddell to Washington in February to "report" seemed to be the usual prelude to hostilities.

But contrary to theory, the gasoline embargo produced a remarkable improvement in the manners, at least, of the Franco regime. The attitude of the press in particular, while still pro-Nazi, improved considerably. By March it was considered possible to make a new move. Mr. Weddell had resigned because of ill health, and Professor Carlton J. H. Hayes, a distinguished Catholic historian of Columbia University, was named Ambassador to Spain just as the gasoline embargo was lifted.

At the same time, under the direction of the Board of Economic Warfare, we embarked upon a more practical and less ambitious course toward Spain. Leaving the question of Franco's policy toward the war to be determined by future events, we began trying to obtain commodities, such as cork and tungsten ore, which we need for our war industries. Our opportunity to apply pressure had always been considerable, and Franco's dependence on us for gasoline, raw materials, and machinery, and upon England for coal and for the navicerts to pass the Argentine food that he needs, gives us considerable bargaining power. We are even challenging Lazar's dominion

---

containing posters instructing the public to "reject" (*rechazar*) the lice-ridden. My wife and I were given the injections and thereafter travelled over Spain with a feeling of security which we now know to have been without foundation.

by setting up a full-blown propaganda office, and at the end of August President Roosevelt announced the plan to help Spain preserve her old masters and develop her tourist trade.

A few days later, still another trade agreement, worked out by Serrano Suñer, was signed between Spain and Argentina. This provided a credit of 100,000,000 Argentine pesos, which Spain agreed to pay back in warships and other commodities that are far from plentiful in Franco territory but might just possibly be built at El Ferrol if Hitler supplies the engineering staff and machinery. It was an excellent reminder of our success in bringing Franco Spain and Argentina together to oppose us.

## *Chapter* XVI

### SPAIN AND THE SECOND FRONT

On November 8, 1942 the Allied landings in French North Africa burst like a bombshell upon Franco and the Axis world. We had been careful to bypass Spanish Morocco, and President Roosevelt assured the generalissimo that we have no aggressive designs on Spanish territory. He replied that he had received these assurances with satisfaction. But we need not be deceived as to Franco's real opinion of this admirable step. For the North African operation, if successful, will completely alter the balance of power in the Mediterranean, destroy all Franco's hopes of taking Gibraltar and French Africa, and surround Spain with a ring of Allied military force that he will find it difficult to break. The *Imperio* will be confined, as at present, to the unsatisfactory territories held already, and all Franco's dreams of making Spain a great power will be dead.

Unless we encounter a serious reverse, however, Franco's obvious course is to lie low. Contradictory reports concerning his intentions, seeming to indicate at one moment that he is veering away from the Axis, and at another that he feels bound more strongly than ever to his fascist patrons, have reflected his frustrated anger.

There are a number of reasons why Franco, always assuming that the Axis is unable to resist in Africa, may await a more favourable opportunity to strike. In view of the improvement in Allied prospects he may no longer be so confident of an Axis victory, and certainly he can have little hope that it can be obtained quickly. And Spain's resources are inadequate for more than a short campaign.

Moreover, the fact that all except two countries of Latin America have sided with the United States, and that Brazil in particular has declared war on Germany and Italy, is another reason for caution. Now that the danger of a German attack from Dakar appears to have been removed, we are stronger in Latin America than ever in our history, and Franco would be ill advised under present conditions to fight us there too determinedly.

Above all, the success of the British offensive in Libya, coinciding with the occupation of the French colonies in North Africa, promises to restore Allied control of the western Mediterranean to the position held by England and France before the latter's capitulation. Again the Iberian Peninsula is virtually an island, and Franco's poverty-stricken regime is at the mercy of the Anglo-American blockade. But it is also an island to which the Nazis have access through France. If Franco defies us, only a quick Axis victory can save Spain from starvation. If he defies the Nazis, their military strength is so overwhelming that Spain probably would be overrun in a flash. By comparison the choice between the lady and the tiger was child's play. Franco has, unfortunately, a predilection for the tiger, but if we act more skilfully than we have thus far it may be possible to show him the less dramatic but safer course.

Provided it is skilfully carried out and there is clear understanding that it is only an interim policy, our buying program in Spain is a welcome approach toward a realism which hitherto has been lacking in our dealings with Franco. If we can obtain badly needed cork and tungsten ore from him in exchange for gasoline, we should get it by all means. Sir Samuel Hoare's policy of always obtaining some sort of quid pro quo did much to make good other failings, and at last we also appear to have given up worrying about political pledges from Franco—

which, in view of Hitler's dominant position, would be worthless if they were obtained—and have begun to seek tangible benefits. As we want to buy from Franco more than we sell him, the question of further credits should not arise.

There is, to be sure, the objection that some of the goods we supply Franco will leak through to the Axis, or will make Spain a more valuable prize when Hitler takes over. Details of our trading must be kept secret in order to avoid helping the Germans cause trouble, and we must depend upon the vigilance of those carrying it on to see to it that we get at least an even break.

A greater danger is the possibility that those carrying on the negotiations may become so engrossed in their work of obtaining valuable materials for our war industries that they lose sight of larger considerations. As I noticed when Hoare's aides were negotiating with the Spaniards, the slightest concession that one obtains from a hostile government tends to assume exaggerated importance. Spaniards are excellent bargainers, and as give and take is essential in such transactions, only the most determined can avoid the temptation to strain a point in order to complete a deal. It was for this reason that the Spaniards succeeded in obtaining large extra amounts of gasoline to fill their storage tanks when the British experts were confident that they knew Spain's consumption down to the last gallon. To be conciliatory in small things but adamant on vital issues is extremely difficult.

On balance, it is likely that the United States stands to gain by keeping Spain out of the war as long as possible. There are two sides to this question, for the usefulness to the Axis of Franco's diplomatic and propaganda agents in Latin America—and possibly in the United States—is beyond dispute. On the other hand, our supply lines to North Africa are vulnerable, and until we can provide adequate air and naval forces for their defence, it probably would be better to keep Franco on the bench rooting for his side.

Yet there is no question that excessive concessions, such as we have tried to make heretofore, defeat their own purpose. It is possible, of course, that take-it-or-leave-it methods, which could have been and should have been employed before the Nazis reached Hendaye, would now be too precipitate. But Franco must be made to realize that we have the power, if he behaves too badly, to shut off his supplies of food, gasoline, and coal and destroy his regime in a matter of weeks. Possibly fulfilment of such a threat would bring in the Germans. But Spain would not be sheer profit for them; almost every ounce of food, gasoline, and other supplies would have to be carried hundreds of miles through a desolated country, and the Nazis would be burdened with the task of feeding and governing a famine-stricken and ungovernable people.

That a firm policy need not necessarily cause Franco to invite in the Nazis was demonstrated by the fact that he made no move when the British cut off Spain's gasoline imports in 1940, or when we did the same thing in 1941. There is, in fact, little question that the comparative success of our present efforts to obtain vital materials from Spain is largely due to the wholesome fear that we may repeat this action. (No one concerned with our policy toward Spain should ever lose sight of the fact that we must inspire respect if we are to get anywhere.)

And so our interim policy is worth carrying on for the moment, so long as Franco is made to realize that we are making these deals purely in our own interests, not because we are frightened by his loud talk or have a lurking sympathy with his or any other brand of fascism. Naturally such practical dealings must not be allowed to dilute our zeal for a people's war or our hatred for fascism wherever it shows itself, and we must always keep in mind that no matter how skilfully we endeavour to make up for the errors in our past policy, sooner or later Spain is almost certain to be drawn into the war.

For this reason, if for no other, we cannot compromise with

the Franco regime. Even the liquidation of the Spanish fascist party would not advance us appreciably toward this end—assuming the Germans are too engaged elsewhere to prevent it. I do not believe, however, that Spain is the place for the opening drive on Hitler in Europe. Browsing through the history of the Peninsular War should not give us the impression that by copying Wellington's great campaigns we can fight our way from Cadiz or Lisbon to Berlin, or even to Paris. Even in the days of sailing ships, when British sea power was unquestioned, and the redcoats could effect a landing anywhere on the continent of Europe, Napoleon's well-disciplined armies defeated Sir John Moore's expeditionary force; its evacuation from Coruña was almost as great a setback in those days as Dunkirk in ours.

Norway demonstrated that without an umbrella of shore-based planes no continental bridgehead can be held today, and Spain is too distant from any Allied bases now available to make it possible to extend this protection. Portugal is no solution, because it also could be overrun by the Germans before we had a chance to establish ourselves. Neither are the Azores, which are nearly 1,000 statute miles from Lisbon, out of range of fighter planes.

With the possible exception of an air and land expeditionary force in the Gibraltar area, however, there will be no occasion to land troops in Spain until much farther along in the war. A glance at a relief map will show why. Assuming that a bridgehead, corresponding to Wellington's lines at Torres Vedras, could be established in Portugal, there would, it is true, be few natural obstacles barring the invasion of Spain. The Tagus and most of the important Spanish rivers flow into Portugal, and their valleys provide excellent invasion routes into Spain. But once established in Spain, the task of reaching France would still present extreme difficulties. Except for a narrow shelf at either end of the Pyrenees, the great barrier is impassable. On the Atlantic side, where Allied air and naval units might be of some assistance, the highway and the railroad descending precipitously from Vitoria to San Sebastián unquestionably would be blown up by the Germans. Aside from difficulties with supply lines, and attacks from German planes based in Spain and in southwestern France, there simply would be no means of reaching Irún. Nor would it help matters to land at Bilbao or other points along the Basque coast; the Cantabrian coastal range permits communication by highway or by narrow-gauge railway only with the greatest difficulty, and it would be simpler to land in France and avoid the bottleneck at Irún.

The approach to France via the Mediterranean end of the Pyrenees presents fewer natural obstacles, but there we would not be able, at least for some time, to bring our aviation and naval units into action. And if our strength had reached that point, we would do far better to land at Marseille and advance up the valley of the Rhone, or strike directly at Italy. Such pleasant developments, however, are all far in the future, and the important thing now is that the airplane has altered the military geography of Spain and considerably reduced its usefulness as an advance base against the Nazi version of Napoleon's Empire.

A still more important reason against the selection of Spain as our initial front in Europe is the temperament of the Spanish people. With the exception of the fascists, and a considerable number of Army officers, all classes and regions of Spain detest the Nazis. If Spaniards were like Americans, this would mean that they are equally strong partisans of the democracies. But this is Spain, where centuries of isolation behind the Pyrenees have produced a general dislike of foreigners and a sturdy liking for things Spanish. From time to time such diverse influences as French rationalism, the Anarchist doctrines of Bakunin, Gladstonian liberalism, Russian Communism, Italian and German fascism, and even a touch of American go-ahead, have occasionally made themselves felt even in isolated Spain. But Spanish individualism has remained essentially unaffected. With all its troubles, Spaniards still place their own country above any other. A century ago Richard Ford, in his *Gatherings from Spain,* quoted a Castilian proverb which admirably reflected this feeling of superiority to the outside world: *"Si Dios no fuese Dios, seria rey de las Españas, y el de Francia su cocinero* (If God were not God, he would make himself king of the Spains, with him of France for his cook)."

The frame of mind which found expression in this saying exists today, and if the democracies should put themselves in the position of imposing alien control upon Spain, the hatred that Spaniards feel for the Germans possibly would be transferred to us. Most Spaniards are against Hitler primarily because at the moment he constitutes the most dangerous threat to their national isolation, but if we made the first move to take over Spain, skilful Nazi propagandists very probably would use it to turn against us this same untamed force. The average Spaniard, having endured continuous privations since 1936 as a result of the civil war, is strongly opposed to fighting *for* either the Axis or the democracies. If it could be made to appear that it was the democracies, rather than the Nazis, who were forcing another war on Spain, there would be a revulsion of feeling against us.

Any realistic policy toward Spain must take these factors into account, and every principle of psychological warfare requires us to allow the Germans to make the first move so that there will be no doubt which is the foe that has forced another war on starving Spain. We must look elsewhere for a place to land the first expeditionary forces that will begin the long and costly task of freeing Europe.

But this is a long way from ruling Spain out of our calculations. We must begin at once to assemble and train the military forces that will be required to expel the Nazis should they finally move in. No matter what we do, we cannot stop them from overrunning Spain, and Portugal as well, but Gibraltar can and must be strengthened to hold out and provide a base for subsequent movements. And since the number of troops that we can send to Spain will necessarily be limited, we must do everything we can to win the support of the Spanish people, whose guerrillas did so much to help Wellington expel Napoleon's armies from Spain.

It is apparently the belief of our government that if Hitler moves into Spain, a Spanish Darlan will arise to combat the foe. We have been given no inkling whether Franco is cast for this role, or Don Juan, or some anti-*Falange* general. But if this should come off we may suppose that it would be justified by the same "realistic" arguments employed in the case of Darlan. To the man in the street, at least, our policies toward Vichy France and Franco Spain seem to have been cut from the same cloth. Since we are now told that every move in our Vichy policy was intended to prepare the way for the North African operation, supposedly a similar claim would be used to defend our policy toward Franco.

I do not think that objections to either Darlan or Franco, as such, should be allowed to block any move that will really help win the war. Although Darlan failed to deliver either Tunisia or the Toulon fleet, his adherence to our cause undoubtedly facilitated our occupation of French Morocco and Algeria, and it may have been due to his influence that the commanders at Toulon, while unwilling to join us, at least scuttled their ships and prevented the Germans from getting them. It remains to be seen whether the gains from the Darlan deal outweigh the difficulties it has caused with the Fighting French and with the other patriots who were courageously fighting the Nazis while Darlan was still an ardent co-worker with the enemy.[1]

[1] The assassination of Darlan at the end of December 1942 may have far-reaching consequences. As this book goes to press, it is still too early to know whether it will benefit or injure the North African operation.

A deal with Franco or his equivalent, however, is another matter. Of the three possible choices, Don Juan has much to recommend him, for he is at least not a fascist. The monarchy, furthermore, has a strong following among the upper classes, and almost any Spaniard would prefer Don Juan to Franco. It may be doubted, however, whether there are many who would be willing to fight for it, and the political usefulness of Don Juan, even in coalition with the Army, is limited accordingly.

Several generals suggest themselves, although, in view of possible bad effects upon any negotiations that we may be carrying on with them, it is just as well not to name them. If we could find one, the pattern of the Darlan deal would be reproduced almost exactly. An Army dictatorship, such as was originally intended by the *Junta* that began the Nationalist revolt, certainly would be preferable to the present state of affairs. It would be more reasonable, just as the Junkers in Germany were more reasonable than the Nazis. But it is difficult to find a general with sufficiently high prestige to win over the remainder of the military caste, and it must be remembered that many Spanish Army officers are pro-German at the same time that they detest the *Falange*. It is doubtful, moreover, whether the Army, as one of the ancient vested interests of Spain, would arouse much enthusiasm among the common people.

Franco himself, therefore, would seem to be the most available leader of the nation's resistance. We can, if we like, point to such events as the dismissal of Serrano Suñer as evidence that the generalissimo does not want to bring Spain into the war. That may be, but it is still an open question whether he would fight Hitler if the Nazis came in despite his protests.

It is likely that the method used would be the undramatic infiltration of German "tourists," which it would be exceedingly difficult for an amorphous government to counteract. Once the Germans were in command of key transportation and military points, it would require a tremendous effort of will for Franco to halt the movement. Moreover, the Germans and Italians won the civil war for Franco, and he has reiterated his solidarity with them on numberless occasions. It may be, as some contend, that these expressions were lip-service, intended to ease German pressure. But the Spanish people may not understand these subtleties, and to fight the Germans would destroy the entire ideological basis of the Franco regime. Franco may fight them after all, but if he does it will be to defend the right of even a pocket dictator to retain some control over his own country. And it seems more likely that he would follow the example of Pétain, who offered no resistance when the Nazis took over the unoccupied zone in France.

But even in the event that a deal with Franco would guarantee his wholehearted resistance, he has much less to offer than did Darlan. For while the latter did render a considerable service, Franco's usefulness is very limited. The combined military strength of Spain is inadequate to do more than hold up the Germans for a few days, and it is to be assumed that Nazi intrigues would prevent at least part of the armed forces from obeying the order to resist. Presumably the Nazis would at once outlaw Franco and substitute Serrano Suñer—or someone of that type—as head of a new puppet government. The xenophobia of Spaniards doubtless would produce some underground resistance to the Germans, but it is hardly likely that the leader of the fascist movement in Spain would rally Spanish Republicans to his standard.

And Darlan, after all, had been called many harsh names but nobody could accuse him of being a fascist. We might think of him as a royalist, a time-server, an Anglophobe. But he attached himself to the Germans when they were in the ascendancy, and left a failing cause, without any particular preference in ideologies. Franco, however, has been a protégé of Germany and Italy since 1936. His ambitions for Spain and his regime are incompatible with the survival of any of the democracies as great powers. This is known to the Spaniards, if not to us, and we can be sure what his real feelings are toward our cause no matter what words of solidarity he may speak.

And while the deal with Darlan could be said to be a temporary expedient, no such qualification may be imposed upon any negotiations with Franco. At the time of his death Darlan's authority was still limited to a part of the French Empire. But Franco has been recognized by England and the United States as the rightful ruler of Spain, and if he aligns himself with us now, we can certainly do no less than guarantee his continuance in office until the end of the war and probably some time thereafter. It would be ironical if Franco, who since June 1940 has stayed in power under the protection of the Germans, should now come under our protection. It is likely enough that the Spanish people will turn him out the moment that his foreign patrons cease to protect him. But this does not alter the unwisdom of doing anything more to confirm his hold upon Spain.

Much more is involved in this question than Spain alone. Many nations of the world groan under the Axis yoke and look to us as their liberators. If they are confident of the sincerity of our intentions, they can strike many a powerful blow in the cause of freedom. But are we to disregard their sufferings and accept any quisling who turns up within our lines? Darlan was the first, and Franco might be the second collaborator with Hitler to decide that the Axis cause is lost and it would be more comfortable to make a deal with us. Each time the plea of military expediency can be brought forward, and it might be argued that a deal with Göring, for example, would be justifiable on much the same grounds as one with Franco.

But it can hardly be supposed that the conquered nations of the world will give us much help if we are willing to come to terms with all the oppressors who now flee a sinking ship. Such deals threaten to forfeit our opportunity to repeat the success of Wilson's Fourteen Points, which supplemented military action so powerfully in the World War. And from a larger point of view, a war for freedom will not have been won if regimes such as Franco's are left in existence. If we do not win the peace we shall have lost the war no matter how far our armies have advanced. It is of the utmost importance that we prove to the Spaniards and the world that we really are fighting the people's war proclaimed so eloquently by Vice President Wallace.

For the aid of the Spanish people, which we can still obtain despite all our errors in the past, is of far greater importance than exclusively military considerations. Only the ingenuous, of course, could expect a nation that has suffered so much from the errors of the democracies to fight for us merely because we have now discovered that we need her. When the millions who are now biding their time rise again, it will be to overthrow the citadels of privilege which defied the Republic but will not always hold out. But for the presence of German troops at the frontier, the Franco regime already would have gone the way of Primo de Rivera's earlier experiment in fascism. Once they are assured of the outside military help that they require, we can rely upon the Spanish people to wage an incessant guerrilla warfare against the Nazis and whatever quisling they use. It will grow more unrelenting as the Gestapo intensifies its reprisals.

But they will not do this merely to help us, or to restore a "reasonable" government by oligarchy, no matter whether it is to be administered by a chastened Franco or by a restored Bourbon. To be sure, as was proved by the mourning banners that were displayed from the hovels of Madrid to salute the passing of Alfonso, they prefer even the monarchy to the present regime. But more far-reaching aims are imperative if we are to mobilize the strength of Spain on our side. We are fighting a people's war, but the common man of Spain will fight for us only if he knows that he is also fighting for himself and his hungry children. It was with this conviction that the people of Spain, attacking Napoleon's dragoons with knives or their bare hands, broke the force of an earlier Blitzkrieg. Thus it was possible for Wellington to cleanse the entire peninsula and finally lead his armies of liberation into France.

For this reason all dealings with Franco must be on an hour-to-hour basis, and meanwhile we must give the Spanish people clear assurances that a popular government will be their reward when the common enemy is dispatched. The means to attain this objective are available today. Indalecio Prieto, the Basque Socialist who is the ablest of the Spanish Republican statesmen, is in Mexico; in London is Juan Negrín, the last Prime Minister of the Republic, who displayed an energy that might have saved it if he had been in power at the start of the Franco uprising. Alvarez del Vayo, Foreign Minister of the Republic, is in the United States, José Antonio de Aguirre, President of the Basque Republic, is in Chile as this is written, but is expected back in New York soon. With the exception of Luis Compañys, President of the Catalan Republic, who was caught in France, most of the Republican leaders escaped to Mexico, Chile, or other American countries [1] and can be quickly assembled to form a government-in-exile.

This is a step that should be taken at once, for the Germans may invade Spain at any time and it will be much easier to convince the Spanish people of our desire to help them if we set up such a government before, rather than after, the Nazis take over. The Spanish Republic, like the democratic governments of Czechoslovakia, Norway, the Netherlands, and other European countries, was overthrown by international fascism; a Spanish government-in-exile has the same right to speak for its people as the other governments that will be restored after the war.

We must not, of course, imagine that by the mere sponsoring of such a government we can cancel the results of persist-

[1] Largo Caballero and Casares Quiroga were caught by the Germans when they took over the former unoccupied zone of France. The fate of the two former prime ministers is unknown.

ent blundering since Franco first raised the standard of rebellion. Spain, like Singapore, the Philippines, and other strong points that we have thrown away, can be recovered for our cause only by the loss of thousands and possibly hundreds of thousands of lives. And it would be useless to minimize the other difficulties which we must surmount in order to regain what never should have been lost.

Those who still think that the fascist regime is "reasonable," and that we need only to get rid of the fascist party, will argue that to set up a Spanish Republican government in the United States would alienate Franco and drive him into the war. That such an action would enrage Franco, and Hitler as well, is obvious. Even if the government were launched under the auspices of Mexico, which is now on our side, we should be held responsible. But the cry of wolf has been heard every time that we have taken any kind of firm action toward either Franco Spain or Vichy France. We have enraged Laval, and Hitler as well, with each reluctant step toward recognition of General Charles de Gaulle as a friend rather than an enemy. But if our firmer action prior to the North African operation had any effect on Germany's attitude toward Vichy, it was to delay the overthrow of Laval's government.

The same considerations apply with regard to Franco: he will stab us in the back when he thinks the right moment has come, or Hitler will invade Spain anyway when it suits the Nazi strategy, and we must not risk a Pearl Harbor. To be sure, Franco Spain is something of a special case, for it is always possible that the recklessness of the fabled Spanish parachute jumper may drive it to its own destruction. For this reason it is inexpedient to arouse Franco needlessly. But the establishment of a government-in-exile would provide us with so many counter-advantages that we must ignore the possibility of the fascist regime's committing hara-kiri.

A far more serious obstacle is the disunion among the Spanish Republican leaders. In the bitterness of exile they have continued the quarrels among themselves which played a tragic part in the failure of the Republic either to carry out its reforms or to suppress the Franco uprising. The Communists are split into Stalin and Trotsky groups, and there are further divisions among the Socialists, Anarchists, Basque and Catalan nationalists, and bourgeois liberals. Some, apparently, despise General Miaja and Largo Caballero almost as much as they do Franco.

But despite these divisions, which are proof that Spanish individualism is not to be eradicated by a mere change of government, it should be possible to form a coalition government and agree upon a minimum program. The forces that eventually brought down the monarchy did conclude such a program in the Pact of San Sebastián, in 1930, and they were probably just as much divided then as the exiled Republican leaders are now. The details would have to be left to the Republicans themselves, but certainly the Charter of Liberty would include complete co-operation with the other United Nations until fascism throughout the world has been defeated and the third Republic is set up in Spain. Naturally, it would be incumbent upon us to provide the food and the means of rebuilding Spain which in the past we have pressed upon Franco.

Once such a government-in-exile was established, we should have a means of combating Hitler under perhaps the most favourable conditions existing anywhere outside of Russia, whose people are the only rivals of the Spaniards in the art of sabotage and guerrilla warfare. The Republicans possess an underground organization in Spain which would be the nucleus of resistance; when at last the day came that we could land troops, we would have allies in every mountain fastness and every sun-baked *pueblo* the length and breadth of Spain.

To restore free government to the Spanish people, who for centuries have been crushed by the weight of special privilege, is itself an aim of the first importance in a people's war. But with it there is also the opportunity to enlist in the battle for human liberty men who are not afraid to die, whose hatred of the oppressor transcends differences of time or place.

The black-shawled women waiting in the dawn outside the empty food stores, the Republican militiamen held without trial in Franco's jails, need only help from us to renew the total war against fascism that began in 1936. If they knew the works of an English Protestant who also fought for freedom, they would repeat his defiance of the powers of darkness:

> What though the field be lost?
> All is not lost; the unconquerable will
> And study of revenge, immortal hate
> And courage never to submit or yield,
> And what is else not to be overcome.

# *Bibliography*

So far as I know, an adequate account of the issues at stake in the Spanish civil war has still to be written. The best account in English of the Republic's stormy existence is to be found in E. Allison Peers's *The Spanish Tragedy, 1930–1936* (London, 1936), although it is very anti-Republican and wastes upon details of parliamentary manœuvres the space which should have been used to discuss the fundamental conflict between the privileged and the mass of the people. Probably the most satisfactory account is Melchor Fernandez Almagro's *Historia de la República Española, 1931–1936* (Madrid, 1940). This was written with an eye only too clearly fixed on Franco's censors, and it is diverting to go back to his *Historia del Reinado de Don Alfonso XIII* (Madrid, 1934) and see the difference that a few years and a different government make. For a one-volume history taking in the outbreak of the civil war it is necessary to go to the violently pro-Franco *Nouvelle Histoire d'Espagne* (Paris, 1938), by Maurice Legendre.

Even the military history of the civil war is yet to be told satisfactorily, but Luis Maria de Lojendio's *Operaciones Militares de la Guerra de España, 1936–1939* (Barcelona, 1940) will do for lack of a better.

Although a number of books have been written in English on events in the war, the most complete history, containing valuable source material, is Julian Zugazagoitia's *Historia de la Guerra en España* (Buenos Aires, 1940).

In addition to books cited in the text, the following will be useful to anyone interested in the origins and development of Spanish fascism:

JUAN APARICIO: *JONS*. Madrid, 1939. An account of the earlier fascist movement which later merged with the Phalanx.

JOAQUIN ARRARAS: *Francisco Franco, The Times and the Man*. Milwaukee, 1938. The official biography

GENERAL MILLÁN ASTRAY: *Franco: El Caudillo*. A eulogy by the officer who organized the Spanish Foreign Legion with Franco as his second-in-command.

FRANCISCO BRAVO: *Historia de Falange Española de las J.O.N.S.* Madrid, 1940. An account which ends with the merger of the fascist and Carlist groups on April 19, 1937, when *Tradicionalista* was added to the official title.

——: *José Antonio, El Hombre, El Jefe, El Camarada*. Madrid, 1939. Revealing glimpses of the Founder of the Phalanx and those associated with him.

ERNESTO GIMÉNEZ CABALLERO: *Roma Madre*. Madrid, 1939. Awarded the San Remo prize by the Royal Italian Academy for the best account by a foreigner of contemporary Italy. Emphasizes the Catholic and Mussolinian version of fascism which has since been supplanted by the Nazi school.

RAMIRO LEDESMA RAMOS. *Discurso a las Juventudes de España*. Madrid, 1939. Exhortation by the zealot who, along with Giménez Caballero and Onésimo Redondo, fashioned the ideology of Spanish fascism.

——: *La Conquista del Estado*. Edited by Juan Aparicio. Collected articles from the fascist newspaper of that name.

JOSÉ ANTONIO PRIMO DE RIVERA: Collected *Obras*. Volumes I, II, III, and IV. Madrid, 1941.

——: *Antología* of his works. Edited by Gonzalo Torrente Ballester and published by the Phalanx party. Madrid, 1940.

Onésimo Redondo: *Antología* of his works. Published by the Phalanx. Madrid, 1940.

Guillen Salaya: *Historia y Anécdota de las Juntas de Ofensiva Nacional-Sindicalista.* San Sebastián, 1938.

A. Alcázar de Velasco: *Serrano Suñer en la Falange.* Madrid, 1940. An attempt to show that Serrano Suñer was a good fascist from before the civil war.

The imperialist aspirations and general ideology of the Franco regime may be examined in the following:

Alfonso de Ascansio: *España Imperio.* Avila, 1939.

José Ibáñez Martín: *Hacia un Nuevo Orden Universitario.* Madrid, 1940.

——: *Hacia una Nueva Ciencia Española.* Madrid, 1940. Two speeches delivered by Franco's Minister of Education, devoted to the thesis that knowledge must hew to the party line.

José María Pemán: *Poema de la Bestia y El Angel.* Cadiz, 1939. An epic poem on the civil war.

——: *Historia Sencilla de España Contada Con Sencillez (Para Niños . . . y Para Muchos Que No Lo Son).* Cadiz, 1940. A child's history, used in all Franco schools.

Antonio Tovar: *El Imperio de España.* Madrid, 1940. By one of the most brilliant and prolific of the younger fascists. A Serrano Suñer protégé, he was Undersecretary of Press and Propaganda until his dismissal in the anti-Suñer movement of May 1941.

The Franco censorship is so severe that little information on Spain is available in the American press. *La Prensa,* a Spanish-language newspaper published in New York, gives a considerable volume of news from Spain and some interesting information occasionally slips through. Spanish newspapers and the *Boletín Oficial,* which reprints government decrees with their lengthy explanatory preambles, are almost the only means of following developments. The *Bulletin of Spanish Studies,* a quarterly published by the Institute of Hispanic

Studies of the University of Liverpool, and edited by E. Allison Peers, contains a useful digest of news revealed by these sources. Excellent information on factional quarrels within the regime occasionally is to be found in the *Tablet,* a London Catholic weekly. *The Spanish News Letter,* published in London and edited by Charles Duff, is strongly anti-Franco but frequently contains valuable uncensored reports.

For the reader who has time for only one book on Spain, however, the work to be recommended above all others is Richard Ford's *Gatherings from Spain.* Few nations have been so fortunate in their interpreters. Ford travelled for years in a land laid waste by the First Carlist War, and his account of the misery which bad government brought to a superb people is as valid today as it was when it was published a century ago. It is available in Everyman's Library (published in the United States by E. P. Dutton & Company).

THE material in this book was obtained mainly during my two years in Spain as correspondent for the *New York Times,* beginning in August 1939. Here I wish to express my appreciation to the management of the *Times* for granting me the leave of absence that made it possible to get this book on paper. The *Times,* of course, is in no way responsible for any of the views that I have expressed.

I am grateful also to Dr. Howard P. Johnson, of the History Department of Tulane University, for his invaluable aid and advice. The authorities of the Library of Congress, who placed at my disposal the slender written material in English on post-civil-war Spain, were most co-operative. Without the help and encouragement of my wife the undertaking would have been impossible.

Thanks are due to a host of friends, both Spaniards and foreigners, who must go nameless because they are still exposed to reprisals by the Nazi-Franco government. I regret keenly that I am unable for this reason to give the source of some of the most important facts in this book. But anyone who knows the treatment that those "disaffected to the regime" receive in Franco Spain will understand the necessity for discretion. Let us hope that the day of liberation, when the friends of democracy and decency will be able to speak, is not too far off.

*Thomas J. Hamilton*

# *Index*

Abdel-Krim, Riffi chieftain, 111, 276
Abetz, Otto, German Ambassador to Occupied France, 228
*Africanista,* Franco's interests as, 257
Agriculture, policy of Franco regime toward, 74, 99, 158
Aguirre, José Antonio de, President of Basque Republic, 320
Alarcón de la Lastra, Colonel Luis, Minister of Industry and Commerce, 139
Alba, Duke of, Spanish Ambassador to London: believes his palace destroyed by Spanish "Reds," 28; attacked by Spanish fascists, 100; rebuked for calling on Franco in a lounge suit, 116 n.
Alfaro, José María, dismissed as Undersecretary of Press and Propaganda, 124
Alfonso XIII: gives up throne without a struggle, 55; opposed by Carlists, 57; Franco opposes restoration, 67; material progress of Spain under, 83; offer to stand aside in favour of Don Juan rejected by Franco, 101–2; dies, 102
Algeciras, strategic position of, 4
Allen, Robert S., on American credit offer to Franco, 297
Alvarez del Vayo, J.: on preservation of Spanish paintings by the Republic, 29; declares José Antonio Primo de Rivera and General Sanjurjo conferred with Hitler before the Popular Front election, 65; on British connection with Casado *coup d'état,* 276
American Embassy in Madrid: hit by Franco shell, 28; desired by Franco as residence, 114; fascist demonstration against, 295
American Red Cross: food shipments to Spain, 188; are alternative to credit, 296; activities of its representatives, 298 et seq.
*America's Strategy in World Politics,* 266
Anderson, Jane, American, agent for Franco and Hitler, 16
Anual, Spanish defeat at, 77
Anti-Semitism: borrowed by Phalanx from Nazis, 73; Franco regime's policy toward Jewish refugees, 219, 225
Appeasement, 10, 271 et seq.
Aragon, home-rule movement in, 76
Aranda Mata, General Antonio, part in Army move against Serrano Suñer, 123
*Arbeitsdienst,* Franco's version of, 151
Areilza, José M., 10
Argentina: efforts of Franco to win over, 260; partnership with Franco in opposing U. S. policies

in Latin America, 268; effect of a firm American policy toward Franco, 269; United States underwrites credit to Franco, 297; Franco receives additional credit, 307
Aristocracy: views on civil war, 52 et seq.; regains privileges, 99; attitude toward Franco, 117
Army: opposition to Serrano Suñer and the Phalanx, 91, 123; position in Spain, 104, 163; possibility of its resisting Nazis, 315, 316
Arrese Magra, José Luis de, Secretary General of Phalanx, helps bring down Serrano Suñer, 128
*Arriba,* organ of Phalanx, 72, 98, 240, 247
Associated Press, representation in Spain, 205
Asturian miners: revolt of, 39, 53; special food rations for, 183
*Auslandsdienst,* Franco's version of, 258
Autarchy, efforts of Franco regime to install, 131, 139
Auxilio Social, fascist relief agency, 47, 149 et seq., 192; and American food gifts, 301; feud with Feminine Section of Phalanx, 107, 229
Aznar, Manuel, Franco press spokesman, demands return of Gibraltar, 283

Baker, Josephine, appearance on Madrid stage, 211
Balearic Islands, strategic importance of, 5
Barcelona: damage to during civil war, 31; food shortage, 143, 195
Basque provinces: home-rule movement in, 52; fascist attitude toward, 75; discrimination against by Franco, 94
Behn, Colonel Sosthenes, president and chairman of the board of the International Telephone & Telegraph Corporation, 120, 185; regains control of Spanish telephone system, 293
Beigbeder y Atienza, Colonel Juan: dismissed from Foreign Ministry, 108, 124, 286; Serrano Suñer takes over his mistress as well, 129; sanctions abuse of diplomatic pouch, 142; and refugees, 218; remarks on Himmler, 286
Belgium, Franco breaks diplomatic relations with, 219
Benavente y Martínez, Jacinto, Nobel prize winner, 206
Benavides, Marshal Oscar R., Peruvian Ambassador to Spain, 260
Bérard-Jordana agreement, 278
Besteiro, Julian, gets thirty-year prison term, 92
Biarritz, favoured haunt of Spanish aristocracy, 24, 55
Big business: helps bring in Primo de Rivera dictatorship, 59; dissatisfaction with Franco regime, 94
Bilbao, little damaged by civil war, 31
Bill of Rights, 58
Black list of American film stars, 207
"Black legend," its "invention" bv foes of Spain, 84
Black markets, 172 et seq.
Blasco Ibáñez, Vicente, 264
Blue Division, fights for Nazis on Russian front, 237
Blum, Léon, Prime Minister, covert assistance to Spanish Republic, 12

Board of Economic Warfare: checks up on Franco's oil supply; commercial dealings with Franco, 306, 309
Bolívar, Simón, 87
Bonnet, Georges, French Minister of Foreign Affairs, 278
Bonney, Therese, American photographer, 227
Boothe, Clare, 207
Bowers, Claude G., United States Ambassador to the Spanish Republic: opinion of José Antonio Primo de Rivera, 61; opinion of Franco, 276
British and Foreign Bible Society, its publications confiscated by Franco, 97
Budget, of Franco regime, 134
Buck, Pearl, 265
Bullfights, poor quality of, 206

Cadiz: famine in, 188; incidents involving American Red Cross Mission, 299
Calderón de la Barca, Pedro, 206
Caldwell, F. T., general manager of Spanish telephone system, 293
Calvo, Luis, London correspondent of *ABC,* 241
Canary Islands, strategic importance of, 5
Carceller, Demetrio, Minister of Industry and Commerce, 154
Cardenas, Juan Francisco de, Spanish Ambassador to the United States, 200
Carlist wars, 19, 36, 55
Carlists: capture Irún, and intercede in behalf of Republican prisoners, 49; origins and doctrine, 55 et seq.; "united" with Phalanx, 66
Carmona, food conditions in, 192 et seq.
Carol, former King of Rumania, arrested in Spain, 217 et seq.
Casado, Lieutenant Colonel Segismundo, heads *coup d'état* in last days of Madrid, 27, 276
Casares Quiroga, Santiago, Republican leader, views on Spanish fascist movement, 64; caught by Germans in France, 320 n.
Castiella, Fernando M., 10
Catalonia, home-rule movement in, 52 et seq.; fascist attitude toward, 75; Franco's discrimination against, 94, 168
Catholic Church: damage to church property during civil war, 24, 30; intercedes for Republicans, 49; fascist attitude toward, 75; Franco's policy toward pro-separatist priests, 95; relations with Franco regime, 96 et seq., 128
*Caudillo,* honorific title of Franco, 52
CEDA, Rightist party, 53
Censorship under Franco, 199 et seq.
Cervera y Topete, Admiral Pascual, 82
Chamberlain, Neville: policy toward Hitler and Franco, 271 et seq.; his government overthrown, 282
Charles II, 86 n.
Charles V, Holy Roman Emperor, 72
*Cheka,* 42, 43
Chesterton, G. K., 52
Chiang Kai-shek, General, 8
*Chicago Tribune,* representation in Spain, 205
Chicote's Bar, 203
Chile: shelters Spanish Rightists during civil war, 44; Franco

breaks relations with, 258; American influence in, 264 et seq.; a firm policy toward Franco would strengthen our position in, 269
China, failure of the United States to aid sufficiently, 8
Churchill, Winston, views on Spanish civil war, 17
Civil Guard: transferred to Army, 104; recruits "volunteers" for Blue Division, 238
Civil marriage, virtually abolished by Franco, 96
Class prejudice, influence on policy of democracies toward Spain, China, Russia, 8
Coca-Cola, reason for shortage of, 165
*Cold Harbor,* delivers American Red Cross food to Spain, 188 et seq., 303
Communism, fear of, by democracies exploited by Hitler, 16
Company stores, Franco requires establishment of, 187
Compañys, Luis, President of Catalan Republic, executed by Franco, 45
Concordat with Vatican, 96, 99
Conquista, Marchioness de la, Franco emissary in Peru, 260
*Conquista del Estado, La,* 59
Costa, Joaquín, 82
Council of the Indies, 85
Council of Hispanidad, fights United States in Latin America, 125, 260
Counter-Reformation, 55; Spain's virtual return to days of, 97
Crockett, Colonel Cary I., head of American Red Cross mission to Spain, 299 et seq.
Cuba: forbids Franco diplomats to cable dispatches in code, 250; dispute with Franco over Cuban Phalanx leader, 259
Czechoslovakia, maintains semi-official relations with Franco, 219

Daladier, Édouard, policy toward Franco, 271, 281
*Dama de Elche,* sculpture taken from Louvre and given to Franco by Hitler, 31
Dario, Rubén, Nicaraguan poet, 262
Darlan, Vice Admiral Jean, our deal with in North Africa, 315 et seq.
Daudet, Léon, editor of *L'Action Française,* 16
"Day of the Race," 84
*Defensa de Hispanidad,* 85
De Gaulle, General Charles, 321
*Depuración,* process of, 46
*De rerum novarum,* use of by Spanish fascists, 71
*Devonshire,* British cruiser, carries Franco emissary to demand surrender of Minorca, 275
Diplomatic corps: its special privileges regarding food, 163; sun bathing, 206; gasoline, 208
*Dirección General de Regiones Devastadas,* 24, 94, 108
Disillusionment with Franco regime, 134, 211
Divorce, abolished by Franco, 96
Dollar Line, sells two ships to Franco company, 292
Don Carlos, pretenders of that name to Spanish throne, 56
Don Juan, son of Alfonso XIII and pretender to Spanish throne: disliked by Carlists, 57; application to enlist in Franco army refused, 67; father offers to step aside in favour of, 102; Phalanx opposes

restoration, 103; possible deal with by democracies, 315, 316
Don Quixote, 180
Dos Passos, John, 265
Drake, Sir Francis, 284
Duval, General Maurice, 13

Economic policy of Franco regime, 131; faulty administration, 135 et seq.
"Education and Rest," 93
England, policy of toward Franco during civil war, 21, 272; attitude of Spanish fascists toward, 71 et seq., 85 et seq., 137; policy toward Franco since 1939, 273 et seq.
Escobar, Dr. A. C., Argentine Ambassador to Spain: courted by Franco, 260; negotiates credit to Franco, 297
Escorial, fascist rallying-point, 50; burial of José Antonio Primo de Rivera, 122, 123
Estella, Marquis de, *see* Primo de Rivera, José Antonio, *and* Primo de Rivera, General Miguel de
*Estraperlo,* 172 et seq.
Executions, 36; by Republicans, 39; by Franco, 44
Export-Import Bank, United States, grants Franco cotton credit, 279

*Face to the Sun,* Phalanx hymn, sung at demonstration against American Embassy, 295
*Falange, see* Phalanx
*Falange Exterior,* fights United States, 258 et seq.
*Fascio, El,* 60
Feminine Section, division of Phalanx, 106; feud with Auxilio Social, 107, 229
Ferdinand and Isabella: emblem adopted by Phalanx, 69; expulsion of Jews, 73
Ferdinand VII: leaves throne to daughter, 56; and Latin American independence, 87
Fernandez Cuesta, Raimúndo, fascist leader: escapes from Republican zone, 43; becomes secretary general of Phalanx, 67; exiled as Ambassador to Brazil, 118
Fiestas, fascist additions to list, 121 n.
Fifth column: during civil war, 43; German agents in Spain and Portugal, 243 et seq.
Finland, United States continues diplomatic relations with, 8
Food situation: supplies ample for wealthy, 164 et seq.; starvation for poor, 177 et seq.
Ford, Henry, 52
Ford, Richard, 314
*Fortune,* too heavy for Franco postmen, 198
Foss, William, 143
Fourteen Points, propaganda value of, in World War, 318
France: attitude of Carlists toward, 58; of Phalanx, 71, 85 et seq.; influence in Latin America, 264; policy toward Spanish civil war, 272; policy since 1939, 273 et seq.; Vichy government confiscates two American Red Cross ships, 298
Franco regime, military strength of, 5 et seq.; solidarity with Axis, 10; vengeance on Republicans, 39, 44; conflict within, 91; economic aims and muddling, 131 et seq.; special privileges under, 162 et seq.; famine under, 177 et seq.; policy toward refugees, 215 et

seq.; German activities in, 234 et seq.; activities in Latin America, 255 et seq.; relations with foreign powers, 271 et seq.
Franco, Señora Carmen Polo de, pro-Catholic influence of, 97; ties with sister, Mme Suñer, 109, 130; activities, 117
Franco, Señorita Carmencita de, daughter of generalissimo, 117
Franco Bahamonde, Generalissimo Francisco: his victory a setback for democracies, 3, 10, 311, 320; suppresses Asturian revolt, 39; revenge on defeated Republicans, 44; adopts fascist program, 52, 66; gives Serrano Suñer leading role in Phalanx, 67; and Moorish bodyguard, 70 n.; hands-off policy toward warring supporters, 91; sole unifying element of government, 107; his career, 109 et seq.; Latin-American program, 256; fascist sympathies, 274; joins anti-Comintern pact, 276; rejects reconstruction credit by democracies, 279; fails to move when France collapses, 284; meeting with Hitler, 287; and American credit offer, 296; defiant speech, 304; accepts our assurances regarding Spanish territory, 308; possibility of deal with, 315
Franco Bahamonde, Nicholas, Spanish Ambassador to Portugal, 110
Franco Bahamonde, Major Ramón, leads anti-monarchist plot, 38; 110; goodwill flight to Latin America, 257
*Freedom's Battle,* 29, 65, 276
Freemasons: held responsible for loss of Latin America, 87; law against, 96
*Fueros,* 76
*Führerschule* of Phalanx, 167, 203

Galán, Captain Fermin, leads Republican uprising, 38
Galarza Morante, Colonel Valentín, Minister of Government, 126; dismissed, 130
Galicia: home-rule movement in, 75; use of, by Germans, 251
Gambara, General, Italian Ambassador to Spain, 236
Ganivet, Ángel, 82
García Hernández, Captain Ángel, leads Republican uprising, 38
García Valdecasas, Alfonso, director of Institute of Political Studies, 11; co-founder of Phalanx, 61
*Gatherings from Spain,* 314
Generation of '98, 82
*Genio de España,* 86
Geopolitics, employment by Spanish fascists, 78
Gerahty, Cecil, 143
Germany: wins war for Franco and sells arms to Republic, 21; a model for Spanish nationalists, 71; Franco's war debt to and commercial relations with, 140; advantages derived from backing Franco, 237 et seq.; conditions under which Hitler might decide to take over Spain, 254; relations with Franco, 271 et seq.
Gestapo, activities in Spain, 245
Gibraltar, its position with regard to the Strait, 4; Spanish moderates not interested in regaining, 77; Serrano Suñer's statement of Phalanx aspirations regarding, 80; imports of food from, 156; censorship, 200; return de-

manded by Franco press spokesman, 283
Gibraltar, Strait of: strategic importance, 4; virtually closed by Axis land-based planes, 254
Gil Robles, José Maria, Catholic conservative, 53
Giménez Arnau, Ricardo, chief of *Falange Exterior,* U. S. refuses to accredit to Washington Embassy, 295
Giménez Caballero, Ernesto, fascist leader, 59 et seq.; views on Spanish policy, 86
Gomá y Tomas, Cardinal Isidoro, Archbishop of Toledo and Primate of Spain: assigned leading role at state ceremonies, 96; death brings to a head quarrel between Franco and Vatican, 98
Good Neighbor policy, 265 et seq.
Göring, Marshal Hermann, 33, 107; trip to Spain cancelled, 279; undesirability of deal with, 318
Goya, damage to two paintings by, 29
Greco, El, his paintings, undamaged, 29, 30
Greece: comparison of conditions in, with those of Spain, 177; Minister in Madrid withdrawn, 219
Grey, Zane, 265
Guadalajara: Italian defeat at, 70; General Queipo de Llano's taunts, 209; damages Italy's influence in Madrid, 236
Guernica: destruction of, 32; plans for rebuilding, 94

Hamlin, John, American consul in Seville, 191
Haugwitz-Reventlow, Count, a refugee through Spain, 220
Hay, John, 50
Hayes, Carlton J. H., named American Ambassador to Spain, 306
Hedilla, Manuel, fascist leader, 65; attempted putsch, 68
Hiett, Helen, N. B. C. correspondent, 205
Himmler, Heinrich, visits Spain, 243, 286
"Hisma," Nazi agency for trade with Spain, 244
Hispanidad: origin and program, 85, 261; Spain's appeal to Latin America, 267
Hitler, Adolf, use of Spanish civil war to confuse and divide democracies, 20; Hendaye interview with Franco, 113, 286; circumstances under which he might decide to take over Spain, 254
Hoare, Lady Maud, remains faithful to appeasement and Chamberlain, 283 n.
Hoare, Sir Samuel, British Ambassador to Spain, 282; carries on delaying action, 283, 284, 289 et seq.; proposes American credit to Franco, 294; changes mind, 297; obtains satisfaction for attack on British Embassy, 303 n.; United States takes over direction of appeasement program, 292
Horst Wessel, similarity of José Antonio cult to, 73
Hotel Florida, damage to, 27
Hull, Cordell, and credit offer to Franco, 296

Icaza, Carmen de, heads Auxilio Social, 152
Immaculate Conception, Murillo's painting of, given to Franco by Hitler, 30

Inquisition, 58, 261
Inter-American Affairs, Office of, 260; its activities in Latin America, 265
International Telephone & Telegraph Corporation: its claims ignored when United States grants cotton credit to Franco, 280; finally regains control of Spanish telephone system, 293
Irún, damage to, 22
Isabella II, 56
Italy: Franco's war debt to, 140; diminished prestige in Spain, 236

Jacobite uprisings, 56
Japan, Franco's solidarity with, 234, 235
Jefferson, Thomas: influence on Latin-American independence movement, 264; and French and Spanish Bourbons, 273
Jesuits: readmitted to Spain, 96; missions in Far East as link between Spain and Japan, 235
*JONS, see* Phalanx
Jordana y Souza, Count Francisco Gómez: Foreign Minister during civil war, 118; returns to office, 130
José Antonio, *see* Primo de Rivera, José Antonio

La Linea, strategic position of, with relation to Gibraltar, 4; hunger in, 156
Land reform, fascist promises concerning, 74; not carried out, 99
Larraz Lopez, José, Minister of Finance, 100; dismissed, 128; conversion of government debt, 133
Las Casas, Father Bartolomé de, 84
Latin America: fascist ambitions with regard to, 76; Serrano Suñer on, 81; Spain's improved relations with, after Spanish-American War, 83; Franco's activities in opposing United States, 255 et seq.; limitations on Republic's influence, 257; strength and weakness of United States in, 264
Laval, Pierre: parallel with Serrano Suñer, 109; Hoare-Laval deal, 284; prevents French government from continuing fight on Germans from Algiers, 284; dismissal by Pétain, 287
Lazar, Hans, German press attaché in Madrid, 238 et seq.
*Leçons de la Guerre d'Espagne,* 13
Ledesma Ramos, Ramiro, fascist leader, 59 et seq.
Lenin, V.: prediction regarding Spain, 64; and cult of José Antonio Primo de Rivera, 73
Leo XIII, Pope, 71
Lope de Vega, Felix, 206
Lothian, Lord, British Ambassador to Washington: opinion of Sir Walter Maxwell Scott, 11; confers with Sir Samuel Hoare on American credit to Franco, 294
Louvre, Franco's accessions from, 30
*Love Lasts Two Thousand Metres,* 207
Louis XIV, 86 n.
Loveday, Arthur F., 74 n.
Loyola, Ignatius, 55
Luca de Tena, Marquis, Franco's Ambassador to Chile, 253 n.
Lupescu, Mme Magda, arrested in Spain, 217
Luxury restaurants, 168 et seq.

Madariaga, Salvador de: views on loss of Cervera's fleet, 82; on in-

fluence of France in Latin America, 264
Madrid, damage from civil war, 25 et seq.; food supplies, 184; living conditions in, 205
Maeztu, Ramiro de, 85
Manila Bay: Germany supports Spanish squadron, 72; effect on Spain, 82
March, Juan, 136
Maritime Commission, approves sale of two ships to Franco by Dollar Line, 292
Mayalde, Count José Finat y Escriva de Romani, head of police, 46
*Mein Kampf:* reveals Hitler's technique in dividing democracies, 9; first published in Spain, 60; Phalanx rejects Hitler's racial doctrines, 73
Mendelsohn, private bank of Amsterdam, sponsors credit for Franco, 279
Menendez y Pelayo, Marcelino, Spanish scholar, 264
Merry del Val, Pablo, chief of Foreign Press, 144, 179, 201; accompanies Mrs. A. W. Weddell on camera tour, 228
Miaja, General José, Republican general, 322
Ministry of Government, powers of, under Franco, 105
Miranda de Ebro, Franco concentration camp at, 221
Mistral, Frederic, Provençal poet, effect on Catalan home-rule movement, 75
*Mocedades del Cid,* 206
Model Prison, 65
Mola Vidal, General Emilio: captures Irún, 23; part in organizing revolt against Republic, 59 et seq.
Molina, Miguel de, *flamenco* dancer, 206
Molotoff, Premier V. M., 251
Monarchists: their aims in civil war, 52 et seq.; slight influence on regime, 101; lack of fighting spirit, 316
Montaña barracks, 39
Moore, Sir John, 312
Moors, form Franco's bodyguard, 70 n., 115; kinship with Spaniards, 78
Moscardo Stuarte, General José, defender of Toledo Alcázar, 49
Motor transport, effect of civil war on, 34
Mosley, Sir Oswald, 63
Muni, Paul, blacklisted by Franco, 207 n.
Muñoz Grande, General Agustín, dismissed from party post, 123; commands Blue Division, 238
Murillo, Franco obtains painting by, 30
Mussolini, Benito, furnishes model for Primo de Rivera dictatorship, 59; generous war-debt terms, 140; North Africa demands conflict with, 236, 287; appeals to Franco for help, 288

Napoleon, mistake in invading Spain, 254
Navarre: supports Franco, 22, 76; food plentiful in, 188
National debt of Spain, 134
Negrín, Juan, 320
*New Republic,* on Serrano Suñer's domestic difficulties, 129
Non-Intervention Committee, 3 et seq., 272 et seq.
North Africa: importance of Spain in relation to our landing, 4; Franco's reaction, 308

One-dish day, 169
Ortega y Gasset, José, 82
*Osservatore Romano,* Vatican newspaper, banned in Spain, 97

Paderewski, Ignace, arrested in Spain, 215 et seq.
Paine, Tom, influence on Latin-American independence movement, 264
Pardo, former royal palace, selected by Franco as residence, 114
Pearson, Drew, on American credit offer to Franco, 297
Peman, José Maria, Franco emissary to Latin America, 261
Peninsular War, 312
Peru, efforts of Franco to win over, 260
Pétain, Marshal Henri Philippe: French Ambassador to Madrid, 12; arranges emergency imports of French wheat, 157; career in Spain, 277 et seq.; returns to France and takes over government, 282; asks for armistice through Franco, 284, 285; does not resist when Germans take over remainder of France, 317
Peterson, Sir Maurice, British Ambassador to Madrid: attitude toward Franco regime, 276; relieved by Sir Samuel Hoare, 282
Phalanx: persecutes "Reds," 49; foundation, 52 et seq.; selection by Franco as official party, 59, 66; borrowings from Italy and Germany, 69 et seq.; its place in regime, 106 et seq.
Pierlot, Hubert, Belgian statesman, arrested in Spain, 216
Pierson, Warren Lee, president of Export-Import Bank, visits Spain, 280
Pius XI, Pope, 71
Pius XII, Pope, slighted by Serrano Suñer, 97
Philippines, Phalanx activities in, 236
Pietri, André François, Vichy Ambassador to Madrid, 282 n.
*PM,* N. Y. newspaper, campaigns against oil exports to Franco, 306
Poland, refugees from, in Spain, 224 et seq.
Police, inefficiency of, 45, 149, 225
Popular Front, significance of February 1936 victory, 15
Population of Spain, increase between 1930 and 1940, 37
Port Mahon, strategic importance of, 5; occupation urged by British Tories, 273; handed over to Franco by British, 275
Portugal, attitude of Spain to, 54, 234 et seq.; protests *Arriba* editorials, 75; semi-protectorate of England, 77
Prado, its collection intact, 28
Prescott, W. H., 84
Presentation, right of, 98, 204
Price-fixing, 133; inadequacy of, 177
Prieto, Indalecio, 320
Primo de Rivera, Fernando, negotiates with Army leaders, 65; killed, 65
Primo de Rivera, José Antonio: ridiculed by Gil Robles, 53; career and death, 60 et seq.; cult of, promoted by Serrano Suñer, 121
Primo de Rivera, General Miguel: his semi-fascist dictatorship, 20, 35, 38, 52, 59; policy toward Catalonia, 76; toward Latin America, 257
Primo de Rivera, Miguel (brother of José Antonio): civil governor

of Madrid, 125; dismissed, 127; becomes Minister of Agriculture, 128
Primo de Rivera, Pilar, head of Feminine Section of Phalanx, 106
Public amusements, 206 et seq.
Punta del Este, fascist agitation over, 262

*Quadragesimo anno,* 71
Queipo de Llano, Lieutenant General Gonzalo: holds Seville for Franco, 37; Republican sympathies, 51; exiled to Rome, 108; his remarks there, 209

Ramsay, Captain Archibald, M.P., British Franco supporter, 16
Railroads, damage to, during civil war, 34
Reconstruction program, slowness of, 23, 94
Redondo, Onésimo, early fascist leader, 60 et seq.
Refugees, Franco's treatment of, 215 et seq.
*Reivindicaciones de España,* 10, 14, 78, 79
Republican fleet: seizure of, urged by British Tories, 273; handed over to Franco, 278
Requetés, *see* Carlists
Reuter's news agency, representation in Spain, 205
Riestra, Genaro, Phalanx leader in Cuba, 259
Rights of Man, 58
Rio de Janeiro, conference of, effect on Hitler's intention to take over Spain, 253 n.
Rio de Oro, strategic importance of, 5
Romanones, Count, 55
Roosevelt, President Franklin D.: appeals to Franco for release of Ignace Paderewski, 216; announces plan to preserve Spanish works of art, 128, 307; attacked by Franco propagandists, 262; and Good Neighbor policy, 266
Roosevelt, President Theodore, attacked in Franco press, 262
*Rouge et le Noir, Le,* 57
Ruiz de Alda, co-founder of Phalanx, 61; killed, 65
Russia, sole ally of Spanish Republic, 3; receives inadequate help from United States, 8; Franco sends Blue Division to fight against, 237

Salazar, Prime Minister Oliveira, *see* Portugal
Salamanca, German foraging bands in, 154
Sampson, Admiral W. T., 82
Sanchez Mazas, Rafael, dismissed from party post, 123
Sanjurjo, Sacarnell, General José: leads plot against Republic, 38; remains exhumed, 48; commander of Civil Guard under General Primo de Rivera, 59; confers with Hitler, 65
San Martín, José de, 87
San Sebastían: undamaged by civil war, 24; beach set aside for diplomats, 206; bathing customs, 211
San Sebastían, pact of, for overthrowal of monarchy, 86, 322
Santiago de Compostella, 70 n.
Santiago de Cuba, defeat of Cervera's fleet off, 82

Sanz Bachiller, Mercédes, head of Auxilio Social, 149, 150, 152
Schacht, Dr. Hjalmar, methods imitated by Spanish fascists, 132, 137
Schley, Commodore W. S., 82
"School and Larder," 82
Schools, religious instruction made compulsory in, 96
Scott, Sir Walter Maxwell, 11, 291 n.
S.E.U. (*Sindicato Español Universitario),* fascist university students' organization: national congress, 50; *Führerschule* of, 167, 203; appeals to students of Latin America against United States, 262
Second Front, Spain's importance in, 308 et seq.
Segura, Cardinal Demetus Carceller, Archbishop of Seville, dispute with Phalanx, 97
Serrano Suñer, Ramón: interview in *Völkischer Beobachter,* 3, 80; escapes from Republican zone, 43; given party post, 67; becomes Foreign Minister, 124, 287; dismissal from office, 68, 108; visits Rome, 97, 279; career, 117 et seq.; regulates excesses of Auxilio Social, 151; ignores American help to Auxilio Social, 153; his cook's quarrel with government butcher, 164; affronts to American Ambassador, 209; persecutes refugees, 218; has himself photographed by Jewish refugee, 225
Simon, Viscount, policy toward Japanese aggression in Manchuria, 8
Singapore, 4, 320
Sitzkrieg, policy of democracies toward Spain during, 282
Snyder, Dr. John C., Rockefeller Foundation typhus specialist, 305 n.
Social customs, little changed by civil war, 210 et seq.
Sotelo, Calvo, Rightist leader, 39
Spaak, Paul Henri, Belgian statesman, arrested in Spain, 216
Special privileges, prevalence of, under Franco, 162 et seq.
Spanish-American War, effect of, on Spain, 56, 82
*Spanish Arena, The,* 143
Spanish art treasures, damage to, during civil war, 28 et seq.
Spanish civil war: importance of, to democracies, 3 et seq.; ill effects aggravated by length, 19; property damage, 22; loss of life, 36; aims of Franco supporters, 51 et seq.
Spanish fascism, *see* Phalanx
Spanish government-in-exile, formation proposed, 320
Spanish Morocco: strategic importance of, 4; moderates' lack of interest in, 77; Franco makes military career there, 110; is *Africanista,* 256, 257
Spanish Republic: excesses committed under, 15; failure to crush military uprising, 19; Leftist terror under, 39; alienates ardent reformers, 51
Spykman, Nicholas John, 266
Stalin, Joseph, 8
Starkie, Dr. Walter, British propagandist, 290
Stendhal (Henri-Marie Beyle), 57
Stohrer, Baron von, German Ambassador to Spain: halts anti-Suñer purge, 128; hold on Franco, 238 et seq.; demands Spain enter war, 288
Stohrer, Baroness von, 116; arrested by Franco police, 205
"Strength through Joy," 93

Tangier, annexation of, by Franco, 125, 257, 297
Telefonica, damage to, 27
Thomsen, Dr. Hans, German chargé d'affaires in Washington, 228
Toledo Alcázar, 30, 48
Tories, British, awaken to Franco's threat to the Empire, 273
Totalitarian economy, 131; malfunctioning of, 158 et seq.
Tovar Llorente, Antonio, Undersecretary of Press and Propaganda, 125 et seq.
Traditionalists, *see* Carlists
Tribunal of Political Responsibilities, 106
Tuberculosis: prevalent before the civil war, 180; subsequently, 194
Turkey, Allied concessions to, 271
Twenty-six Points of Phalanx: adopted by Franco as official program of new state, 66; provisions, 73 et seq.

Unamuno, Miguel de, 82
United Press, representation in Spain, 205
United States: policy toward Franco during civil war, 21; attitude of fascists toward, 71, 85, 137; recognizes Franco regime, 276; extends cotton credit, 279; attacks on in Franco press, 293; stoning of U. S. Embassy, 295; offers Franco $100,000,000 credit, 296; helps underwrite Argentine credit to Franco, 297; donates food through American Red Cross, 298; cuts off oil shipments to Franco, 306; attempts to buy strategic materials, 306, 309
University City, damage to, 25
Uruguay, denies cession of Punta del Este to United States, 262

Valencia: damage to during civil war, 31; home-rule movement in, 76
Van Zeeland, Paul, contact man for reconstruction credit offer, 279
Varela Iglesias, Lieutenant General José Enrique: converted to fascist imperialist doctrines, 79; dismissal as Minister of War, 108, 130; part in anti-Suñer move, 123; attempt made on life of, 129
Vidal y Barraquer, Cardinal, Archbishop of Tarragona, barred from Franco Spain, 96
Vigon Suerodiaz, General Juan, Minister for Air and confidant of Franco, 117
Vitoria, Bishop of, barred from Franco Spain, 96
*Völkischer Beobachter,* interview with Serrano Suñer, 3, 80

Wallace, Vice President Henry A., and a people's war, 319
Wavell, General Sir Archibald, 254; offensive in Libya halted, 287
Weddell, Alexander W., American Ambassador to Spain, 276; orders American Embassy children home, 289; and stoning of American Embassy, 295; offers Franco $100,000,000 credit, 296; called to Washington to report and resigns, 306
Weddell, Mrs. Alexander W.: tries to find alternative Embassy, 114; supervises fitting out Auxilio Social orphanage, 152; work in be-

half of refugees, 223; insulted by Franco press, 226
Welles, Sumner, Undersecretary of State, 297
Wellington, Duke of, drives Napoleon's armies out of Spain, 312; aided by Spanish guerrillas, 315
Weygand, General Maxime: a Franco supporter, 13, 14; and Wavell's offensive, 254, 287
Whitman, Walt, 265
Willkie, Wendell: presidential candidacy supported by Hitler, 286; and Franco, 294
Will to empire, fascist desire to restore, 81
Windsor, Duke and Duchess of, 220
*Women, The,* Spanish version of, 207
*World War in Spain,* 74 n.

Xavier, St. Francis, 235
Xenophobia, Spanish, 58, 314, 317

Yaguë, General Juan, 108; dismissed from Air Ministry, 123

Zabala, Dr. Pio, rector of University of Madrid, 262
*Zam Zam,* survivors from, pass through Spain, 23 n.

## A NOTE ON THE TYPE

The text of this book was set on the Linotype in Baskerville. Linotype Baskerville is a facsimile cutting from type cast from the original matrices of a face designed by John Baskerville. The original face was the forerunner of the "modern" group of type faces.

John Baskerville (1706-75), of Birmingham, England, a writing-master, with a special renown for cutting inscriptions in stone, began experimenting about 1750 with punch-cutting and making typographical material. It was not until 1757 that he published his first work, a Virgil in royal quarto, with great-primer letters. This was followed by his famous editions of Milton, the Bible, the Book of Common Prayer, and several Latin classic authors. His types, at first criticized as unnecessarily slender, delicate, and feminine, in time were recognized as both distinct and elegant, and his types as well as his printing were greatly admired. Four years after his death Baskerville's widow sold all his punches and matrices to the Société Littéraire-typographique, which used some of the types for the sumptuous Kehl edition of Voltaire's works in seventy volumes.

COMPOSED, PRINTED, AND BOUND BY H. WOLFF, NEW YORK